Pinstripes and Penance

The Life Story of
Ex-Yankee John Malangone

Michael Harrison

Jarndyce & Jarndyce Press

Pinstripes and Penance

Michael Harrison

Jarndyce & Jarndyce Press
Published by Cincinnati Book Publishing
Cincinnati, Ohio
www.cincybooks.com

Anthony W. Brunsman, president and CEO
Karen Bullock, assistant editor
Andreya Carlson, assistant editor
Amelia Stulz, assistant editor

———————————————

ISBN 978-0-9910077-7-6 softcover
ISBN 978-0-9910077-8-3 ebook

Library of Congress Control Number: 2014944041

———————————————

Printed in the United States of America
First Edition, 2015

To purchase additional copies online, visit
www.cincybooks.com

Discounts available on quantity orders.
Email: info@cincybooks.com or call 513-382-4315.

This book is dedicated to the memories of

Orlando Panarese
Paulie Tine
ARon Weiss

When we meet together again in heaven,
it will be to the cry of "Let's play ball."

John Malangone

Table of Contents

PART II: Penance

Acknowledgements

This biography proved to be a difficult challenge in terms of research. Many of the key people in John's life, including family members and professional athletes, have passed away. Italian East Harlem and the social and cultural ways of life associated with it have all but vanished into New York City's historical records. Still, there are written records that have been left behind that shed light on the era in which John Malangone grew up. Our Lady of Mount Carmel Church, Jefferson Park, the Boys Club on East 111th Street, Rao's Restaurant, and Patsy's Pizzeria remain vibrant and popular landmarks in East Harlem, and many old-timers still remember the legend of John Malangone, the ex-Yankee ballplayer.

The wonderful spirit and cooperation of the extended Malangone and Panarese families have made this book possible with photographs, newspaper articles, and stories that illuminated the events that transpired over time. John's brother, Sal, and his wife, Dolores, were invaluable in supplying vital information and archival material, as well as arranging meetings with other family members. Anna Malangone, John's sister, and his aunts Yolanda and Margaret, all provided firsthand accounts of neighborhood and family life.

Special thanks go to three former educational colleagues from Lynbrook High School in Lynbrook, New York. Louise McCartin and Carla Gentile, members of the English department, provided much inspiration, encouragement, and well wishes to me at the start of this project. Ken Barrett, a retired social studies teacher and old Brooklyn Dodger fan, also gave insight and suggestions for the book.

Three special people who previously authored stories about John deserve gratitude for their willingness to consent to interviews and therefore make themselves part of the ongoing saga of John Malangone. I give thanks to Wayne Coffey of the *NY Daily News*, Gary Smith of *Sports Illustrated*, and Bruce Spiegel, editor and producer for the CBS broadcast show *48 Hours*.

Special thanks also go to Mark Van Overloop, founder of A League Of Our Own (ALOOO), for supplying information about the league and John Malangone's pitching statistics. Anyone wishing to listen to more stories about John can meet with Mark and his colleagues most Sunday afternoons in the Park Ridge Diner in New Jersey during baseball seasons.

A special shout-out goes to a group of baseball-minded guys, including ex-Yankee scout Brian Collins, who attended some of John's interview sessions just to hear some stories about past ballplayers and life in East Harlem. These gentlemen, from all over the New York metro area and beyond, engaged in entertaining conversations with John, and they provided information for the book in many instances.

Translation of some phrases and conversations from Neapolitan to English was provided by longtime friend Vincent Carotenuto, well-versed in the nuances of Italian-American cultural expressions.

Special thanks go to Devonie Clark and to Rod Price, for taking time to read and assist in editing this manuscript.

I am especially grateful to Ron Weiss, who supplied some of the research materials, support, and insight into John's story. Weiss spent many long hours sitting in on interviews conducted with John and other people acquainted with both Malangone and Weiss.

I must acknowledge Andreya Carlson, assistant editor, Karen Bullock, assistant editor, and Tony Brunsman, publisher, of Cincinnati Book Publishing | Jarndyce & Jarndyce Press, whose professional expertise and interest in John Malangone's story helped to make this book a reality.

Completion of this story was also made possible with the assistance of my daughter, Jasmine, who provided much insight and encouragement.

Extraordinary gratitude goes to Ron Lacey, friend, softball competitor, and now baseball teammate, who attended many of the interviews conducted for the book and supplied advice on all phases of the project. At times I would confide in him about how frustrating the research effort had become when trying "to get to the bottom" of John Malangone's story; the events and occurrences in John's life appeared to be endless. Ron counseled, "Just enjoy the ride, wherever it takes you." That advice proved priceless.

What a ride it was... and still is.

Mike Harrison

Foreword

Anthony Belli

When asked to write this foreword, I accepted with eagerness because John inspired me and so many others in ways he never really knew. As someone who grew up on the mean streets of East Harlem in the late 1950s and 1960s, I can say this with certainty—you had one of two paths to choose from: be a wise guy or be an athlete. My path was spoon-fed to me by my older brother Vinny, who thought he was the baseball great Willie Mays. So baseball it was.

Every day, after ten hours of stoopball, stickball, punch ball, and baseball, we ended up on the stoop talking more baseball. The stoop chatter was always Mickey Mantle vs. Willie Mays or Sandy Koufax vs. Juan Marichal. Then the conversation would always turn to, "What about that guy Malangone?" You see, none of us neighborhood guys ever played with John, but everyone knew the legend of John Malangone.

The conversation would sound like this: "I hear that he was better than Berra and Dickey." "Yea, he had the strongest arm and hit the ball hard and far like Mantle." "So why didn't he play in the majors?" "Oh, he was crazy or something." That's all we knew!

Occasionally, we would have stoop talk with someone who actually played with John and we would demand validation of Malangone's talent and craziness. Both topics were always corroborated. We really didn't care about the craziness part because we took pride that one of our own was as good as the best in baseball. That was enough for us.

East Harlem, during the time of my youth, was in decay and surrounded by crime and poverty. In such times people need hope, and John was ours. He made everyone believe that it was possible to run with the "big boys." If only we could be a little better, stronger, faster, smoother, we would have our meal ticket out of the ghetto and up to the Bronx at Yankee Stadium. John never knew that he allowed us to dream big. We didn't care that he was considered a flake and didn't go all the way. Actually, we fantasized about John being kept from the big leagues. Like Frank Sinatra, we believed that John did it his way or the East Harlem way—that is, fight back. So we admired his no-nonsense, fight back attitude regardless of the consequences. Little did we know, he was haunted by personal demons.

As you learn John's story, you will laugh, cry, and understand these demons. You will also learn of a man with incredible guilt and a sense of unfulfilled promise. I guess it is true that he could have been one of the greats in a unique tradition of Yankee greats. There is no doubt he did not fulfill his promising baseball career. But I use a different scale to measure greatness.

Each spring I invite John to visit the City College of New York during the school's annual sports alumni reunion. I am a graduate of CCNY, and I always ask John to speak with members of CCNY's baseball team. What does an eighty-three-year-old former professional athlete have in common with aspiring collegiate baseball players? The love of a special game! Recently, I saw John mesmerize twenty or so members of the team with interesting and humorous stories. These athletes, of many ethnicities and three generations removed from John, listened with rapt attention to every word spoken by the East Harlem icon.

What was so special about his presence? Physically, John at eighty-three still resembles a block of stone, but his ability to speak from the heart allows his words to penetrate like lasers. John has been to hell and back, and his story is about how the fragility of life can bring even the most talented to their knees. But in the end, John showed he had much more than just physical talent. He possessed the strength to turn his personal adversity into triumph and be a role model for other people. John's speeches and pep talks about his life's experiences have inspired others to be better.

Shouldn't this be the true watermark for success? When John was speaking to the City College baseball players, a passerby who was taken by the passion and tone of his words asked, "Who is this guy?" Before I could answer, one of the players replied, "He was almost a great baseball player with the Yankees."

Anthony Belli, author
The Street-Smart Salesman

PART I
Pinstripes

"We will never win the pennant with you."

Yankee infielder and legend Billy Martin to rookie John
Malangone, on several occasions in the early 1950s

"Whaddya doin'?"

Johnny Blanchard, Yankee catcher and friend to John Malangone,
during a key moment in Yankee rookie school in 1955

"Anything you would like to talk to me about, John?"

Legendary Yankee Scout Paul Krichell to rookie John
Malangone, on several occasions in the 1950s

Prologue

NBC Studios
Rockefeller Plaza, NYC
December 1997

One mistake can ruin your life forever. Do people who make tragic mistakes that alter their lives deserve a second chance? That was the premise for this episode of the television show *Maury* which featured, among other participants, an ex-Yankee baseball player named John Malangone. The popular talk show host Maury Povich introduced John as the first guest at the show's opening.

Povich explained to his television audience that John Malangone's life was changed for sixty years after one mistake John had made when he was a child. Beginning his interview with John, he inquired, "We have to go back to when you were five. What happened?"

At that instant, he felt the pressure mounting inside of him. Wearing a baseball jacket, John smiled nervously, and paused after saying, "Well..." He proceeded to explain what happened next, before a captivated audience.

As he finished his story, John's face suddenly changed from calm to visibly upset. Sensing John's emotional distress, Povich interrupted at that point. Taking control of the conversation, he said, "And this event has never left you. I mean, I can tell right now. Sixty years later, you get very emotional when you talk about it."

John took a deep sigh, closed his eyes, fighting to hold back tears, and quietly answered, "Yeah..." John proceeded to talk about experiencing shame while his family gave him love and support; they never reminded him of his mistake and they never spoke openly to anyone of it. Povich informed his audience how John became a great athlete and was signed by the New York Yankees, with the possibility of becoming a successor to Yogi Berra, already a renowned player on the team. Povich continued, "And you were scared the whole time. What were you scared of?"

John replied with one word: "Recognition." He explained

that attaining any fame would allow anyone interested in his background to find out his childhood story. He was afraid his secret would come out, and he explained what would happen next: "You get sick, it wipes you out, you lose sleep, and it's tough to play." Povich continued to guide the conversation, saying to John, "You thought about it all the time." John replied, "It never left."

Povich reminded the viewing audience that most people grow up fearful of failure, whereas his guest was afraid of success. Turning his attention directly back to John, as if verbalizing John's thoughts, he said in amazement, "You can't be successful."

John answered, "No." He remained visibly upset and looked away from the cameras. He thought to himself,

Success is a scary thing...

John had a vacant look on his face. I remembered that look from forty years ago, when we had worked together. It was a distant, faraway look. I could sense an emotional eruption that was brewing over key words in his mind.

Confusion... camera light is red... green light you are on one... or was it two? Two and two fastball... odd, even, breaking ball... what sign was that? You gotta be a rocket scientist to figure this out. Just throw anything, I'll catch it. I can't take this...

Povich retained control of the conversation, gently asking his guest, "Did the Yankees know about this?" John answered no, saying that he did not feel "worthy of this [playing ball with the Yankees]." He talked about self-destruction, and playing the role of someone considered flaky by other ball players. "You start doing things and start to hold yourself down, I guess." The pressure eased a little bit. He started to appear a little more relaxed as the interview progressed.

Povich reinforced the point about self-destruction by telling John that he was trying to put himself down all the time:

...because of this one, big secret you've held since you were five years old, this one mistake you made in your life. It is the car and the engine that drives your life. Have you ever been able to get rid of it?

John simply said, "No... you never get rid of it, but it's much better now." Povich then asked in what way things were better.

Wiping his forehead, John pointed to Ron Weiss, sitting in the first row of the audience. He explained how encounters with Ron led to a renewal of an old friendship and how Ron wanted to know about his personal secret. John described himself to Ron as a "Yankee problem child" and how he decided he wanted to take his secret to his grave. He stated he eventually changed his mind and told Weiss his secret. Holding back tears, he continued...

Once I told him that was it. I felt like a piano coming off my back, and wide angle vision...

Povich extended his arms outward with a smile, interrupting John with reinforcement, "Once you opened up..." He continued, reminding everyone that John never told anyone about his background and the tragedy.

John continued talking to Povich and the audience about Ron. He explained that Ron asked him what he would like to do, now that the secret was no longer secret and that this great burden of guilt was now lifted from his back. John recalled his answer, "Now that I have a clear mind, I would like to go back to playing ball." John described how the two men went back to playing baseball together and how they had traveled to a Roy Hobbs Tournament in Florida. Grinning before the camera now, he further commented, "We won the championship in '94."

At that moment, the audience erupted in applause and enthusiastic approval. Prior to this, John's demeanor throughout the interview had easily evoked compassion and understanding from everyone in attendance. Povich, smiling, said,

It's remarkable. There was a huge, several-page story several weeks ago in Sports Illustrated, *on you... on you! All your life, you're reading about these sports heroes. You think you're never going to get there, and you end up being a big story in* Sports Illustrated.

While television monitors flashed a visual of *Sports Illustrated* author Gary Smith's "Damned Yankee" article, the interview continued with a discussion about several Yankees who John knew from his playing days with the team. John explained that he told ex-teammate John Blanchard what happened, and no one else. Povich stated that some former Yankees were probably wondering what happened to John. He continued,

Guess what, you are not alone today, John. We got a lot of people in this studio today. A lot of our guests are looking for the same second chance that you were looking for because of one mistake.

Povich's show did not end there, as six other guests recalled stories of how they each made a single mistake that altered their lives. The guests, all from different backgrounds, discussed topics that included substance abuse, custody issues, criminal charges, and a driving accident. When all the personal stories were completed, Povich interviewed another guest, Steve Viscusi, who was a radio talk show host giving advice to listeners on career topics. Viscusi listened to each of the show participants and then weighed in with his own observations on their stories. Starting with John, he stated that his story was unusual and that it was less a career story and more of a personal tragedy. Viscusi summarized,

I am sure everyone in the audience agrees. John has a story that was a true American tragedy and a real hero to all of us in what we heard today.

It was a classic made-for-television, feel-good moment. In approximately ten minutes, John's life was neatly packaged to show how he endured and overcame a personal tragedy, and presumably was now happy. The reality was something else; a lifetime of events and obstacles was omitted in the process, and memories of those moments were still sitting in the back of John Malangone's mind. He was fortunate that the glare of studio lights and questions did not cause him to have an emotional meltdown. A follow-up offer to appear on the Oprah Winfrey show was rejected because he felt he would not have survived the spotlight a second time.

What I didn't understand forty years ago, I understand now while writing this book. Still, I am totally amazed by John Malangone's journey through life.

How does a man live his life and survive when guilt, post-traumatic stress disorder, panic attacks, chronic headaches, murder, domestic violence, beatings, dyslexia, illiteracy, suicide, racial prejudice, divorce proceedings, gangs, truck hijacking, mobsters, inexplicable behavior, social workers, psychiatrists, loss of a child, straitjackets, illegal contracts, gambling, alcohol, misunderstandings, bad luck, and plain and simple failure are permanently embedded in his life's memories?

I thought about that look again. It was 1969. John and I worked together in a Sears Automotive garage, on Fordham Road in the Bronx. He was my night manager. I asked him about a rumor that he played ball with the Yankees. He acknowledged the chitchat by saying "Yeah." Then he dropped the conversation and looked away. The look was vacant, as if he wasn't inside his body, but simply gone. He was oblivious to any noise from air guns or tire machines or loud conversations around him. I never raised the subject of Yankee baseball again.

At other times during work hours, John was exhuberant. He would often joke, tell entertaining stories, and be the center of attention during conversations.

At any given moment, with an imaginary flip of a switch, the vacant look on his face would return and he would withdraw into total silence.

Despite possessing mood changes, John was like a godfather figure in that garage, managing people, controlling the ebb and flow of service transactions, and troubleshooting any problems that arose during normal work days. I admired the way he handled and communicated with people. He was astute at reading people's motives and behavior. It was a survival skill, honed over time to compensate for a reading disability. More importantly, he used any knowledge that he gained to give constructive advice and to assist everyone around him.

One evening he stood outside the garage, pointed to the train rambling by on the old Third Avenue El, and recalled how one winter night, he nailed the motorman on a similar train with a snowball through an open window. He was boasting about his throwing arm; I didn't believe him then, but I do now.

I stopped working with John in Sears in 1972. After graduating from nearby Fordham University, I went on with my life, but I never forgot the positive impression he had made on me. My memories of the time spent with him were revived in December of 1994 with a *New York Daily News* profile of John Malangone, as an ex-Yankee. I attempted to contact him, without success. The information in the article stuck in my mind, however, and in 2009, I made a determined effort to locate and meet John once and for all. When I finally tracked him down, he stated that he remembered me, and when we reunited, I found him to be more open and communicative than during the years we spent together in Sears. I quickly realized my past recollections of John were missing major details; I heard stories and background information that I, like most other people, never knew about. We met in the home of his longtime friend and teammate, Ronnie Weiss.

Weiss, the calming presence for John in the front of the

Povich television audience, always had another take on his friend. He would offer insights and put everything into perspective with John Malangone by saying,

Truth is stranger than fiction...
You're not gonna believe this...
You can't make this stuff up...
Unbelievable!
Just listen to the man...

Chapter 1
Fond Memories

Yogi Berra Museum & Learning Center
Montclair State College University Campus
Little Falls, New Jersey
Winter 2012

The Yogi Berra Museum & Learning Center is an interesting and informative site that promotes Major League Baseball history; its spacious design holds a number of photographic exhibits and memorabilia displays covering Yogi's Hall of Fame career with the New York Yankees. The museum includes a glass-enclosed cafeteria with "Yogi-isms" painted on one of its walls and an elevated view of the home baseball field of the Montclair State Red Hawks baseball team. The museum also houses a cozy theater room for film projections. The site has received a steady stream of visitors since its opening to the public in 1998.

John Malangone entered the front entrance of the museum, warmly greeting two men at the front desk with his trademark smile, and intoned, "Howse everybody doin' today?" Slowly walking a few more steps in the front lobby area, John stopped to admire larger-than-life black and white photographs that captured special championship moments of Yogi and other Yankees. John, sporting his now weather-worn and beloved Yankee cap, stood for a few moments, smiled broadly, and recounted his own memories. The men in the photos reminded him of things that were said so long ago...

I want you to stay away from my brothers...
Why you clowning around?
I did it, skip...
You need to calm down...
Whaddya doin'?

John broke his momentary silence and shared his thoughts when another visitor stood next to him. This baseball conversation was like so many others that John had with countless listeners over the past fifty years. The give-and-take always included, "I knew these guys. I used to be with the Yankees myself..." Expectations of a brief, passing conversation were not possible; nothing in "Malangonespeak" was ever explained in ten words or less. Eventually ambling around the corner behind the photos, John all but disappeared into the interior of the facility. If anyone needed to look for him, it wouldn't have been hard to find the old-timer; one could always locate him by the sound of his deep voice. Possessing an affable demeanor and a commanding presence, John would usually engage in conversation with anyone willing to listen.

He moved slowly from exhibit to exhibit. Time had taken a toll on John's strength. In the early years of his life, John Malangone was an above average physical specimen, having incredible power and quickness that easily surpassed that of his peers. His undefeated boxing career (sixteen first round knockouts) was testimony to that; a photo of his final fight against Tom Peoples at a U.S. Army boxing championship at Fort Dix, New Jersey in 1954 reveals enormous, muscular thighs and legs. One can only imagine the sledgehammer-like force that knocked Peoples, a successful fighter, out cold.

His physical abilities and skills would be showcased in other areas, especially on a baseball diamond. He would describe, in his unique baseball vernacular, hitting a baseball "outta sight," or "a frozen rope, so tight, you coulda hang your clothes on it." He possessed gigantic wrists that were not the result of any drugs or steroids, but the result of hard work and repetitive physical exercise far beyond what most men would be motivated to do. He could throw farther than almost anyone else during his time as a ballplayer.

Speed was another asset; stories from the old neighborhood in East Harlem always included John Malangone "taking off and running for days" to downtown lower Manhattan on food errands for local mobsters. John's physical prowess in East Harlem was legendary, especially after literally flipping over an automobile—albeit a small model Crosley—for out of town guests. Since John could do anything except leap over tall buildings in a single bound, he was considered just the man for any occasion that involved displays of physical bravado. In spite of his limited leaping ability, he did throw a baseball onto the roof of a thirteen-story project building, for the same out of town visitors.

Even though numerous accidents and injuries slowed John down over time, it would take a broken neck, obtained in a freak accident at seventy years of age, to finally end his playing career as a pitcher. Now at the age of eighty-three, more than a decade later, the man is still pushing himself and enjoying life as much as possible. The exhibits in the museum gave him an instant spiritual charge and rejuvenated his thoughts and feelings about the game he loved. He stood in the museum and talked about the Yankees and the 1950s because he had been there, briefly sharing time and space with some of the most famous Yankees that ever played the game of baseball. One of them was Yogi Berra himself.

The lives of John Malangone and Yogi Berra intersected in 1955 spring training in St. Petersburg, Florida. John was a heralded rookie catcher who would, according to Yankee manager Casey Stengel, eventually take Yogi's position as the starting catcher. What happened next sent both men in opposite directions, as far away from each other as possible. Yogi went on to be an icon of Yankee history and success; John, on the other hand, spiraled downward into obscurity. He became the antithesis of the Yankee brand of success.

During the past decade, and prior to the publication of this book, John felt he had come full circle in his life. He wanted people, including the famous Yogi Berra, to know why and how things happened to him. He was, and still is, willing to admit that he was his own worst enemy.

Both men shared similarities with some sharp distinctions, even as they veered off in opposite directions in 1955.

Both were descendants of Italian immigrants and lived in Italian-American enclaves. Yogi hailed from "The Hill" section of St. Louis, while John came from "Little Italy" in East Harlem, NY. Yogi dropped out of school to work and support his family; John worked but remained in high school, in "hammer and nails" classes. He never graduated.

Both served in the armed forces. Berra served for three years in the Navy during World War II, while John was drafted into the army for two years at Fort Dix, New Jersey. Both signed with the Yankees: Yogi in 1942, and John in 1949, albeit illegally, as he was underage. Both played the catching position. Berra started out in the outfield, while Malangone was converted from pitcher to catcher because he was a power hitter with a "valuable bat." Both were coached by Yankee Hall of Famer Bill Dickey, who assisted one (Berra) to become a great catcher, while frowning on any possibility of the other (John) becoming successful. Both were nicknamed "Yogi" and both employed unusual verbal sayings. Yogi would become famous for his quotes, while John's sayings would eventually be forgotten. Both would be covered by the media. Yogi would do commercials, books, and other activities too numerous to list here. He remains in the public limelight. John received limited exposure in *Sports Illustrated* and other various publications, a video documentary, *Long Road Home,* and an appearance on *Maury.*

Despite the geographical proximity of the two men that has lasted decades, no reunion between the men ever took place, for reasons unknown.

Ironically, in 2007, a documentary about John's life was shown to a packed house in the Yogi Berra Museum's theater. The film, *Long Road Home*, would receive much praise for its depiction of John and his time with the Yankees.

This book is not about Yogi Berra, since both his career and his life have been thoroughly documented. Mr. Berra has received numerous awards, acknowledgements, and accolades. He still makes public appearances, does autograph signings, and remains visible in media circles. The museum itself is a wonderful testimony to the Hall of Famer's accomplishments.

This book is about the other "Yogi," the guy who didn't make it in the "big leagues." Some people may have regarded John Malangone in a negative light for various reasons, and perhaps that could be well understood.

He didn't adhere to the written and unwritten guidelines necessary for achieving success in his time, allowing others to regard him as a troublemaker and loser. However, the mental distress, pain, and suffering that held the man back for most of his life was hidden for decades. These setbacks were a result of a personal tragedy, and overcoming them made John Malangone a winner in the game of life and a hero to others who sought comfort and strength from his heartbreaks and triumphs. He would ultimately inspire many individuals to overcome their own obstacles and personal difficulties. His trademark grin and his love of baseball have enabled the man to survive life's curveballs.

Standing in the museum and observing everything around him, John smiled and relaxed. The anguish he suffered through was now diminished. Unburdened, he is able to converse freely about his life and his days as a Yankee...

Chapter 2

The Neighborhood

East 114th Street
East Harlem, NYC
1930s

    John Gerard Malangone was born May 9, 1932, and was raised in the neighborhood of East Harlem in New York City, dubbed "Little Italy" because of its heavy concentration of Italian immigrants, most of whom passed through immigration procedures at Ellis Island, located in New York City's harbor. The first Italians arrived on 115th Street in East Harlem in 1878, and by the 1930s decade, the numbers of immigrants had swelled to nearly ninety thousand, coming from every area of Italy. First and second generation Italians occupied the areas between Lexington Avenue and the East River, and between 96th Street and 125th Street, east of Lexington Avenue. Although there were other "Little Italys" in New York City, including one in lower Manhattan, East Harlem contained the largest concentration of Italian American immigrants anywhere in the region.

    Most people lived in poor, run-down tenements. The majority of housing units in the area lacked central heating, tubs or showers, and even private toilets. The area was home to the working class and the poor, and it was severely overcrowded. The area was hit extremely hard during the Great Depression, and a third of the work force still suffered unemployment by the time of the 1940 census.

    In 1931, following a neighborhood courtship, John's parents, Sylvester Malangone and Josephine Panarese, were married. Josephine was the eldest daughter of Sylvia and John Panarese.

    The couple resided at 336 East 114th Street, between First and Second Avenues, in the heart of Little Italy. A year later, Josie bore her first child, christening the boy John. Over the next several years, a daughter named Anna and another son named Sylvester (Sal or Junior) were added to the family.

    Residing on the top floor of the building, above the

Malangone family's apartment, was the Panarese family, including Josephine's parents, brothers, and sisters.

The Panareses lived in two apartments that were connected by a doorway constructed to facilitate family movement between the units. The family was headed by John Panarese and his wife, Sylvia, whose maiden name was Bozza. Both were Neapolitans, who had emigrated from Sant'Arcangelo Trimonte, in the Avellino province of Campania, Italy. The region was referenced in the HBO television series *The Sopranos*, with the main character, mob boss Tony Soprano, tracing family roots back to Avellino. Both John and Sylvia came from prominent families in the area. Sylvia, who lost her mother at an early age, was schooled by Catholic nuns. Her future husband, educated and considered a risk taker, wanted to see what America was like. John immigrated via Ellis Island and eventually began work with the New York Central Railroad, fueling locomotives with shoveled coal. John and Sylvia knew each other from their hometown. When John temporarily returned to Avellino, the couple began a romance that blossomed into marriage. She was nineteen and he was thirty-one. Sylvia became pregnant with the couple's first child, Josephine. John Panarese left his wife and unborn child behind in Avellino and returned to his job on the railroad in New York. Following Josephine's birth, Sylvia relocated from Italy to America and joined John in New York. The couple eventually settled into the combined double apartment on East 114th Street in East Harlem, surrounded by fellow paisans who all hailed from the Naples region of Italy.

The Panareses lived modestly but managed to raise a large family, eventually having nine children: five boys and four girls. The daughters were Josie, Lena, Margaret, and Orlanda. The boys were Delfino, Grant, Orlando, and Joseph. The boy named Orlando was killed at the age of six when he was hit by a truck. Sylvia's ninth and last child was then named Orlando, with a middle initial A for Anthony to distinguish him from the first one.

The parents were stern but fair with the children. Holidays were celebrated with John providing accordion talent and piano accompaniment for family sing-alongs. Sylvia Panarese slowly evolved as the family matriarch of her children and their spouses, and later her grandchildren. With the passage of time, she would become controlling of her daughters, while giving free reign to the male children. Sylvia was afraid of no one in the tough neighborhood, and she was known for carrying a kitchen knife or a rolling pin on her person when navigating the crowded streets surrounding the apartment.

By all accounts, fulfilling the typical American dream of newly arrived immigrants, John and Sylvia Panarese worked hard and raised their children as best they could. John Panarese, like most of his neighbors, made an honest living in providing for his family.

Some neighborhood paisans, however, took a different approach to success, choosing the life of a criminal organization known as the Mafia, whose roots extended all the way back to Italy. The Mafia dominated the area of East Harlem, having a firm grip on the economic and social aspects of neighborhood life.

The web of criminal activity covered the Malangone family's arrival in America. Some members of the clan were already schooled in organized crime and had experience as members of the infamous Black Hand, predecessor to the Mafia. John's grandfather, Giovanni Malangone, married a Neapolitan immigrant, Anna Ventri, who bore him three sons: Rudolph, Harry, and Sylvester. Giovanni changed his name to John as part of his transition to American culture. John Malangone eventually moved from Little Italy in lower Manhattan to the new, growing Little Italy in East Harlem. Malangone set up a barbershop in his name on Second Avenue, although there were never any haircuts given in the store; John and his associates carried on criminal rackets in the back room of the shop, behind the neatly painted red, white, and blue "John Malangone Barbershop" letters on the glass window. Neighborhood residents knew enough to avoid the place.

John's wife, Anna Ventri Malangone, would die of gangrene after a tragic accident. She was replaced by a second wife of Polish ancestry, also named Anna, who was reputed to be a victim of white slavery, a common mob racket.

Only one of the three Malangone sons, Rudolph, would ply a legitimate trade as a barber. Harry and Sylvester followed in their father's footsteps and engaged in questionable activities outside of the legal system. Sylvester was involved in the numbers racket and gambling, especially card games.

Sylvester's sons, John and Sal, grew up understanding that their relatives did not maintain checking and savings accounts; any monies earned and not spent were deposited in shoeboxes. The boxes were stashed in loose brick openings down in a "dungeon," wine cellar, or some other basement setting, where no one thought to look for it. As John remembered:

The money was stashed in shoeboxes in the wall. The shoeboxes looked like little coffins in the wall. It looked like a concrete vault, a mausoleum down there... even down there the money wasn't always safe. Uncle Harry came down one day, looking for his money, and screaming "What the fuck? Sonuva bitches!!" The fucking rats ate all the money and left shit all over the place. Sometimes building supers would come downstairs and plaster over the gaps and loose bricks and then you didn't know where the hell the shoeboxes were.

For better or for worse, the young Malangone boys would become immersed in Mafia culture, but John especially would become involved in various mob activities for much of his life. He would later boast that a miracle allowed him to escape the clutches of known associates and their neighborhood boss, a powerful and influential man known as Dom Bepp.

Chapter 3
A New Birth Certificate

Little Italy
East Harlem, NYC
1940s

"Dom Bepp," as he was nicknamed for this book, was a prominent member of Little Italy's Mafia. John, always speaking deferentially about Dom Bepp, would say the man controlled a large area of East Harlem between 112th and 120th streets. Dom Bepp frequented several mob social clubs that were located on 114th Street, including the Seahawks Club. The mob was allegedly headquartered on East 112th Street, not far from the Malangone residence located on East 114th Street. According to John, the headquarters was the focal point for Mafia activities nationally as well.

The beginnings of the New York Mafia can be traced to an Italian immigrant named Giuseppe Morello. Known as the "Clutch Hand," Morello oversaw the evolution of the Mafia from its early origins as The Black Hand. Morello's criminal enterprises originated during the 1890s in lower Manhattan's Little Italy. Within a few years, his gang was centered in East Harlem, which experienced a heavy influx of immigrants from all over Italy. Despite the eventual expansion of the Mafia into four and then five families in New York City, the center of power for Morello's successors remained in the East Harlem enclave of Little Italy.

The mob's presence was felt everywhere in Italian East Harlem. While numerous Italian immigrants struggled to make an honest living and stayed away from criminal activities, many residents found it difficult to avoid the omnipresent wise guys on the streets. The wise guys made it their business to know everybody else's business, and secrets were hard to keep. Fear and occasional gunfire were necessary tools to keep the racketeers themselves in line and to follow orders from Dom Bepp and other mob bosses.

Despite this, rub outs of fellow mob members were common in East Harlem. John's Aunt Yolanda once remarked, "We saw more murders than we saw on TV." Yolanda recalled observing a dead mobster on a bloody snow bank one winter morning across the street from the family apartment. She and her sisters alerted Grandma Panarese of their discovery, but she was unimpressed; the woman just philosophically shrugged her shoulders and said, "I wonder who is next?"

Dom Bepp and his associates always strived to maintain a low-key presence and not attract the glare of law enforcement if at all possible. In the latter part of the 1940s, a few racial disturbances occurred in the neighborhood when black students from West Harlem traveled to Benjamin Franklin High School to attend classes. John explained that most kids prided themselves on getting along with each other, but the problems originated with the "sons of wise guys" who felt a need to assert their presence. Tensions between students were defused over time, thanks to the collective efforts and superb leadership of Dr. Covello, the school principal, and U.S. Congressman Vito Marcantonio. Both men worked to assure parents and students involved that any issues would be resolved to the satisfaction of all. At one point, Frank Sinatra and Paul Robeson visited the school in a display of unity. Not mentioned publicly, according to John, was the fact that Dom Bepp was using "enforcers" to maintain the neighborhood peace and to ensure the safety of students walking along 125th Street and down Pleasant Avenue to the school. His explanation for keeping peace was simple: "We don't want no trouble here. We don't want the Feds coming here, snooping around..."

John remembered Dom Bepp as a "good looking guy, like the movie star Tyrone Power." Maintaining good public relations with a display of generosity, Dom Bepp would often walk down neighborhood streets with an entourage, passing out samples of Charlotte Russe and other pastries to children and families gathered around the stoops in front of the tenements. Occasionally, the Malangone family would receive such treats, and this kindness on Dom Bepp's part left a lifelong impression on young John. The relationship between the mob leader and the troubled young neighborhood boy would grow and last on and off for years. Mercifully for John, that relationship ended without any acrimony or retribution from Dom Bepp. John's past errors in judgment while dealing with Dom Bepp did not come back to haunt him later in life.

Dom Bepp was aware of the Malangone boy since he was five years old. He knew from fellow associates that the kid had been nicknamed "killer," but over time he tolerated John's presence around the local clubs and would employ the kid in various odd jobs. Tormented by a personal secret, John would "punish" himself by doing strenuous jobs that left him physically exhausted. He carried large blocks of ice to local apartments. He would shovel endless truckloads of coal into carts and barrels that were then distributed to tenement houses on nearby blocks. The kid gradually strengthened his upper body not only by lifting shovelfuls of coal, but also by learning to swing the shovel and swat vicious horseflies that were commonly present around the equine population in the area. Swinging the shovel meant turning over one's wrists, an acquired strength that would make John Malangone a feared power hitter in baseball later on. The youngster also spent hours in the wine cellars learning how to squeeze and crush the grapes that were necessary for the production of various wines.

Although cleaning Dom Bepp's horse stables was a priority, snow shoveling became another punishing physical activity and a way for John to earn some money. Oftentimes he would shovel both sides of his block on 114th Street, being rewarded with fruit and other items from food and pushcart vendors who were grateful for the cleared street space, especially on the corners. Such foods were often given to Grandma Panarese for distribution to the Malangone and Panarese households. Driven by mental torment and guilt, John would strive to please Sylvia in any way possible. Although Sylvia understood the boy's emotional pain, she would never discuss the topic with anyone, deepening John Malangone's secret and extending the mysterious origins behind his behavior for another fifty years.

Malangone's secret anguish morphed into obsessive and compulsive behavior in all of his physical activities. It was especially obvious at the Boys Club gyms on 111th Street and in the Seahawks Club, a mob-operated casino and gym. The young teenage boy's nervous energies and wild streaks were channeled into relentless punching of the speed bags in the gyms. It was here, before the influence of Major League Baseball, that the mobsters and others began to notice the boy's physical potential. During his childhood and adolescent years, John spent hours hammering away at the speed bags and annoying Dom Bepp with excessive noise. The kid would not stop. Reflecting on the times, John commented, "I could play music with the speed bag and I could hit that thing for an hour without ever getting tired."

However, Dom Bepp was not amused. The annoying "thumpa thumpa thumpa" finally made him lose patience one day and he instructed his bodyguard and chauffeur, Jerry, to tell John to stop; if that didn't work, then "shut the lights off." The response that came back to Dom Bepp was twofold: no, the kid would not stop and "he hits the bag in the dark."

Jerry approached John a second time.

Jerry: *Dom Bepp is offering you twenty-five dollars to fight.*

John: *Jerry, I don't wanna fight...*

Jerry: *You sonuva bitch! I gotta go back and tell him you refused him? Huh? Is that what you want me to do?*

John: *Jerry, I don't wanna fight...*

Jerry: *Why are you doing this?*

John: *I love to train, that's all...*

John was wild and lacked self-discipline much of the time, but he was not the bullying type and he tried to avoid fights of any variety. However, the mean streets of Little Italy on occasion would force him to think differently. John was very protective of the Clydesdale horses in the stable and found spiritual comfort in caring for the gentle animals. One day a mob associate's son, trying to show how tough he could be, entered the stables and punched a horse squarely between its eyes. The beast yelped and buckled under the force of the blow. John, enraged, called the assailant "a fucking coward." Verbally challenged, the punk raised his arm and attempted to land a blow on John, but was decked by a counterpunch from John that knocked him out cold. The boy's father arrived a short time later, with a pistol in hand, demanding an explanation from John for what had occurred. John was saved by a girl who witnessed the fight and told the father simply, "It was a fair fight."

Another altercation, however, landed the young Malangone in trouble with Dom Bepp himself. One day John spotted his mother and his sister, Anna, scurrying for the entrance to the tenement.

I could tell my mother was pretty upset. She ran down the block. I asked her what happened. She said two guys, twin brothers, had pinched her. I knew who they were... wise guys sent here from Italy, who spoke broken English. I ran to the corner to Rita's bar and found them. They looked at me and knew right away why I was there. They said, "Whaddya gonna do?" They started moving at me. I hit both of them with one punch and knocked them out.

One guy hit the floor and the other fell down outside on the curb. I knew I was gonna be in trouble with Dom Bepp because I was not supposed to fight these guys. I got scared...

For reasons unknown, it would be three weeks before John was summoned to meet with Dom Bepp. During that time, he stayed out of sight, venturing only downstairs to the alleyway out back where throwing a baseball night and day was reasonably safe. He wanted no contact or additional trouble with these wise guys. When the time came for a meeting of both parties with Dom Bepp, John was accompanied by Grandma Panarese.

Dom Bepp made it clear to the twin wise guys: "You gotta respect family. If you had pinched my mother, I woulda put a fucking bullet in your head! Family comes first!"

Turning to John, Dom Bepp asked Sylvia to step away, so he could make his point to John very clear.

John, you got no respect. You gotta respect these guys, whether you like them or not. You can't do what you did. You can't hit these guys, that's against the "rules." You will be punished. Don't you understand? These guys have the brains and the minds of Frankenstein, they can't think too good.

Dom Bepp dismissed all those directly involved in the altercation, and no apologies or handshakes were issued. With that, John was free and clear knowing Dom Bepp's word was good. But Dom Bepp did not forget the end game, which was making a boxer out of the boy. Several weeks passed with John still pounding at the speed bag. The next time John was summoned to see Dom Bepp in the club, he was asked to come alone. A Catholic priest, Father Joseph, whom John nicknamed the "hoodlum priest," was standing beside the boss. Entering the room, John noticed a wad of cash on the table in front of the two men, and Dom Bepp explained that the money was for the kid's first fight. The sight of the cash immediately stressed John out. Recalling the meeting years later, John explained what that offer meant:

Now you can't refuse. This is the way they were. What he did for the neighborhood... everybody ate. A whole lotta people never understood this... we ate good. Everything came from hijacked trucks.

Realizing he was trapped in a hopeless situation, John consented with the stipulation that no one would tell his parents or grandmother. Dom Bepp replied, "I'll tell you what. We'll change your name. Father Joseph, isn't that right?"

To which the hoodlum priest answered, "Yeah, we'll make a new birth certificate."

Dom Bepp was satisfied. He wasted no time seizing the opportunity presented to him and cashed in on it immediately.

Chapter 4

I'll Kill Him

Little Italy
East Harlem, NYC
Mid 1940s

He became John Mallo when he started boxing at the age of sixteen. Over the next six years, he would fight in sixteen matches, starting under the guidance of Dom Bepp's associates. He would end his career in a ring on the grounds of the United States Army base in Fort Dix, New Jersey. Additionally, there were two matches where the scheduled opponents did not show. His early fights were booked in the local social clubs, the Red Shield Club, and venues in lower Manhattan, Brooklyn, and Queens. He would have first round knockouts in every one of these fights, utilizing a vicious left hook for which his opponents had no answer. He made large sums of money for Dom Bepp and later generated much excitement and publicity for the U.S. Army during the Korean War. His fastest fight was just thirty-two seconds against a soldier named Tommy Boyle. He would end his boxing career by winning the heavyweight championship in the U.S. Army at Fort Dix, New Jersey in 1954.

Uncle Harry, Uncle Grant, Paulie Tine (John's best friend), and Father Joseph were always present to support the young champ's prowess in the ring. Grant was a Golden Gloves prizefighter who commanded everyone's respect for his skills and knowledge. A *New York Daily News* article in February of 1942 described Grant as "one of the classiest middleweights to show in Gloves competition in many a moon." Of all the relatives in John's life, Grant would emerge as the closest to John. The nephew admired his uncle as a fighter, a classy and well-groomed guy, and a ladies man. Even Uncle Harry, though he was a great street fighter with nicknames like "Hurts" and "Demo," acknowledged Grant's pugnacious reputation. Grant did much to enhance his nephew's boxing skills.

He wasn't, however, able to soothe his nephew's anxieties and fears that arose from hitting opponents.

Incredibly, John's father, Sylvester, was not aware that

John Mallo was his son until after the first four or five bouts. Dom Bepp was partially successful in shielding John's identity from immediate family members. Sylvester became aware of the situation after being offered a chance to make an "easy thousand" on a fight. He understood the offer after showing up for a fight and witnessing his son's devastating left hook.

Silvio Fiorello, an East Harlem resident and lifelong friend of John, was not personally at ringside for the fights, but he still knew John's state of mind at the time:

He was always punching like a professional on the speed bag in the Boys Club on 111th Street. No champion could punch a bag better in the whole city. Maybe two or three guys could punch a bag like John. He was always training like crazy, hand over hand, legs sticking straight out, rope climbing in the gym. Looking for John, you had to look up at the ceiling. If he hit ya, he'd kill ya... [the mobsters] knew he was a flake, but they couldn't control him. They would pay him $225 to $250 to fight while betting thousands on him. Nobody knew who the hell he was. Even though these guys were halfway decent fighters, they didn't stand a chance. He reminded me of [Mike] Tyson at that age.

Yet the love of punching a speed bag did not transfer over into the satisfaction of hitting other fighters. John Malangone, despite his success, was not a pugilist at heart. Defending a stable horse and his mother's honor were exceptions that were governed by overriding emotions. He suffered anxiety and panic attacks in and out of the ring and was haunted by fears that he would kill someone during a fight. These attacks would usually follow the end of a fight, with an opponent down and his mouthpiece laying several feet away on the floor. Hitting the speed bag was one thing, but punching opponents was another matter. Hitting the speed bag was an obsessive-compulsive kind of "fun" that allowed John to forget about his troubling inner thoughts. Boxing success did not produce the same personal satisfaction. The boy did not think of sports in the same competitive way that others did. It didn't help the kid's psyche when he was nicknamed "Lefty Long" because mobsters said that if the kid ever hit anyone with his right hand, he would kill that person.

A past image of a neighborhood mobster would surface in his mind...

We gonna call you a killer, kid...

Fear and panic attacks would surface because of these comments. The fear also extended to neighborhood situations outside of the ring. John, despite his immense strength, avoided confrontations where arguments usually escalated into street fights. Near the horse stables there was an empty lot that was home to open-air mob crap games and people playing stickball with a water-soaked Spaldeen tennis ball. Too often, John would fire fastballs at a chalk marked strike zone on the brick wall, and some opponents regarded the unintentional "brushback" throws as too close for comfort. Occasionally one would get upset and try to taunt John into a fight. Despite the provocations, John would turn and walk away, past the crap games and Brownie's Candy store, and onlookers would relay word to Sylvester Malangone, who in turn vented his rage at his oldest son.

Whatsa matter? The fucking scumbags come to me! They said you were pushed around like a fucking baby! You embarrassed me, ya fucking coward! Get out and fight the goddamn bastards!!

John's brother Sal also couldn't understand his brother's reluctance to defend himself. After being the object of a few beatings by bigger neighborhood punks, Sal turned to John for help, urging him to go "beat up these guys." Help never came, and the response was usually a "go home and forget it." No one understood what John was really thinking.

Uh uh, I can't do it. No way. I am afraid if I hit him, I'll kill him...

John, fearful of his "killer" right hand, switched to his left hand to finish off his opponents when boxing. From a practical standpoint, the left hook turned out to be just as effective, if not more so, than the "lethal" right hand. On one occasion, after a typical bout, John wanted to check in on his opponent:

I would go in the other locker room and see if the guy I just knocked out was okay. I mean, I hit him good. The trainer or some other guy would say "Whaddya doin'? Whaddya want?" I said, "I wanna know how he's doing, that's all." The guy reached for a gun and said "Get the fuck outta here!" Father Joseph and Paulie come running in, grabbing me, "Whaddya doin'?" I explained while I felt a nervous twitch forming around my lower lip. They said, "You don't do that, for Chrissakes!" After that fight I had one more bout "fooling around" with some guy in the ring. One left hook to the ribs and the guy yelled, "Fuck you!" He walked outta the gym sideways [laughing].

Father Joseph was the first to hear the teenager's pleas that he needed to stop. John initially complained to the priest that the gloves that he had to fight with were too big. The priest explained that large gloves were necessary for safety reasons. Father Joseph's response was proper and correct, but unfortunately he unintentionally inflicted damage on the kid's already troubled psyche when he replied, "No, you will kill somebody." For John, that was enough. Fear would well up inside of him at the very thought of the priest's words. John also remembered Uncle Grant saying, "He can fucking hit like thunder." He didn't understand Grant's words at first, but after being in the ring, he was able to comprehend the meaning and its possible implications. Grant himself didn't realize the powerful effect of his words on the teenager.

Yet another flashback...

Youse gotta notch on your belt, kid...

Memories kept the panic attacks coming.

He explained to Father Joseph he could no longer stomach "legs that were shaking and the foam that was coming out of the fighters' mouths." The priest was not happy; he hinted that John "might get hurt" by people in Dom Bepp's social circle if he didn't continue to fight. Father Joseph eventually relented, reluctantly agreeing—perhaps with Dom Bepp's blessing—that maybe it was time to stop. Whether the hoodlum priest was making money on the betting of John's fights is not known. John's boxing career came to a halt, but only temporarily. Dom Bepp was not happy, but he eventually relented—for the moment.

The flashbacks were in the back of John's mind every day and in nightmares every night. Images replayed in the troubled youngster's head would always motivate him to participate in a frenzy of strenuous activity, which resulted in drawing the attention of the New York Yankee organization. His mind would always replay the fateful events that occurred one warm summer evening in late June of 1937...

Chapter 5

No One is to Speak of This Anymore

Little Italy
East Harlem, NYC
Summer 1937

John had just turned five years old in the summer of 1937. Two of his aunts, Yolanda and Margaret Panarese, both recalled that their nephew was a "tough kid" for his age, being a little bigger and stronger than the average five-year-old. John was always willing to challenge or defy authority, feigning indifference to spankings or any implied threats to tell his mother about being disobedient. When Margaret discovered that pinching and twisting the boy's cheek proved to be effective behavior control, the boy realized that he had met his equal. Pinched cheeks were painful, so toeing the line was a preferred option for John, who remained fun-loving and energetic. His best buddy was his uncle, Orlando A. Panarese, seven years old and the youngest child of John and Sylvia.

Orlando A. Panarese was the baby of the family and loved by everyone. He was a very handsome boy, with stunning features not shared by the rest of the family. His blond hair, topaz eyes, and pleasant disposition earned him the nickname "Sunny." In a family photo, the boy radiates a photogenic aura, posing in a saddle on a neighborhood pony. He had an innocent demeanor, and his general behavior never warranted punishment. This contrasted sharply with his nephew John's behavior, which attracted physical punishment and constant scolding. Despite the contrast between the boys, John and Orlando were best friends and always played together. Their bond had been unbreakable, until fate intervened one warm June evening.

At the time, East 114th Street between First and Second Avenues was an extremely busy thoroughfare, jammed with horses, occasional automobile traffic, and pushcart peddlers, who were selling pots, utensils, clothing, and just about anything considered edible and desirable for the local Italian clientele. In the middle of the block were the stables, where Clydesdale horses were housed and maintained. The din of noise and confusion of street activities at times made it an unsafe environment for the children of the neighborhood; their activities often required adult supervision. Children typically played in apartments or up on the rooftops, where playing space was sometimes shared with pigeon coops.

John and Orlando were usually watched by all the Panarese girls: Lena, Yolanda, and Margaret. That particular evening, the girls and their mother, Sylvia, had left the building to sing in a church choir at Our Lady of Mount Carmel Church. As Margaret and Yolanda recalled, "It was the feast of the Immaculate Conception or some saint or other. There was always a celebration going on." John Panarese was at work on the railroad. Josie, John's mother and Sylvia's eldest daughter, was in a neighbor's apartment, indulging her reputation for neighborhood gossip. Anna and Sal were with her at the time. John's father, Sylvester, was busy gambling in a card game with known associates in the nearby candy store hangout. The elder Malangone (a.k.a. Doc Holiday) had developed quite a reputation playing poker, hearts, and pinochle, and enjoyed letting his opponents know what cards they were holding during the games.

This left Delfino (a.k.a. Duffy), Sylvia's son and Orlando's older brother, watching the boys in the Panarese apartment. Delfino was in a window watching the street below, waiting for his brother Grant to return home with a horse-drawn peddler cart used for selling tomatoes, onions, and other assorted produce. Grant's return home sent Delfino scurrying downstairs, with John and Orlando right behind him. Despite the prohibition of playing downstairs, the two boys seized the opportunity to go outside without any admonishment from Delfino. Grant busied himself securing the mare in the neighborhood horse stable next to the apartment building. He did not notice John and Orlando. When finished, he went upstairs with Delfino, but the boys remained in the alleyway beneath the building.

John, ever playful and imaginative, spotted a broken umbrella in the alleyway and pulled a loose wire from the apparatus. Taping the loose wire to a broken broom handle, he now envisioned himself as a track and field athlete tossing a javelin. The boy had watched people throw "spears" at nearby Jefferson Park. Moments after emerging onto the sidewalk from the alleyway, John took a few steps back and then threw the contraption towards a sand pile in the front of the stable. For a guy who would later be the legendary "rifle arm from Little Italy," and who would possess uncanny accuracy, he was about to make the worst throw he would ever attempt in his life. Instead of landing in the mound of sand, the "javelin" struck someone in a group of boys standing next to the pile. A scream of pain and a chaotic commotion ensued, and suddenly two feet, protruding outward from the crowd, were visible upright on the sidewalk.

John knew he was in trouble the moment he released the makeshift spear, but now his fears were compounded by the color of the socks on those two feet on the ground. The socks did not match, but John knew they belonged to his uncle, Orlando; the mismatched socks were the same combination that was on John's feet. John was already wishing he could have outrun the spear and caught it before landing. An adult neighbor who witnessed the scene removed the wire from the side of Orlando's head. Despite the initial shock and pain, Orlando appeared mostly fine with some minor bleeding, and he was escorted upstairs. Sylvia and the girls returned home from church and administered cleanup and tender loving care to the injured boy. Matters settled down, at least temporarily.

The calm following the accident didn't last. Yolanda and Margaret explained what happened next.

We didn't understand the injury. How deep could it go? It looked like a tiny pinprick. After one week in bed, Sunny began complaining of pain and headaches behind his ear. Our mother [Sylvia] tried a home remedy, thinking the tiny cut would heal, but the infection must have been much deeper. She took him to Beth David Hospital blocks away. The doctors cut open the tiny hole and blood shot up in the air. We think the doctors cut an artery and made things worse. They stopped the bleeding and Orlando came home again.

Another week passed, but Orlando got worse with more pain and convulsions. He was in such dreadful pain. Sylvia took the boy to Little Flower Hospital on 96th Street, but nothing helped. One day, we [Yolanda and Margaret] went to the hospital and snuck up to his room to check on him. We knew right away something was wrong. He was delirious. He told us, "Tell Delfino I wanna go on the horse downstairs." We told him Delfino is not there. He [Sunny] started screaming "Don't you say it! Tell him I wanna go on the horse now!" We were kids, but we realized he was not right. We ran home and told Sylvia, "Something is wrong! It doesn't make any sense!" She dropped her wash boarding and hurried to the hospital. She watched her son convulsing in his bed and screaming in pain...

That was the last time any family member would see Orlando alive. The next day, on July 10, 1937, the beloved Panarese boy took his last breaths and passed away. The news hit the close-knit Malangone and Panarese families like a thunderclap. Reeling from shock, no one could believe what happened. Years later, family members would always say the antibiotic penicillin would have probably saved Orlando's life. Unfortunately, in 1937, the drug was still a few years away from being used in clinical trials and being heralded for its medicinal properties as an antibiotic.

The Panareses decided to place their son's body in an open coffin in their apartment. Various family members were assigned to watch John and prevent the youngster from entering the room where his uncle was laid out for the wake. The intent of the adults was to shield John from the obvious, but despite everyone's best efforts, the mission failed. Fiercely determined to discover what was happening upstairs, John finally managed to slip past everyone responsible for watching him and keeping him out of the Panareses' apartment. Having just turned five years of age, he did not initially grasp the reality of seeing his best friend lying in the coffin.

U´zi! Scètate!! Sòssate, jamme fore a jucà! U´zi...
Uncle! Wake up!! Get up, let's go out and play! Uncle...

Sensing no response, John slowly stepped backward away from the body. Suddenly there was a loud scream from Sylvia Panarese, horrified that John was in the room. John became immobile like a statue and deaf to any sound. Sylvia then dragged her grandson into another room, which housed pictures of both Orlando boys and lighted candles. John described what happened.

I was frozen. She grabbed me. I didn't hear any sound after that. She pulled me into the "church" where there was a shrine with lighted candles. I started to hear again, nice and easy... I heard her say out loud, "God, please don't take this one!" I lost some hearing after that. Being in that room, I started to believe in sanctuaries. That's why I would also go to churches for relief.

Sylvester Malangone was Orlando's godfather, and it didn't take him much time to start verbally attacking and screaming at his wife, Josie, for her negligence. After all, he wasn't going to take any responsibility for being absent from the scene; it was the woman's job to manage the children. Playing cards "with the boys" was a male entitlement. Family members, understanding the accidental tragedy, pleaded with him to back off and leave his wife alone, but to no avail. John's mother maintained her silence through the entire ordeal. Following the burial rites, in a belligerent display of frustration, Sylvester dangled his son John by both ankles, upside down and outside of a fifth story window in front of Sylvia Panarese and screamed, "Do you want me to even the score?"

Reflecting on the terrifying moment years later, in his standard wisecracking manner, John commented,

I was upside down watchin' the number of clotheslines, tryin' to decide which ones to grab on the way down [hee hee].

Sylvia Panarese, all business and meaning what she said, quickly put a stop to the bizarre incident by warning Sylvester:

Put the kid inside before I throw you down.

For Sylvia, the matriarch of the Panarese clan, Sunny's death was a huge blow, and it would be a long time before she got her authority and composure back to the level that she was accustomed to having. She never expressed anger at John, realizing the tragedy was an accident. However, it didn't stop her from demanding answers from her daughter Josie, exclaiming, "Where were you?" The relationship between mother and daughter was forever altered, with guilt now a major and influential component in their daily lives. Other family members would regard Josie as beholden to her mother's wishes at all times after the funeral.

Margaret and Yolanda recalled some startling behavior on the part of their mother.

We were shocked. He was the baby. I [Margaret] dropped out of the choir, I was so angry at God. How could this be allowed to happen? My mother would go downstairs, show the young boys out on the street Orlando's photo and tell them that he would be coming out to play. She went on tranquilizers and lay down all day long. She got pregnant again, but had a miscarriage. Our father would sleep during daylight hours because sometimes he worked night hours on the railroad. Everybody got silent, nobody wanted to talk. We were all on our own. We learned to survive because we were strong.

Sylvia Panarese eventually rallied, and as if anyone needed a reminder, she then placed numerous photos and candles along one apartment wall commemorating the deaths of both Orlando boys. Her children had always been reminded of the first Orlando's passing with an empty hook on the apartment coat rack. Now, they would be constantly reminded of two Orlandos. The room began to resemble the shrines and alcoves with lighted candles that were an integral part of nearby Our Lady of Mount Carmel Church. Orlando's death preceded the annual Feast of Our Lady of Mount Carmel street procession, where over one hundred thousand Italians would gather and pray for various miracles. There was no religious miracle in store for Orlando's death or John's suffering. Every time John entered the Panarese residence, he saw the pictures and they constantly haunted him. Even worse for the five-year-old was his grandmother's dictum that "no one is to speak of this anymore." This declaration, according to many family members years later, originated from another one of Sylvia's dreams, in which the recently deceased Orlando admonished his mother, "Mommy, leave Johnny alone. Don't bother Johnny anymore."

Family members would assure each other that the tragedy was an accident, but no one spoke to John and reassured him. The result was a growing demon in John's mind, fueled by the guilty assumption that he murdered his uncle. John remembered (with a sense of humor),

I used to wet the bed. I was ashamed. My mother used to hang the sheets out. It was target practice for the pigeons [laughing].

Sylvia would attempt almost daily to soothe her grandchild's suffering, not understanding that her mandated silent treatment was making matters much worse. Word on the street that Malangone was a killer only reinforced the growing psychological trauma that governed the boy's behavior. The boy had nowhere to turn for help or guidance. The name-calling would drive the boy off his block and into hiding. By the time a mischievous John Malangone crossed paths with Joe DiMaggio at Yankee Stadium one summer day in 1946, his behavior was out of control.

Chapter 6
The Redcoats are Coming

Yankee Stadium
Bronx, NYC
Summer 1946

One point during John's recollection of early Yankee memories was emphasized very clearly...

I didn't know anything about the Yankees. I heard of Joe DiMaggio because people in Harlem were always talking about him. I heard "Jolting Joe, Joe D, DiMag." People in East Harlem were betting on him and Ted Williams and Stan Musial to combine for a total of six hits in the same day. Hundreds and hundreds were bet every day. Not many were winning that one... it wasn't easy to get six hits between those three guys. Some people were losing their shirts.

Breaking into a familiar ear-to-ear grin, his black eyes lit up as he started laughing about the mathematical odds of those three famous players being able to pull off that minimum number.

Reminiscing over a cup of black coffee in Craig's Deli in Little Ferry, New Jersey, a favorite spot close to his home and heart, John Malangone continued with a story of events that unfolded one summer day in 1946.

After the war, a Mr. Harrington ran the predominately black Red Shield Club [a youth club] up on 147th and Lenox in Harlem. He loved me, Mr. Harrington... thought I was a great athlete and great fighter. Hey, I've been hitting the bag since I was six, ya know?

John explained that cultural exchanges between black kids in West Harlem and Italian kids in East Harlem through youth clubs were not uncommon; defusing racial tensions at that time was a priority.

Me and Paulie were always looking for freebies, so we would go to shows and stuff with the Red Shield Club. We saw Edward G. Robinson in 17 and Oklahoma, with guns going off on the stage. This kind of cooperation went on for close to a year. One day we go to Yankee Stadium. All the kids sat in the right field bleachers. Like I said, I didn't know who the Yankees were, I had no idea. I heard of Joe DiMaggio, but didn't know where he played on the field. I started to get involved in the game. While I am watching, I am learning.

Late in the game, me and Paulie snuck out of the bleachers, and ended up near the railing where first base was. Nobody stopped us from going down to empty seats by the railing. The ushers in redcoats didn't pay attention to us. I don't remember exactly how it happened, but [Phil] Rizzuto, stretching a single into a double or trying to steal second base, was tagged out while sliding into the bag. The inning was over, and the players started switching sides.

At that point, Joe DiMaggio trotted across the infield and stepped on second base, headed for his usual spot in center field. He was unaware that a fourteen-year-old kid was causing a commotion by following behind him and sliding into second base himself.

While everybody was switching sides, I jumped over the railing, ran to second base, and slid funny. I hurt my leg. I didn't know how to slide. I got up and started running for the bleachers, where Mr. Harrington and the other kids, ya know, were sitting. I passed by the guy in centerfield, who was DiMaggio, but I didn't know it at the time.

He said to me, smiling and shaking his head, "Ya better get outta here, the redcoats are coming." When I turned to look, boy, a whole lotta ushers really were coming!

Recalling what looked like an army of redcoats chasing after him, John began cracking up, with that loud, easy laughter of his...

I headed for the bullpen because a Yankee pitcher opened the gate to let me through and I kept going to the back of the bullpen, where two other guys opened another door and I ended up under the bleachers, but not outside the stadium. The redcoats were all old men and they had to make an effort to catch me, but nobody was gonna catch me. I was too fast, even with the hurt leg. They opened the bullpen gate and door because no one was gonna tackle a fourteen-year-old.

The area [under the bleachers] was jammed with people buying cotton candy and soda, so I jumped a turnstile, but a cop stood right there and yelled, "Hey you! Whaddya doing? Why did you do that?" He wasn't angry, just concerned, and he didn't know anything that happened on the field. Then Paulie showed up, so I told the cop, "We're going home, officer..." He left us alone, and nobody arrested us, or bothered looking for us. Paulie came around the same way we snuck out, using a catwalk across the bullpen to get back to the bleachers and come down to the turnstiles. Paulie laughed, saying, "You coulda teached them how to slide." I said yeah, but I hurt my leg. I didn't know how to slide...

Then John said something very telling, exposing a truth about himself and his dark secret:

I could run with pain! I could do anything!

He was referring to coping and surviving with his mental pain and anguish; for John, the suffering was both physical and mental. He would often say, time and again, "I don't know how I did it." He switched back to the story.

Harrington didn't know that was me. Me and Paulie waited for the group to return to the bus to go back to Harlem. Never knew. He was like a father, but didn't always have control... no clue. If he did, he never said anything to me about it.

"Me and Paulie" was a phrase heard by everyone whenever John told a story or discussed any part of his life. Truth was, John and Paulie Tine were inseparable from the day they met; they did anything and everything together, seemingly destined to be lifelong buddies.

The kid had no appreciation, never mind respect, for meeting the famous "Yankee Clipper," Joe DiMaggio, or any of the other players in the bullpen. They were all accomplished icons in their baseball world. The irreverent, wacky, and tough kid from the mean streets of Little Italy met the famous businesslike athletes in constant pursuit of excellence. John's sacrilegious antics on the field that day in Yankee Stadium, a divine cathedral for baseball's heroes, resembled a baseball version of "encounters of the third kind."

Incidents where fans enter the playing field are not

uncommon, but usually they are quickly forgotten. Not on this particular occasion. The incident was an opening chapter between a neighborhood boy and a famous sports franchise. With each passing day, the kid with the black tousled hair, dark eyes, and that silly grin was developing into an exceptional athlete with tremendous strength. In time, the Yankees would take notice. Unfortunately for the organization, no one would have the insight or knowledge necessary to handle and shape the teenage prodigy. The kid, haunted for nearly a decade by his dark secret, would be back in Yankee Stadium, reappearing like a human boomerang and driving himself and the organization crazy.

Chapter 7
John's World

East Harlem NYC
1940s

John's behavior at Yankee Stadium was no different on his home turf in Italian East Harlem. The neighborhood of East Harlem has showcased many famous Italian eateries over the years, such as Rao's Restaurant and Patsy's Pizzeria. For generations, numerous photos of celebrities and politicians have adorned Patsy's interior walls. Since its inception in 1933, the restaurant has enjoyed immense popularity with customers from all over the New York metro area. During John's time as a teenager, well known Yankee ballplayers frequented Patsy's for dining. Many of them were Italian themselves and were familiar with the surrounding area, so it was no surprise that Joe DiMaggio would visit the famous restaurant often. As fate would have it, the "Yankee Clipper" was sitting in Patsy's one evening, enjoying his meal, when he paused for a brief moment. He spotted a familiar face in the young kid sweeping the sawdust on the floor and cleaning out spittoons. DiMaggio said nothing, simply eyeballing the kid. John did likewise to the baseball legend, and returned to his tasks at hand. No words were spoken and there were no smiles of acknowledgement that evening. DiMaggio would represent the first Yankee contact with John in his neighborhood, and others from the Yankee organization would visit soon.

The baseball scouts would return to the neighborhood looking for talent, but John's potential would not be apparent to Joe DiMaggio that night. The Yankee centerfielder would possibly only see a teenage troublemaker in John, that or a smart-ass kid who had fifteen seconds of fame in Yankee Stadium and then faded into oblivion. A potential ballplayer? No one would have given it a second thought.

Unbeknownst to him, DiMaggio shared company with plenty of other observers in East Harlem who viewed the Malangone kid as a wild teenager. The entire neighborhood around the Malangone household on 114th Street was aware of the boy, his reputation for having killed someone, his enigmatic habits, and his puzzling behavior. John often disappeared from everybody's sight, only visible when entering and leaving the building where he lived. Stares, whispers, and taunts from neighbors haunted the young boy, who found hiding places outside his immediate neighborhood that helped him escape the daily torment. Yet at times, he would wear that silly grin of his and appear absolutely carefree about situations that should have mattered, or at least been taken seriously.

There was another brush with the Yankees that was not related to baseball. John operated a bicycle cart for the Jacob Ruppert-owned brewery down on 98th Street and Lexington Avenue. Ruppert was a beer baron who owned the Yankees. Although Ruppert passed away in 1939, ownership of the brewery remained in Ruppert family hands. The employment opportunity proved temporary when, in a moment of inattentiveness, the kid turned to watch his cart roll downhill four blocks to 94th Street, hitting a variety of objects along the way and crashing into a car. Flashbacks of Orlando were continuous...

That javelin, hurtling through the air... over and over and over again... Like an endless video loop, I couldn't get it out of my head.

The Malangone kid would often stay in the alleyway beneath the family's old tenement building, where many apartments shared a common hallway bathroom. The Malangone family was fortunate that its residence had a bathroom, but the toilet and tub shared space with the tiny kitchen. There was little privacy for family members. When he wasn't in the alleyway, John would hang out on the rooftop of the building watching flocks of pigeons leave and return to his father's cages.

He was rarely ever seen on his 114th Street block, preferring to leave the neighborhood by scaling wooden and wrought iron fences behind tenement buildings and emerging onto 113th Street. Often his destination would be across Third Avenue, a few blocks away. That area included his grandfather's place, the John Malangone Barbershop, and the Seahawks Club. On occasion, John and Paulie traversed Third Avenue by entering a sewer tunnel beneath the street. The elevated train line was nearby, and turnstile jumping at station entrances became a Malangone trademark for traveling out of the neighborhood. Hazards were seemingly unavoidable; numerous accidents would characterize John Malangone's life, and falling out of a tree and impaling his leg on a wrought iron fence proved par for the course. The wild teenager would eventually have more scars than most people sporting full-body tattoos. When not climbing alleyway fences, the kid would jump tenement rooftops as an alternative method of moving from one place to another. John nearly slipped one day on a rain-slicked tile cap on the edge of a roof; a woman standing in an alleyway below screamed hysterically, with word rapidly traveling to the Malangone residence.

Though the kid had difficulty learning or focusing on tasks in general, he nevertheless managed to absorb some essential street knowledge—to keep his mouth shut and not ask questions about any activity occurring in certain places. After all, this was Mafia territory, with its members often serving as the only role models for neighborhood youngsters. His grandfather's barbershop, constantly cleaned by John and brother Sal, was merely for show. Secret meetings were always held in the back of the store, and they were off-limits to John and Sal.

Gambling was everywhere. The coffee shops, the backrooms of local businesses, apartment hideouts, basements, and even the confessionals in the churches served as staging areas for collecting wagers on everything from the daily numbers to horses to boxing matches to the number of hits by baseball players during a given contest. There were no limits to the stakes of gambling or what could be gambled. Young John watched his peers bet money on racing cockroaches that were identified by painted dots. Winning roaches were kept by bettors for future races, while the losers were simply hammered out of existence.

The teenager was used occasionally as a "gofer," running errands and delivering numbers slips or mysterious packages (usually cash). Sometimes the recipient was not a person, but a heavy ash can that was bottomless and covering a drainpipe in the sidewalk. The pipe would lead down into a basement where money and betting slips would be counted. Fake chimneys (dropouts) were also used on rooftops, where the pipes led to an apartment on the top floor of the building. John often operated as a gofer out of a men's hat and suit place on Third Avenue. In that store, he developed his friendship with Silvio, whose father-in-law owned the "business." The store, like others in the area, never sold anything to anyone. While Silvio became lifelong friends with John, it would take decades before he or anyone else, including Paulie Tine, would understand the inner workings of John Malangone. What Silvio remembers reflected a universal point of view of John at the time:

Nobody knew what was wrong with him... he didn't even know what was wrong with him. Every time he got close to doing something well [like the Yankees], he'd blow it. He would do stupid things.

43

John often annoyed people around him by having a smart mouth when it suited him. One incident involved his Uncle Harry. Harry owned a laundromat, but none of the washing machines actually worked. He was a tough guy who was widely respected by neighborhood associates because he would demolish any opponent in a street fight. John's brother, Sal, recalled the incident involving his beloved uncle and John:

My uncle's name was Enrico [Harry] Malangone. We called him Uncle Harry, although his street name was "Demo" because he reminded everybody of Jack Dempsey. He was always punching somebody. He loved us, looked over us, and used to say, "Where are you going? Need money? Here's a dollar." One day he came out of Sloppy Mike's Bar and saw one of the racketeers hit my brother. My uncle was short, but he beat the hell outta this guy. What started it? I dunno... but my brother was a little ballbreaker when he was a kid. He was wild and must have gotten under the guy's skin.

The young Malangone was exposed to violence on a daily basis, not only on the streets but in the home as well. Domestic violence was a Malangone family trademark that was well known throughout the East 114th Street block, as many people heard the family fighting on a daily basis. Discretion was absent as the neighbors witnessed firsthand fisticuffs, squabbling, and flying objects in the street, the hallway, and even out apartment windows.

Sylvester Malangone Sr. was a hot-tempered father who thought nothing of beating John with a leather barber strap. There was a long list of imagined and real transgressions committed by John during his childhood and early teenage years, and the boy would accept what was happening because he felt deserving of his father's unmerciful punishments. Guilt, as it would be revealed later in John's life, was a powerful force within the Malangone family.

I tried so hard to please my father, but I couldn't do anything right. I didn't fight... I felt I deserved it; the beatings were never enough.

While the Boys Club of New York branch on East 111th Street provided a respite from his unhappy surroundings, the block was dangerous as mob violence and shootings were not uncommon. Despite repeated admonitions from his parents to stay away from the area, John frequented the club and practiced his boxing skills.

The coal yard was also on East 111th Street, providing the shoveling work that teenaged John was eager to handle. Here too, the violence was inescapable. Next to the coal yard was Thomas Jefferson Park, built by New York City for the benefit of the neighborhood. John enjoyed playing in the park when few people were around so that he did not have to hear any tormenting insults from other kids in the early morning hours. One morning at sunrise, John and Paulie were climbing a steep pile in the coal yard to retrieve a batted ball that flew over the high fence bordering Jefferson Park. The stillness of the dawn was shattered by rapid-fire gunshots in an adjacent parking lot. The victim of the shooting had tried to dodge behind a car, but to no avail. His body was partially sprawled under the car and on the street curb. The rubout was witnessed by both boys, who remained hidden on top of the coal pile. News of the shooting sent John's mother screaming hysterically to the scene because it was rumored that the victim resembled her son. John was safe of course, but the incident would continue to influence the teenage years of the boy who had witnessed the murder from the top of the coal pile.

Besides Jefferson Park, there were other outlets when the teen needed mental relief from his personal troubles. One was the East River shoreline, which provided escapes from the grim realities of life that were weighing down the young man at the time. The pier at 107th Street, according to John,

...was a sanctuary of escape. It was great therapy. Everything was gone from my head, especially when the water was cold. Getting the shivers didn't matter. It was a great place to throw fruit at the passing ships.

However, the real challenge was for John and Paulie to traverse a crossing of the river near a wire factory, located at 119th Street near Randall's Island. Despite repeated warnings from marina cops about the inherent dangers of riptide currents in the river and whirlpools swirling under the Triborough Bridge, the teenagers swam there on numerous occasions.

The bridge itself attracted John for another reason. He would, on occasion, flirt with the idea of suicide as a way of ending his problems. His first jump was as a result of rejection by a waitress, who was flattered by John's puppy love overtures. The waitress had the same name as John's mother, Josephine. This appealed to the young man, who showed respect and kindness to the young lady, but that was not enough for the girl's mother. While shielding her daughter from John, she bluntly warned him, "Stay away... you already got one under the ground." John's negative reputation had preceded him, and he would not see Josephine again. Even years after the accident, a few mothers of local girls would always remind John that his past was the reason he was not allowed to date just anyone he found attractive.

His joy erased by the scolding of Josephine's mother, John became depressed and made a futile dive off an entry ramp to the bridge. Matters were made worse when he belly flopped right next to a passing patrol boat. Cops tossed a rope with a hook into the swirling waters, and the tool stabbed the kid's forearm. This enabled the cops to pull John to safety, while giving him another lifelong scar. Saved from serious harm or death, John was hauled into a station house and reprimanded for being a pain in the ass. A blond-haired desk sergeant recognized John and yelled at him for jumping. The kid replied,

Sarge, I didn't jump, I dove...

The sergeant shot back,

You SOB! You gotta be a fucking floater! Not in my fucking precinct... get outta here and stay out of my sight!

Being held for observation at New York's Bellevue Hospital in Manhattan was not automatic in that era.

Thankfully, John still had the church, and religion would provide some psychological relief for the boy. The neighborhood was heavily Roman Catholic, with churches on almost every corner. Our Lady of Mount Carmel, located on 115th Street, is an impressive stone structure built by the early arriving Italian immigrants in the late nineteenth century. The edifice is still standing and includes a bell tower that overlooks the surrounding neighborhood and houses the Statue of the Blessed Mother, officially blessed by the papacy in Rome. Thousands of immigrants over the decades have visited the church and prayed for miracles in times of despair. John and Paulie visited the sanctuary and lit candles every day. Paulie relied on his strong Catholic faith in visiting the church, while John depended on the sanctuary for mental relief.

The mental relief never happened for John. Despite holing up in the bell tower at times, there would be no miracle cure for anything. Unlike the Quasimodo character's grotesque looks in *The Hunchback of Notre Dame*, Malangone's deformities were invisible. Being near the church's deafening bell brought John some temporary inner peace when most anyone else would have been driven insane. Still, his mind was plagued by flashbacks.

The socks, when I saw one stripe and one solid color sticking out on the ground, I knew instantly who it was... I knew I was in big trouble. I wished I coulda outrun that throw and caught it before it came down.

Attempts at being a church altar boy during Masses failed miserably. John's presence was equivalent to being the proverbial bull in the china shop. Nervousness and lack of concentration turned the boy's participation into a comic tragedy. The solemnity of the religious rite was on occasion interrupted by the spilling of communion wafers, misinterpretation of directions from the priest presiding over the Mass, and even setting candle fire to the cloths draped on the altar. The boy did not possess the necessary attention span required of an altar boy.

John became well acquainted with Father Joseph during his stint as a boxer, and through his participation in the church. He had a dark olive complexion, tight curly hair, and although a man of the cloth, he had no illusions about the tough neighborhood of East Harlem. He routinely carried a dagger under his robe while he administered blessings and went about matters of the faith, as even priests were occasional targets in the neighborhood. Father Joseph was known as the "hoodlum priest," a well-earned moniker, for he was often seen in the company of reputed mobsters. However, the priest was a positive presence in John's life, and he oversaw many of the boy's activities during his teenage years, through boxing and eventually, the Yankees.

John's reputation with other local clergy wasn't always positive. Sadly, when the teenager expressed his desire to another local priest about eventually joining the priesthood, he was told, "Hoodlums [meaning John] don't become priests."

School was another part of John's life where miracles were nonexistent. Catholic and public elementary schools alike had trouble managing the rambunctious boy. Being placed in a nearby Catholic elementary school did not help matters. The nuns wasted no time using triangle-shaped wooden rulers to instill discipline in John, but they were not very effective.

They put me in Catholic school for maybe two months. I used to get beat by the fucking nuns. Flat rulers didn't bother me, but the triangle ones hurt. They were made of heavy wood. They used to say, "Put your hand out." When they went to whack my hand, I would move my hand and say, "Do it again." When I left school I took three of dem things with me [grinning broadly].

In junior high, a teacher nicknamed "Father" Hays made a special visit to the Malangone household to tell the parents, "Your son is crazy. There's something wrong with him." By the time he was a teenager, John ended up in the ungraded section of nearby Benjamin Franklin High School. The school was led by Dr. Leonard Covello, the first Italian-American principal in New York City. John admired and respected the man, whose leadership was instrumental to the school earning a national reputation for intercultural education. Even with the institution's credentials, the principal and the school could not improve Malangone's academic abilities. Throughout his life, John would refer to "the hammer and nails classes" that effectively barred him from participation in any school athletic activities. Only students pursuing regular academic courses were permitted to participate in after-school sports activities. Special education was not a term used to describe students with learning disabilities in the 1940s.

You hadda wear helmets and glasses in the hammer and nails classes. When people didn't hit the nails with their hammers square, you didn't know which way the nails were gonna go flying. It was a combat zone in there.

He remembers a group of students his own age being taught and sequestered on the first floor of the building. When asked why the first floor, he would always answer, grinning broadly,

There were some crazy people in there, you don't know how messed up some of them were... if there was a fire drill, I guess they [the administration] figured everybody would go the wrong way.

John's relationships with his teachers were generally upbeat, yet totally frustrating where academic improvement was concerned. The school had outstanding athletic teams, including a baseball team coached by a Mr. Spiegel. Spiegel was well aware of John's physical strength and desperately wanted the kid to play on the team instead of just being a volunteer batboy. The coach eventually approached an English teacher named Mr. Locke for help with John. Locke frequented the Malangone residence on his own time to try to help the boy learn to read. Despite his Herculean efforts, he failed miserably and made absolutely no headway. Even though the results were disappointing, Locke left the teenager with a positive impression of his caring attitude. Mr. Locke was a tall, thin black man who enjoyed the copious amounts of pasta that John's grateful Grandma Sylvia Panarese would prepare for every visit, which always helped ease the frustration of teaching the boy.

In spite of the collective efforts of caring faculty members, John never graduated and never received a diploma. At the age of seventeen, he was finished with secondary education. He never learned how to read, and it would bedevil him during the next five decades of his life.

On the home front, when not being beaten by his father, John would spend much of his time seeking some kind of spiritual solace from his grandmother. The matriarch of the Panarese clan, Sylvia would always play a major role in her grandson's life, and she proved fiercely protective of all the Malangone and Panarese children. Despite the children being exposed to neighborhood shootings, and racketeer social clubs, Sylvia was on occasion given to going along with the hijinks. On one occasion, she had permitted some numbers activity in her apartment. From her window, she spotted a squad of cops entering her building, apparently acting on a tip. But the police weren't fast enough at getting to the top floor. Before they reached her apartment, Grandma Panarese had scooped up the daily numbers receipts in a tablecloth and climbed out onto the fire escape, headed for the sanctuary of the roof.

The woman understood her beloved grandson's unspoken problem and mental anguish, but she could only do so much in giving John love and reassurance. A very religious woman, Sylvia would constantly light candles and recite novenas for her grandson, both in her apartment and at Our Lady of Mount Carmel Church. If John had the beginnings of a panic attack, she would administer ashes to his forehead. She regularly consulted a priest named Father Sal from the church for guidance on all family issues. She had a reputation amongst her neighbors for being a faith healer of sorts and curing various physical ailments. Yet, even the matriarch had her limits of curing with John's behavior. Her deep abiding faith could not stop the boy's frequent headaches and panic attacks or the constant bed wetting habits, which proved to be another family matter that wasn't discussed. Sylvia finally decided to escort John to Bellevue Hospital in downtown Manhattan for observation and some sort of mental therapy.

Bellevue is the oldest public hospital in the United States, having opened its doors in 1736. The facility has evolved through history to be a premier facility in medical care, and it historically pioneered evaluation and treatment of mental illness amongst its other programs.

Despite its reputation, on that particular day the hospital staff was not prepared to deal with the Grandma Panarese and John Malangone combo. Communicating with the pair would have left anyone wondering who was really crazy. John recalled the incident, smiling at the turn of events:

The only way you could get help in dem days was if a member of your family recommended you for help. I heard them [Sylvia and the Bellevue staff] talk about a lot of things that I did, ya know, and I know Grandma was trying to help me, but then I saw two guys in white coats coming towards me with this jacket that had heavy sleeves that reached the floor. I remember seeing a Popeye cartoon where he was strapped with a jacket like that. I saw some papers next to my grandmother that she had to sign with help from an interpreter. They were talking in some fast Italian dialect that I couldn't understand. But I knew once she signed those papers I wasn't gonna get out. She began to realize that while the interpreter was talking.

I said, "Grandma, they are gonna lock me up." I was thinking of Popeye again, this time squeezing a can of spinach and getting out of trouble. I pushed one guy away. As I ran for the door I grabbed my grandmother. She pulled her shoes off because she had high heels and she couldn't run. We started to run out to the lobby and this black guy opened the door for us, ya know, and shaking his head, said out loud to everybody, "They're both crazy…"

Chapter 8

The Alleyway

336 East 114th Street
East Harlem, NYC
1937-1949

While boyish pent-up energy often sent John off of his 114th Street block, he discovered an alternative for activity in the alleyway right under his own building. It was the same alleyway that was garbage-strewn, and the source of the umbrella used in Orlando's accident. The alleyway's layout would provide an ideal facility for John to develop throwing skills essential for playing baseball. Consumed by the surrounding fog of guilt, the distressed boy sought to punish himself and his arm by throwing baseballs, round fruits, and other spherical objects relentlessly, night and day, to the point of exhaustion, through a tunnel against the back wall of the alleyway.

Initially, leftover discarded peaches from local vendors were a preferred fruit of choice for throwing. Although messy, they were easy to grip and throw, and the splattered remains were always mysteriously cleaned up by morning. John would realize afterwards that the building super wasn't responsible for the cleanup; the local pet population was eager to eat the spoils.

This self-inflicted physical punishment became an unintended blessing in disguise.

Eventually acquiring some tennis balls or Spaldeens, the boy learned to throw nearly sixty feet from the open patio area of the alley, through a six-foot-high tunnel, against the back wall, which was made of cement. The back wall was actually part of a narrow walkway behind the building, which led up some steps to the ground level of the neighborhood. Any ball hitting the back wall would most likely bounce or roll back through the tunnel to where John was standing. Baseballs didn't last long, as the covers would quickly shred after smashing into the brick wall. To avoid any waste, baseballs without covers would be taped and tossed until they became useless. This was the Great Depression era, and improvising with scarce resources was a necessary survival skill.

Throwing and hitting the wall was a challenge because the tunnel was narrow and low in height, and it sported a dim light bulb in its ceiling. John soon learned the art of gripping and releasing his throws with maximum efficiency and control. Throwing low and straight to avoid hitting the light became easier as the years passed; young John not only acquired masterful command of his baseball throws, but he also developed his powerful throwing arm.

He often did this two to three hundred times a day. For every throw, the kid placed a marble in a bucket, with the blue ones streaked with white counting as double. John's sister Anna would always count the daily total afterwards.

The area was somewhat sealed off from public view and was private and quiet, eliminating potential stares from people walking outside on the street. It was certainly no field of dreams in baseball parlance, but for young John it was a great escape from the realities of everything around him. However, it wasn't long before the boy's obsessive presence down in the alleyway drew the attention of locals. Even though John had a fervent desire to be left alone, intruders would descend into the alleyway, mainly because they were curious. People wondered why the boy was always there and always throwing baseballs and various objects off of a wall. Word spread that the boy could throw pretty well, bringing Father Joseph, Dom Bepp, and some acquaintances down to see for themselves. The kid did not disappoint them. Some visitors would impart life-changing experiences to the withdrawn John Malangone, who was both impressionable and very vulnerable.

There were tenants in the building above the alleyway who did not care to hear the loud sound of a ball continually thumping against the back wall. The boy heard it over and over.

Ue' Giann!! Va a juca rint'u parc!
Hey John!! Go play in the park!

The complaints quickly vanished whenever Grandma Panarese watched from her bedroom window up on the fifth floor. Tenants learned to swallow their words if they discovered that the matriarch was staring at them.

Behind this alleyway, at ground level, was a high spiked fence that separated the alleyway and the rear of PS 102 elementary school, located on East 113th Street. The fence proved no barrier for a young, small black boy, who scaled the fence one day and made it down to the back of the alleyway. He approached John and asked if he could throw the ball, too.

Evidently, he must have been in the school. I don't know where he came from. I never knew why he came to me. He probably heard the ball banging against the wall a hundred times. It coulda been a week, two weeks, maybe a month... to me it felt like a thousand years, I was so happy. For the first time since the accident, I could play ball without thinking of anything that was going on in my head. This kid was like lightning. We played with the Spaldeen, hitting the ball in the courtyard in front of the alleyway. Using a sharp stone, he would write EH and JM on the wall and keep score. Sometimes I thought it was 3H, because I couldn't read the letters right. Those letters never looked the same. He might have said his name once or twice.

The therapeutic bliss would not last. One day, some "sons of wise guys," as John referred to the neighborhood thugs, appeared and immediately disrupted the playing in the alleyway. John recalled the incident with tears flowing down his face.

I felt terrible and guilty. These guys called him all kinds of names. One tried to kick him in the ass, but missed and got him in the back. He cried out in pain and I started crying. They turned to me and said "Whaddya doin'? What are you, a nigger lover? Whaddya doin'?" I was afraid they were gonna kick me too. I couldn't have a black boy playing with me. I never saw my friend again. Remember, this was 1937. For two or three months, I was wiped out.

Malangone's experience in racial relations did not end there. When he attended Benjamin Franklin High School as a teenager, he would play pickup basketball with some of the greatest black ballplayers of that era, including Floyd Layne, who became a nationally recognized college basketball player at the City College of New York. The strong relationships with some of these athletes spilled over onto the baseball diamonds the rest of his life.

The incident in the alleyway was never forgotten, and John recalled that years later, the assailant "had his ass broken by the mob for something else." John could not remember EH's name until some seventy-five years later, when he would bolt upright in bed one morning, suddenly remembering that EH stood for a boy named Edward House.

The alleyway, however, provided the basis for John to first meet his lifelong best friend, Paulie Tine. Paulie wandered into the alleyway one day, curious to see John after hearing about his throwing ability. Although Paulie was several years older than John, the age difference never mattered because the two boys formed an immediate friendship. Like Edward House before him, Paulie became "lightning" in John's world. Unlike Edward House, Paulie was a neighborhood guy who would not be harassed by local, young, "wannabe" wise guys. John and Paulie were linked by a common social bond. That bond was sharing traumatic experiences that left both boys lonely social outcasts. One suffered emotional distress and tried avoiding people. The other suffered from a physically disfigured face that caused other people, particularly adolescent girls, to try to avoid him. Over the years, Paulie Tine would have a reputation as a very kind person, but there was no getting around the open sores and pustules that covered his face. Young females avoided socializing with Paulie, as if he were a plague. Explanations for the cause of this disfigurement ranged from severe acne to scarring injuries suffered in a house fire. No one associated with Paulie ever knew the real cause. Regardless of the origin, John immediately accepted Tine as a trusted friend.

He would worry about his face night and day. When he talked to you, he would look away. I would touch his chin and move his face to look at me. I said to him, "See? It's alright." It took about a year before he looked at me straight in the eye. Before, he would never look at me. He didn't wanna look at himself in the mirror, and he was like me... I didn't wanna look at myself, either. I would break mirrors with a hammer. After a while we were like brothers.

The alleyway proved to be the basis for not only developing John into a professional athlete, but also for bonding two troubled youngsters into a long lasting friendship.

Chapter 9
Rise of the Rifle Arm

East Harlem, NYC
Mid 1940s

In the aftermath of the boxing spree, John returned to the usual activities that helped shape his physique. That meant shoveling coal and snow, simonizing cars, hitching and pulling carts, tending the horses in the stables, and anything else that would, in his mind, produce punishment and exhaustion. However, by the age of sixteen, the locals had recognized that "Lefty Long" owed his boxing success to his tremendous strength gained from working all those difficult jobs. At one of many of Dom Bepp's block parties, an opportunity arose to showcase that strength again in public. Dom Bepp was entertaining out of town mob associates from Chicago when he decided to impress his guests with some unusual entertainment. John recalled passing by the mob boss, when...

[Dom Bepp] said to me, "Hey, kid... come over here. See that car? The guy just called me and said his car won't turn over. I need you to turn it over. See if you can help the guy." So I go over there, and I knew what he meant. So, I grab the fucking running board and next thing ya know, ka boom, boom, boom, the car is rolling over [motioning with his hands]. Everybody went nuts! They just left it there. Later I heard they took care of the owner of the car...

The car was an American-made lightweight Crosley subcompact with a two-cylinder engine. It was strange in appearance when it was first manufactured compared to other automobiles at the time. The irreverent and wild side of John was exploited for a zany publicity stunt. Amidst all of the shock and eventual laughter and guffaws from Dom Bepp and his onlookers, the little car gave the appearance of an oversized Matchbox toy with broken windows and shattered glass. The boss had utilized the young Malangone's rowdy behavior for his purposes, and everything worked out perfectly. However, Dom Bepp wouldn't be satisfied until John served a new purpose for making money. If boxing wasn't good enough anymore, then perhaps swinging a bat in baseball would suffice.

East Harlem was a neighborhood where baseball and other sports provided a hotbed of activity. Kids played stickball games everywhere, although in John's youth the game was actually outlawed. If cops confiscated the sticks by chance, they would sometimes drop the sticks down sewer drains. After the cops left the area, kids would hold other kids by the ankles and lower them down in the sewers to fish out the sticks. The sandlots of Jefferson Park, the main outdoor recreation facility in the community, were always crowded with baseball games being played around the clock every day of the week. For the most part, John did not participate in these games and stayed out of sight. At the age of sixteen, he had minimal understanding of the game of baseball, but his physical tools allowed him to hit and throw almost better than anyone else. On occasion, he would hit and throw baseballs with Paulie Tine for the farthest distance, rather than for scoring runs against another team. He liked to play for play's sake, not playing to win. Fooling around on the sandlots was about having fun and maybe enjoying some bragging rights about throwing farther than anyone else. John's short attention span wouldn't allow thorough absorption of a baseball game's nuances. However, the throwing skills developed by John in the alleyway were being noticed.

He enhanced his strength and throwing reputation, impressing some neighborhood onlookers with an astounding baseball toss that landed on top of a newly built thirteen-story project building. New York City bureaucrats, intent on breaking up mob influence in the area, decided to tear down a number of tenement blocks and replace them with high-rise project buildings that were populated with newly arrived Puerto Rican immigrants. Regardless of the politics and demographic changes, the young Malangone viewed the newly constructed edifices as just another throwing challenge.

Sal, John's younger brother, knew of John's ability to hit and throw a baseball. One day in Jefferson Park, Sal pitched batting practice to John, but dropped to the ground, lying flat, after every pitch. It was a matter of self-preservation for Sal, who feared being hit by any line drive off of John's bat. Sal lost any control trying to pitch baseballs to his older brother. John, pissed off, gave up trying to swing at bad pitches, and chased Sal out of the park. It was the last time the two brothers would throw and hit baseballs for fun.

If someone had outstanding athletic ability in John's neighborhood, that person was going to be noticed. John looked older than his true age, and weighed over two hundred pounds. He was lean and muscular, sporting powerfully built arms and wrists. By the time the kid was sixteen years of age, he was sought out by Dom Bepp and influential neighborhood people for "money" softball and baseball games, where gambling set the rules for games and determined the competition. Anybody who was a participant in such contests was expected to excel, as too much money was invested in the outcomes to take chances on mediocre talent.

Dom Bepp had arranged a money game of windmill softball against an outstanding team of black ballplayers from West Harlem. He had acquired the services of a first-rate pitcher named Roy Stephenson from the renowned Grumman Aircraft softball team, which was based in Bethpage on Long Island. Stephenson was a five-time All-American windmill player who was later inducted into the ASA National Softball Hall of Fame. The team was managed by Red Borelli, a schoolteacher who later taught a young student named Ronnie Weiss, who would be the future "game changer" in John's own life. The game was played at Jefferson Park on a Sunday morning, a short one-block walk from the Malangone's apartment.

John was normally a batboy, a field liner, or a batting practice pitcher for these money teams. When he wasn't busy, he stood on the sidelines watching the game. Both pitchers dominated the contest that day. The game remained scoreless into the bottom of the eighth inning, when a runner reached first base for the neighborhood's team. Leaning against a chain link fence in a camel haired coat, surrounded by bodyguards, Dom Bepp motioned to and spoke with Borelli, who then inserted John into the contest as a pinch hitter. John got all of the first pitch thrown to him, and, in his words, "hit it into orbit." The base runner easily scored, but John wasn't as fortunate. The batted ball was a line drive, hit so hard that it ricocheted off an oak tree right back to the centerfielder, who promptly relayed the ball back to the cutoff man, whose throw nailed John at the plate. John's base running skills at the time were nonexistent. Recalling the putout, he jokingly said the tree was credited with an assist on the play.

Despite the putout, one run was all that was needed. The team went on to win the game, 1-0, after Stephenson struck out the side in the ninth inning.

Everyone celebrated a terrific win over a tough opponent and hugged John for the key hit. In gratitude, everyone on the team also contributed a buck for a collection for John. Dom Bepp gave the kid a handful of cash as well. The jubilant teenager returned home while the team went to a social club across the street from the field to celebrate. The party turned into a street festival with plenty of food for everybody, and the opponents were invited to join in as well. John explained that "the food was ten times the money," with gofers, as usual, being dispatched all the way downtown to Katz's Deli for fifty sandwiches.

When John returned home, he excitedly presented the winnings to his grandmother. That was a mistake.

Chisti´cà so´ tutt´i sord ch´aggia avuto ogge... accattata nà casa!
Here is all the money I got today... buy a house!

Eying the money in John's hand, Sylvia, eyes widening with consternation, was clearly getting ready to blow up over the cash.

Chi tà rate sti sord? Figl´i zòccola!!
Who gave you this? Son of a whore!!

John explained the softball game and the aftermath, but to no avail. The words "Dom Bepp" were enough for Sylvia to smack her grandson's face. Furious, she wasted no time grabbing a rolling pin in one hand and John's wrist in the other, and marched off to meet Dom Bepp at the club. Titans were about to clash. The respected family matriarch angrily confronted the mob leader. This was a privilege not accorded to male family members, who would have to suffer the wrath of a Mafia boss.

Figl´i zòccola... Lasc´ stà a nipot´ma!
Son of a whore... leave my grandson alone!

Dom Bepp replied curiously,

Che succiess?
What happened?

Sylvia repeated herself,

Figl´i zòccola... Lasc´ stà a nipot´ma!
Son of a whore... leave my grandson alone!

Dom Bepp defended himself.

Nuje limm´a rate i sord pecchè joca ´u bazeball. Stu juaglione joca veramente buon...Isse sape juca...

We gave him money for playing baseball. This boy plays really well. He knows how to play.

Grandma, clearly irate, waved at all the bodyguards and associates and yelled in clear English,

You are not going to do to him what you do with these fucking bums!

Undaunted and still waving her hands, Grandma flung all the loose bills at Dom Bepp, then turned, grabbed John, and stormed away from the block party. Dom Bepp, loving the exchange and watching bills fly all over the place, reflected,

I teng i sord...
I have the money...

Rather than feel offended, the mob boss took the whole scene in stride, and if anything, relished the attention and regarded the conversation with much amusement.

Departing the scene, but looking back at the money on the ground, John said out loud to his grandmother, "Are you crazy? You can buy a house with that money."

That comment prompted another backhand smack from Sylvia.

Dom Bepp was not alone in using John's athleticism to make money. In East Harlem, there was a Puerto Rican barber named Balbosa who often arranged and financed money games between Latin ballplayers who hailed from New York City or Spanish speaking countries abroad. Balbosa approached John about playing in a big money game involving game involving Puerto Rican all-stars in Central Park. John's excitement about traveling out of the neighborhood was tempered, once again, by Sylvia Panarese. She expressed her concerns about her grandson being the only "gringo" participating in an entirely Spanish speaking environment, where winning a baseball game for money was always taken very seriously. Eventually, Balbosa prevailed over the matriarch by respectfully speaking in Italian and reassuring the woman that John would be protected by two bodyguards at all times. Balbosa also sweetened the arrangement by buying John new baseball cleats, a bat, and a glove, since he did not have any equipment of his own. As Paulie Tine's presence was automatic, Balbosa also took care of John's buddy with new equipment.

According to John, the field in Central Park was mobbed with people "with picnics and tents," even lining the outfield perimeter, where a giant rock rested near centerfield. It was a very festive atmosphere. John watched from the sidelines as the game proceeded into the eighth inning, with Balbosa's squad trailing 2-1. The starting pitcher ran out of gas, departing the game with opposing runners on first and second, with one out. Balbosa summoned John to come into the game as a relief pitcher. Big bettors backing Balbosa's team began to fret, asking, "Who is this guy?"

Oblivious to everyone else's concerns, the "gringo" took to the mound. Again, John's athletic ability was initially overshadowed by his ignorance of how to pitch from the rubber embedded on the pitcher's mound; all four umpires yelled "balk" on his first pitch. The runners advanced into scoring position, and vocal complaints started getting louder behind Balbosa. John was then able to wind up and eventually struck out two batters to end the threat. Meanwhile, Balbosa was busy calming down his "investors" on the sideline, reassuring them that the "crazy gringo" knew what he was doing. Balbosa's team didn't score in the eighth inning, but John helped matters by striking out the side in the ninth inning.

In the bottom of the ninth, still trailing 2-1, Balbosa's team managed to place two base runners after the first batter made out. Thinking pitchers didn't hit, John was packing his gear when Balbosa told him he was due to hit. Balbosa had seen Malangone swing a bat for the fun of it on other occasions, so he knew what John could do. He also totally ignored "the brass" clamoring for the gringo to come out of the game. John would remember what happened next for the rest of his life.

I hit the first pitch, outta sight... that fucking ball went over that rock, and everybody standing out there... whatta shot... I couldn't even start running around the bases, people were running everywhere screaming and yelling. I'm looking for Paulie, I'm looking for Balbosa, I can't find the bodyguards. I didn't know where to go, but somehow I ended up heading for third base.

The two runners that scored ahead of John were sufficient for the win, and that proved to be a good thing as far as the winning bettors were concerned because the gringo never made it to home plate. Rounding third base, one of the bodyguards assigned to protect John slammed him with a bench grabbed from the sidelines.

Next thing I remember, I woke up in the hospital. I was in a coma for ten days. One of the bodyguards hit me in the head with a bench. He had money on the game, thousands, for the other team. Balbosa didn't know that... he went hunting for that guy. When I woke up, everybody was there. My grandmother put candles on my chest and ashes on my forehead. I woke up with double vision and said, "A nonna, ma che mè succiess? Grandma, what happened?"

I heard her speaking in tongues, and then she said, "Diu mio, pigliam `a mè! Lascial `a isso, e pigliam `a mè! Nun´tu piglià ghistu `ccà! Pigliam `a mè! Pigliam `a mè!

My God, take me! Leave him alone, and take me! Don't take this one! Take me! Take me!"

Balbosa had to close the barbershop, and he was afraid to face my grandmother. He was brokenhearted over what happened but gave me a fortune from the game.

John was lucky and escaped death. He did not receive a direct, full force blow from the bodyguard's swing. The kid had already experienced some traumatic incidents in his life. There would be more close calls in later years, and somehow he would manage to survive. For the ever-faithful Grandma Panarese, this was simply a miracle, with God answering her prayers.

Chapter 10

Praying for
Another Miracle

East Harlem, NYC
Summer 1949

John Malangone's relationship with Dom Bepp, however "positive" it might have been, took an ominous turn after John took off his boxing gloves. Having just turned seventeen, the kid was summoned to see Dom Bepp and was made an offer.

Wanna make a deuce? I want you guys to go in two vans to Winston-Salem, North Carolina. You're gonna bring back three tractor-trailer trucks. You're gonna drive them to a truck stop in New Jersey. You're gonna leave them there, take the keys, throw them away as far as you can, and run like hell.

John asked, *"What's in the trucks?"*

Dom Bepp replied, *"None of your fucking business. Don't worry about it. It's all legal."*

From Dom Bepp's perspective, John was the perfect recruit for this task. He was young, impressionable, and strong as a bull. He was constantly around Dom Bepp and his associates. John's personal reputation was terribly unfair and erroneous, but that didn't matter. Mobsters were saying what they wanted to say and, although sensitive and irate about the remarks, the kid couldn't do anything about it.

John learned that Jerry, Dom Bepp's chauffer, and several men he didn't know were to be involved in bringing the trucks north. Since Paulie was with John everywhere he went, he was included in the mission as well. The job involved leaving cash envelopes for the truck drivers of the rigs, who in turn left spare keys for Dom Bepp's men routing the trucks to New Jersey. John would not be required to drive, which would prove to be a blessing since he couldn't read road signs anyway. He recalled years later how the whole operation would have blown up:

I would have been asking the wrong people [cops], "Which way was the highway?" I woulda ended up in Chicago or someplace.

Dom Bepp had stated that the date of the trip was two weeks away. The gravity of the matter made John realize that if he were to go, he would be in the mob, and there would be no getting out. He had said yes to Dom Bepp, but there was still Paulie to deal with and John realized he had made a serious mistake. Paulie never said a word in protest to the idea, but he didn't have to because he wore his emotions on his sleeve. Tears were flowing, amidst his silent reaction. He too realized he was about to be trapped in the mob's grip.

John empathized with the desperate feelings that were showing in Paulie's face. The boys needed a miracle, with a deadline looming over them only two weeks away. Finally, John addressed the issue with his lifelong friend.

Paulie, we're gonna run away. Will that make you feel better?

Paulie: *Where are we gonna go?*

John: *Out west, I dunno, anyplace...*

Following the initial conversation, the two met again in Our Lady of Mount Carmel Church to light candles and pray for a miracle. In John's words, "I really fucked up big time." It was almost a betrayal of his best friend. Similar to other situations in his young life, suicidal thoughts began entering his mind.

I was trying to think what to do. I thought about the "shanty" down in Times Square. I talked to the soldier down there [at the army recruiting center] about joining the army. I told him I was eighteen. He said, "Go home, get your toothbrush, your sneakers, come back and you're in the army." I said, "What about my friend?" He said, "Tell him to bring his toothbrush and sneakers and he's in the army. We need soldiers."

The two boys decided that enlistment was the best method for getting away from any further threats to their lives. Before finalizing plans, John told Paulie on that first weekend after Dom Bepp's request that they would go down to Jefferson Park and "throw fruit together for the last time." This made Paulie happy, as it was something that the two boys did together nearly every weekend for fun.

Despite poverty, organized crime, and the daily grind that took a toll on the average neighborhood resident, good things also happened; on rare occasions, even a miracle or two occurred with divine intervention.

Jefferson Park was, and still is, a "crown jewel" of a park for neighborhood residents of East Harlem. Built around the beginning of the twentieth century by the City of New York, the park has endured right up to the present day, providing a source of many recreational activities. When John was growing up, the park was an escape for residents of all ages. Numerous bocce courts reflected the ethnic Italian neighborhood that surrounded the park. Several baseball diamonds and backstops accommodated the baseball frenzy that captivated successive generations of neighborhood kids.

The east side of Jefferson Park faces the Harlem River, and it is now bounded by the highway known as the East River Drive. Back in John's time as a teenager, the area was just a two-lane road; it did not deter youngsters and adults from reaching the piers that were jutting out from the shoreline along the river. The waterfront provided a measure of relief from the summer heat for neighborhood swimmers, and local kids enjoyed throwing fruit and vegetables at passing ships.

Sundays were quiet days in the neighborhood, and often pushcart vendors would look to dispose of unsold foodstuffs. The era of refrigeration had not yet arrived, and unwanted fruit was often used by anyone looking for mischief. It was not uncommon for John and other teenagers to toss the leftovers in any direction at any target of their choosing. Unfortunately, wild teenagers indulging in food fights were not welcome in the tranquil setting that the tree-lined park provided for nearby residents.

Responding to complaints from park users, local mobsters warned anyone wanting to toss fruit to take it out of Jefferson Park and go elsewhere, meaning the waterfront. It was a typical summer day when John and Paulie decided to visit the shoreline with leftover containers of fruit, obtained from the pushcart peddlers doing business along First Avenue. At an early age, John became an expert at hitting "bull's-eyes"; the targets being anything on passing ships in the East River that John considered entertaining or worthy of a physical challenge. The favorite targets were portholes. Peaches and apples were preferred for throwing, as John would later boast, because one could grip and release them like baseballs. Malangone became aware that he and Paulie were being observed by a pair of well-dressed strangers who were visiting Jefferson

Park that afternoon.

I saw the old men. Straw hats, white jackets... I said to Paulie, "They won't bother us." I saw the tugboat coming, and we got busy firing away at the portholes. Suddenly this man is standing there and says to me, "Hey kid, do you mind coming over to the ballpark? I want to see you throw a baseball." I said, "Sure."

The stranger continued,

Hey kid, how old are you? Are you playing with the high school [Benjamin Franklin] baseball team?

John replied that he was seventeen, and no, he was not on the team because the coach had informed him that he did not have enough academic credits. He did, however, pitch batting practice and served a role on the team as batboy. No mention was made of Coach Spiegel's desire and Mr. Locke's extensive attempts to make John a member of the team. The boy's weaker side remained hidden from scrutiny.

On entering the park, all of the youngsters were then encouraged to throw some baseballs as far as they could to the left side of the diamond, where there was plenty of space. There was a sign posted on the outfield fence, along First Avenue, which claimed a distance of 368 feet from the home plate area where everyone was standing. The man suggested the sign as a possible throwing target; he was unaware that John couldn't read and was baffled when the kid asked, "Is that the one with the numbers?" The question provoked both men to exchange glances with each other, wondering what to make of the boy.

Excited at the prospect of showing off his arm, John started throwing as far as he could toward the fence. For Malangone, this was a fun throwing contest, not related to a game of baseball or a potential baseball opportunity. Several enthusiastic attempts later, he hit the 368 foot sign on the fly, not once, but twice.

I threw one over the sign. I put on a show. Hey, this was fun! I told the guy, "Watch me do it again. I told him I can hit the fence on a fly! See the middle number on the sign?" After a couple of throws I hit the sign. "See that ashcan [dumpster]? I can throw one in there!" After four or five tries, it went in.

All those years of throwing in the alleyway and the waterfront, all those years of shoveling snow and coal, all those years of pushing and pulling horses, carts, and anything else that required physical strength and endurance—all those years had created a physical specimen that easily surpassed the talent and ability of the average seventeen-year-old and even most adults. No one realized that this was the result of guilt, and punishment that the teenager had intentionally inflicted on his throwing arm. Reaping the benefit of his extraordinary strength, John now enjoyed all of the attention he was getting when showing off his prowess.

The stranger was certainly impressed by the kid's rifle arm. Taking a card out of his pocket, he handed it to John. The bespectacled man then introduced himself:

I am Paul Krichell, chief scout of the New York Yankees. Please report to Yankee Stadium tomorrow afternoon.

The other gentleman was also a Yankee scout, Harry Hesse. Although flattered, John had no clue about finding the famous ballpark.

Yankee Stadium? Where is that? I don't know how to get there...

Surprised, Krichell offered an alternative.

You live in Harlem and you don't know where Yankee Stadium is? I'll have a limo pick you up right here at the park.

Another much-needed miracle was about to become a reality.

Chapter 11

All of Little
Italy Went Nuts

Yankee Stadium, Bronx, NYC
East 114th Street, East Harlem, NYC
1949

The Yanks, the Yankees, the NEW YORK Yankees—are
arguably the most successful and most famous sports franchise in
America. When the franchise moved to New York from Baltimore
in the early twentieth century, the initial name of Highlanders
soon gave way to Yanks, as it was easier to fit the team nickname
on newspaper headlines. In 1913, Yankees became the official team
name. The original Highlanders played at Hilltop Park at 168th Street
and Broadway in upper Manhattan. In 1913, along with the name
change, there was a field change; the Yankees began using the Polo
Grounds, home field of the New York Giants, a National League
championship team led by the fiery and legendary manager, John
McGraw. The Yankees, based in the American League, played the
role of stepchild to the Giants. Under McGraw's tenure since 1902,
the Giants won eight National League pennants and three World
Series titles, including two titles over the Polo Grounds stepchild,
the Yankees, in 1921 and 1922. McGraw despised his American
League rival, but the Giants' image of baseball dominance in New
York, and McGraw's larger than life persona, would soon make
way for their emerging Bronx rivals and a new showman in a player
named Babe Ruth. The Yankee team, on its third attempt, would
finally win the World Series over the Giants in 1923, in a new home
called Yankee Stadium. A new sports dynasty was born.

The name and field changes were only the first steps.
The franchise would quickly evolve in the areas of ownership,
management, personnel, players, location, iconic marketing
images, and winning traditions.

The players, and the scouts hired to find the players,
ultimately determined a team's reputation and value. The
franchise's increased popularity was owed to its roster always
being stocked with talent, even during off years. Some of the
team's players of the Dead Ball Era (1900-1919) would achieve
baseball immortality. Pitcher Jack Chesbro won an incredible 41

games in 1904. Frank "Home Run" Baker led the American League in homerun totals from 1911-1913. Baker earned his nickname by hitting two homers in the 1911 World Series as a member of the Athletics. He joined the Yankees in 1916 and finished his career in 1922 with the team. But Baker was soon overshadowed by the arrival of a competitor who changed the game, its standards, and everyone's expectations of greatness.

In 1919, one of the Yankees' most famous acquisitions involved a pitcher named Babe Ruth, sent from the Boston Red Sox to the Yankees for cash. The Yankee dynasty was born with the arrival of the most prolific homerun hitter anyone had ever seen. Ruth's presence signaled the end of the Dead Ball Era in Major League Baseball and the birth of a new era where fans paid to see sluggers and the long ball. The Babe's towering homeruns boosted fan attendance in all Major League Baseball parks and at the new Yankee Stadium.

Frank Baker would later comment about Ruth's presence, saying, "I hope he lives to hit one hundred homers in a season. I wish him all the luck in the world. He has everybody else, including myself, hopelessly outclassed." Baker's "hope" almost became reality when Ruth set a new homerun record of sixty in one season in 1927, and finished his career with an astonishing 714 round trippers. He became known as "The Sultan of Swat."

Yankee team success continued during the latter half of the Roaring Twenties, with new nicknames such as "Murderers' Row" (1927 Yankees) and "Bronx Bombers." The team now projected an image of archetypal batting sluggers who could dominate opposing pitchers and weaker teams.

Other monikers would also stick as the team's accomplishments and the ever-increasing fame of individual players would become the stuff of baseball legends. "The New Yorkers," "The Pinstripers," and "The Winners" all exemplified Yankee success and a winning attitude.

The team, with the addition of Joe DiMaggio and other new stars, continued winning right into the thirties and forties, and won five consecutive American League pennants and World Series from 1949-1953. By the time John was permitted to practice at the stadium in 1951, the Yankees had played in eighteen World Series, and had won fourteen of them. It was during this time that the young rifle arm from Little Italy would be exposed to the world of the Yankee organization, its personnel and its corporate business practices. The organization's point man with John would be the renowned chief scout Paul Krichell.

Born in the Bronx in 1882, Krichell found his way to baseball at the major league level, playing an uneventful eighty-five games with the St. Louis Browns in 1911 and 1912. During the early years of the Yankee organization, Krichell signed with the Yankees as a scout and worked thirty-seven years, signing more than two hundred prospects that included Lou Gehrig, Whitey Ford, Red Rolfe, Tony Lazzeri, George Stirnweiss, Tommy Byrne, and Leo Durocher. Krichell answered to Ed Barrow, the general manager and architect of the Yankee dynasty in its early years, as well as the owner, Jacob Ruppert. Krichell was highly regarded as a shrewd judge of talent. He managed to sign Phil Rizzuto after the young prospect was rejected by the rival New York Giants and Brooklyn Dodgers. Casey Stengel, manager of the Brooklyn club, allegedly told Rizzuto he was too small and that "he should go shine shoes somewhere." Rizzuto, of course, had a great career as a Yankee shortstop and became extremely popular in later years in the Yankee broadcasting booth, teaming up with ex-major leaguer Bill White. Rizzuto certainly contributed to the Yankee mystique and will always be remembered for his contribution to the Yankee lexicon with the expression, "Holy Cow!"

Years before watching John Malangone, Krichell watched future Hall of Famer Lou Gehrig hit a monster home run in a game at Columbia University and immediately sensed something special in the kid. Gehrig possessed tremendous power. Krichell was later quoted as saying,

I did not go there to look at Gehrig. I did not even know what position he played. But he played in the outfield against Rutgers and socked a couple of balls a mile. I sat up and took notice. I saw a tremendous youth, with powerful arms and terrific legs. I said, "Here is a kid who can't miss."

Paul offered Gehrig a contract, and the kid became a Yankee legend. Krichell's instincts were equally accurate that day he saw John Malangone in Jefferson Park; the kid had a special arm, no doubt about it.

Limo driver Paul Garcia arrived at Jefferson Park early the next day to pick up John, Paulie, and of course, the hoodlum priest, Father Joseph, along for support and perhaps an official blessing. Garcia was also the manager of a semi-pro team named the New York Oaks, who proudly wore discarded Yankee uniforms. Garcia transported John and company to the original Yankee Stadium, which stood at the time as Major League Baseball's great cathedral. It was also known as "the house that Ruth built" or, as local New York sportscaster Art Rust Jr. once put it, "the big ball orchard in the South Bronx."

Although remembering the ballpark as "bootyful," John was unfazed by the surroundings, and was not aware of the Yankee mystique. He had not been following the professional game as a teenager, despite the neighborhood's passion for Yankee games. Local mobsters would hook up speakers in front of Rao's Restaurant and other storefronts so shoppers and residents would be able to hear live broadcasts out in the streets. Local bookies would take bets on games and the total number of hits accumulated by certain superstars each day of the week. Malangone was oblivious to this entire sports scene. Years later, he would admit his knowledge of baseball, on a scale of one to ten, was probably a three at best under certain circumstances.

Entering the stadium, the kid was unfazed by the glass cases exhibiting the uniforms of Yankee legends, including Miller Huggins, Babe Ruth, and Lou Gehrig, and the monuments dedicated to them in centerfield.

Approaching the backstop area of the playing field, John excitedly anticipated another throwing contest and basically chased everybody else away from home plate. After throwing baseballs into the left and right field stands (300 feet away), he began concentrating on tossing balls into the outfield alleyways (400 feet away). The next challenge was centerfield, where the three monuments were located.

The kid was feeling great, although oblivious to everyone else's priorities. After all, this was an organized tryout with a group of young ball players hoping to make it to the big leagues.

Hey, this was pretty good for a throwing contest! Watch me do it again!

In the midst of this throwing frenzy, he was quietly approached by some bystanders holding bats in their hands. They were looking at the kid and wondering about his odd behavior. Reality began settling in for John. Casey Stengel, the newly hired Yankee skipper at the time, was present for the gathering and uttered his first words to the rookie:

Hey rookie, take it easy! These guys are waiting for batting practice! They need to take a few swings!

During his turn at bat, John ended up hitting one of those iconic monuments on a bounce, nearly 460 feet away. When practice was over, Mr. Krichell approached John about the next day's plan.

Listen kid, with that arm of yours, we are going to put you on the mound. You are gonna pitch the seventh, eighth, and ninth innings in a scrimmage game.

Krichell didn't realize it, but John's euphoria over the whole chain of events began to fade by the time the scrimmage got under way the next day. The forty ballplayers were divided into two squads, confusing John. In his mind this had become anything but a throwing contest, and it made him nervous. John asked Paulie to let him know when the seventh inning was coming. Yankee bird dog scout Ralph Perricone was John's catcher for warm-ups before the seventh inning that day, and he instructed the nervous kid to throw fastballs, nothing else.

Wherever I place the glove, that's where you throw fastballs. Got it?

John felt confidence flowing back into his body and replied with a wide grin,

That big thing? The glove? You kidding me? I can hit Japanese beetles on a wall from 100 feet. Give me three shots.

Perricone stared at John, hiding a variety of thoughts running through his mind while sizing up the kid. John was becoming a source of wonder to everybody. No one knew that the kid had thrown a baseball thousands of times in a hidden alleyway for over a decade.

Entering the game, John struck out the side in the seventh and eighth innings, and retired the side in the ninth, while adding one more strikeout to his total. But the day was not over quite yet. In the dugout, someone yelled,

Hey kid, grab a bat, you're gonna hit now.

Nervous, John picked up a bat and walked to the plate. He recounted the incident again, for the umpteenth time:

This wasn't a throwing game anymore… I started getting nervous again and almost had a panic attack. The pressure was building up. But I hit that first pitch into the upper deck in left field! In the old Yankee Stadium! Nobody does that! The Yankee brass, including Krichell and Ralph Houk [future manager of the Yankees], were getting out of their seats to leave, when they turned and saw the ball land in the upper deck.

At that point, Krichell asked Ralph Perricone, who was emerging from the dugout, to greet John…

Who hit that?

Perricone replied,

That was your rifle arm from Little Italy.

Krichell responded back,

Sign him and give him anything he wants.

The teammates jumped all over the kid upon return to the dugout. From the stands, Paulie cheered wildly, while Father Joseph was simply stunned and speechless.

Signing the contract proved no easy task. The next day, despite the presence of Krichell and Perricone in Little Italy, nothing was signed. Confusion at the sight of a sleek, black car turning the corner onto the block stirred a quiet 114th Street into a state of panic and fear. John's brother, Sal, was playing stoopball with his friends when he noticed the neighborhood racketeers.

They were hanging out on the sidewalks, the stoops, and the corner when the black cars [limos] turned on to the street. All of a sudden, the first two guys disappeared down some steps. Then two more ducked away. As the car came down the street, ding, ding, ding, they all disappeared like roaches. Everybody was thinking someone was gonna get shot. Window shades went down, doors closed and rooftop lookouts popped up all over the place.

The limo pulled up to the Malangone residence. Satisfied there wasn't some sort of attempted "hit" or trouble, some of the mob lookouts slowly reappeared in the street. Dom Bepp approached the limousine and asked,

Who are you…?

Getting out of the car, Krichell responded,

We're from the Yankees. We are here to sign John Malangone.

John was nervous about the Yankees becoming aware of his father's mob activities. Krichell and Hesse sensed that John himself was holding out for some reason; the kid sounded reluctant, perhaps because he felt a change coming that required him to leave the neighborhood. Dom Bepp, acting as an intermediary, facilitated a meeting between the scouts and Josephine Malangone and Sylvia Panarese outside the building near the limo.

Sylvester, John's father, wasn't prepared for the news and did not participate in the meeting. Packing a concealed weapon, he admonished John,

These guys were all bullshit! Phonies! They're feds! Do you believe these bastards? This is a scam! Why are you bringing these crazies around here? You're gonna get us, the whole family, all killed!

It would take the Yankees another trip to the neighborhood the following day to secure signatures and final consent that would allow John to sign with the team. Up to that moment, John did not believe the Yankees would return and negotiate another signing attempt. This time the neighborhood was fully aware of the limo, the visitors, and their purpose. The Yankee representatives brought calling cards and showed letters that authenticated the organization's presence. The limousine bore identifying Yankee logos.

Paulie Tine was present at the time. He went upstairs to the apartments and escorted Josephine, John's mother, and Sylvia Panarese downstairs to meet the visitors.

Sylvester Malangone was angry again, this time because Dom Bepp had wisely summoned him out of a busy card game in Brownie's Candy Store. He finally appeared at the limousine for the actual signing. He became convinced that John was not playing ball with the "Feds" and he agreed to be present.

Paulie, although left-handed, signed for John, Sylvester, Josephine, and Grandma to avoid embarrassment about the family's literacy issues. The signing was conducted on the trunk of the limousine itself; observing the crowd gathering in the street, Krichell and Hesse were not anxious to enter the building where the Malangone family resided.

Despite John's newfound status, Sylvester showed little joy or happiness. Only when fellow mobsters patted Sylvester on the back with congratulations and pressed the idea that he was going to be rich did he begin to show serious emotions that led to tears. Later, when the signing was over with, John discovered his father in the apartment, beating his bloodied fist on a nail embedded in the wall. John understood, with some ironic humor, the emotions that had engulfed his father at that moment.

He was pounding away and stabbing his hand with the head of the nail. The nail was where he kept the barber strap that he beat me with for years. He was mad at the nail, blaming the nail for why he hit me all that time. He didn't blame himself. He was crying. He said to me, "You put us [the family] on the map. I am so proud of you."

John was relieved that he finally made his father happy. It was something he had been trying to do for years, to no avail. While growing up, he continually asked his father to come down to the alleyway and watch him throw. All those years, his father continually rebuffed him, saying things like, "Later, I will be out in an hour" or worse, "Get the fuck outta here." He simply would not come out and support John. The beatings had actually stopped a few years earlier, because Sylvester realized his son was now bigger and stronger than he was. The kid was immune to any pain inflicted by that leather strap. Unfortunately for John, the verbal tirades and emotional abuse by his father continued right up to the actual signing. Despite the newfound peace between father and son, both men would continue to be driven by all-consuming guilt, which for different reasons could not be shaken off or forgotten. Neither father nor son would openly address John's issues, and the teenager did not know that his father was harboring a dark secret of his own; nearly a lifetime would pass before John learned the truth about it. The presence of the Yankees in his life would not present a solution for John Malangone's constant and hidden mental suffering.

Word of the signing rapidly spread through the neighborhood and within a week there was a giant celebratory block party again, this time with a grandstand practically constructed overnight. Dom Bepp and company spared no expense with food and entertainment for this occasion. Loudspeakers and an ethnic Italian band enlivened the proceedings that celebrated a neighborhood son making it to the Yankees. The sound of "oompapa, oompapa, oompapa" was heard everywhere.

John explained years later that the mob left him (and Paulie) alone after the signing, simply because the Italians, as an ethnic group, "owned the Yankees" in that era of baseball. There were a number of ballplayers with Italian surnames on the Yankees, and on the rival Brooklyn Dodgers and New York Giants as well. Dom Bepp's enthusiasm meant John and Paulie were off the hook for the trip to North Carolina—the miracle had come true. John commented, "This was the proudest moment of my life, no doubt about it."

The community's pride knew absolutely no bounds on this subject. Remembering the neighborhood's reaction at the block party, John summed the mood up nicely, smiling and stating, "All of Little Italy went nuts."

While the celebration was going on, a money collection for John was taking place. Dom Bepp, as was his custom, decided to chip in with a contribution of his own. After opening his wallet, Dom Bepp, in John's words, "took everything he had in that wallet and gave it to me."

Feeling anxious, John looked at his grandmother, who was observing Dom Bepp's generosity. She then glanced at John, who inquired if it was ok to take the money. This time, she approved of the gift, then turned, smiled, and bowed respectfully to the mob boss. Smiling as he did so, Dom Bepp returned the gesture. John became jubilant and handed over all the money for safekeeping to Sylvia Panarese. The two titans, mob boss and family matriarch, had finally managed to make peace.

Meanwhile, Father Joseph, present at the stadium, the signing, and the block party, couldn't resist answering an inquiry from someone in the media about all the fruit thrown and wasted by John and others out on the pier in the river. The hoodlum priest shook his head, commenting, "Tell the fucking bums we didn't have refrigeration."

One person was wary of John's signing with the Yankees. Grant Panarese, the respected athlete in the Panarese and Malangone households, held an almost solitary viewpoint about his nephew's future with the Yankees. Grant felt John would have been better off signing with the Chicago White Sox or the Cleveland Indians. The atmosphere on those clubs may have allowed John to survive professionally, whereas the corporate environment of the Yankees would not tolerate John Malangone's antics and wild behavior for long. Grant understood what was coming after the signing. He told his nephew, "You're gonna die there." A clash of disparate worlds was just beginning.

Chapter 12

Hidden Away

Greater NY Metropolitan area
Johnstown, Pennsylvania
Polo Grounds, NYC
1949-1951

The euphoria from the signing did not fade away immediately, and it would further benefit the good sentiment shared by John and his father. John was invited to a celebratory lunch that was hosted by John J. Lyons, the Democratic Bronx Borough President, who served the office for eight terms before stepping down in 1952. Lyons was immensely proud of the new Yankee prospect, and offered John a public service job if he ever needed one. The teenager declined the offer on the grounds that he was now a professional baseball player, and thought to himself, "Are you kiddin'? What, I gotta work? I got a job playing baseball." However, John seized the opportunity to request a job for his father. Lyons agreed and arranged a position for Sylvester in the highway department. Sylvester was listed in the 1940 national census as not having any visible means of support, and nothing had changed since that time. But like son, like father; Sylvester's reaction was, "Are you kiddin'? What, I gotta work?"

The excitement did not end with Sylvester's ultimate employment. Money, in the form of cash, was now being dispensed by the Yankees to John Malangone, albeit under questionable circumstances. The contract was not legal under the rules of Major League Baseball, since John was not eighteen years old. However, clubs looking to lock in promising baseball prospects for future use routinely broke the rules. Joe Garagiola and Stan Musial were two underage stars who exemplified the practice and temporarily stayed on lower level baseball teams, under the major league radar. Yankee management endeavored to keep John off the radar until his eighteenth birthday. Since playing in the minor league affiliates was obviously not an option, moving the promising rookie around various semi-pro leagues and amateur teams in the New York metropolitan area became a necessity for the club. Adding name alteration, similar to Dom Bepp's approach in boxing, was also a consideration.

It should be noted that John was warned, nearly a year before the Krichell and Yankee signing, not to sign with anybody. Among the many people watching John and other teenage baseball prospects during the 1940s was a baseball aficionado named Lou Haneles. Haneles held a unique distinction in baseball: he was a left-handed catcher. Although Haneles never progressed past the Eastern League at the age of twenty-three, he vowed to remain in baseball in another capacity. In 1946, Haneles was one of the co-owners and player/general manager of the Bloomingdale Troopers. He ended that year as owner/player/manager of the Walden Hummingbirds in the same league. Later, in June of 1948, Haneles sued the Brooklyn Dodgers and Branch Rickey for $100,000, claiming that the Dodgers illegally seized the Walden franchise and moved it to Kingston, NY. The Dodgers subsequently sold the Walden team to some Pennsylvania businessmen, but eventually lost the case.

It was during this time that Lou also got involved in running baseball camps, including one in the local New York area at Hunts Point, near East Harlem. The camp attracted local Harlemites, including Paulie Tine, who invited John along to watch the camp proceedings. Before long, Paulie was pestering Haneles to take a look at his friend on the sidelines. Haneles eventually acceded to Paulie's pleas, and was stunned by what he saw from Malangone. In a letter about John in 1995, Haneles commented, "He slugged the ball all over the stadium." Haneles allowed John to pitch batting practice and was stunned by the boy's rifle arm. Lou immediately saw major league talent in the Malangone kid, and inquired, "You are sixteen? Are you sure about that?" He told John any scout who saw him play would try to sign him. John would later visit other Haneles-operated camps in New Farmers Oval in Ridgewood, Queens, and Avon Park in Florida. Lou had advised John not to sign with any big league scout right away without his knowledge. But John at the time did not understand where Haneles was coming from and forgot about the fatherly advice. Krichell's presence in East Harlem erased any thoughts that John may have possessed about using caution. Lou would later recall,

I later found out that Krichell had not put a date on the contract, which is against baseball law. Not only did Krichell... pull the wool over the Malangones' eyes but it is still an illegal baseball contract because John's high school class had not graduated yet. The baseball rule was that no player can be signed to a pro contract unless the boy had graduated or his class had graduated.

To further illustrate his point about the illegality of contractual signings, Haneles claimed the Yankee organization did the same thing to Bernie Williams, who attended the Haneles' baseball school in Cheshire, Connecticut. The date on the Williams contract was not entered until the future Yankee star turned seventeen years of age. In Haneles' opinion, both athletes would have been declared free agents by the Commissioner of Baseball. However, the Yankees at the time of John's signing had an edge that prevented legal hassles or Malangone family objections: the illiteracy issue in the Malangone household. The inability to read often leads to personal intimidation, and John and his family were not about to challenge the corporate presence of the Yankee organization.

The Yankee organization's cash payments to John were not matched by any fiscal discipline, especially when such matters involved shoe boxes. The cash meant freedom to spend because there would be more of it as time went on and John continued his baseball career. The money was more than John was accustomed to seeing, and spending it became addictive. After the signing, John and Paulie wasted no time spending cash for a new Cadillac that was purchased uptown from a dealer on 125th Street. Money was no longer an issue. No driver's license? No issue either, because everybody knew how to drive a car anyway. Wasn't riding around in mob-owned Caddies sufficient instruction in the finer points of safe driving? "Driving school? What, you kiddin'??"

John offered Paulie the keys as "the first to drive my car." No sooner did that happen, when Paulie managed to crash into the safety gate on the nearby Willis Avenue Bridge, between Harlem and the Bronx.

Paulie slides around the corner and vavooooom!! [Hee, hee] After that, that car wasn't worth a dime. So, we walked, and left the car there. We went back to the dealer and said, "Something wrong with that car, it doesn't wanna go." The dealer says, "We'll get it towed." I said, "No, I don't wanna do that, something wrong with that car." He says, "Whaddya wanna do?" I said, "I wanna another one. I'll buy one." The money I got was like chickenfeed, ya know? The Yankees kept sending me bonus money, in dribs and drabs, ya know, not checks, because I wasn't eighteen and they had to hide me.

The second car that was purchased was a Lincoln Mercury, a car that would earn the moniker "Hotel Mercury" during John's minor league years.

Following the contract signing with the Yankees, John also provided money for cosmetic surgery on Paulie's face; the subsequent "scraping" of the bumps left Tine's face no better than before the surgery.

The business of baseball, from the standpoint of Yankee management, became a reality with John's entry into the sprawling world of semi-pro baseball, with numerous teams and leagues spread out across the city's five boroughs and surrounding metropolitan areas. Beginning in the early spring of 1950, John Malangone began his organized baseball career with the Glendale Tigers of the Queens Alliance League. The Tigers were founded and initially managed by Frank Herbert. Frank managed the team to a title in 1945, before stepping down and leaving the team in 1946 for the Yankee farm system. The team had a proud history of famous and semi-famous ball players who went through their organization, some making it to the big leagues. This included the legendary Yankee shortstop Phil Rizzuto. The Queens-Brooklyn area was a hotbed for baseball, with the Tigers' home field, Arctic Oval, actually located at the intersection of Johnson and Varick Streets over the county line in Brooklyn. John joined the Tigers for a weekend, early in the season, in his words, "pitching for a couple of innings under the name of Tipinelli. The Yankees were trying to keep it Italian."

John ended up playing all around the New York metro area, and he developed a reputation as a valuable player. He would occasionally be offered cash to play in some of the games. Playing for a team called the Nebells, he pitched and won one game against a powerful semi-pro team named the Mohawks, whose home field was in Pelham Bay in the Bronx. The team's roster included the Colavito brothers, Rocky and Dominic, and eventually a young pitcher named Stanley Lewis, who would play with John nearly fifty years later in the Roy Hobbs World Series in Florida. Despite the presence of the Colavito brothers and a powerful Mohawk lineup, John recalled "shutting them down in that game." Rocky Colavito later turned pro and played for the Cleveland Indians, Detroit Tigers, Kansas City Athletics, Chicago White Sox, Los Angeles Dodgers, and the New York Yankees.

The team also played several money games in Dexter Park in Woodhaven, Queens, against the renowned Brooklyn Bushwicks, whose origins can be traced to the years preceding World War I.

During the summer of 1950, John and Paulie even briefly

participated in some baseball barnstorming tour games with the Kokomo Clowns, a travel team based in Waterbury, Connecticut. This baseball/basketball outfit was founded by a promoter named Howie Davis. The group eventually became the basis for the Harlem Wizards basketball team. Paulie had traveled everywhere with John, whether he was playing with Malangone or not. When Paulie did get an opportunity to play, he did not disappoint; his talent was above average, and he did attempt a brief foray into professional ball in Nova Scotia. When the attempt proved unsuccessful, he returned to New York and followed John everywhere.

Despite joining the baseball leagues as a pitcher, the Yankees decided on a different approach for the teenager, preferring to take advantage of John's bat and moving him off the mound to catching and outfield positions, with an occasional third base for variety.

The Yankee scouts, Krichell and Harry Hesse, kept watch on John's participation and whereabouts off the field. So did Johnny Johnson, another Yankee executive. The entourage was completed with the presence of a future Hall of Fame catcher, Bill Dickey.

In 1946, Bill Dickey ended his legendary catching career with the Yankees, actually guiding the team as player/manager to a third place finish. Dickey returned to the Yankees in 1949 as a first base coach and mentor to the now famous Yogi Berra. Inheriting Dickey's uniform number eight, Berra would eventually reflect with a typical Yogism on his mentor, "Bill Dickey is learning me all of his experiences."

However, Dickey viewed John in a less than confident perspective. His experiences with John were not positive and would mirror the opinions of other Yankee players who would cross paths with Malangone in future years. Dickey was a "bird dog" scout who was serious about his professional duties. Although John's "demon" was relatively quiet during that 1951 summer, Dickey, according to John, "told me he saw something in me he didn't like." Dickey insisted that his catchers should catch low and learn a series of exercises that would reinforce his point. No one in the Yankee hierarchy seemed to understand that John had never really played the position before, and the adjustment proved somewhat difficult for the boy. Dickey did not limit his personal comments as the summer season got under way. He regarded John as "a little clownish," "someone who lagged behind," and asked, "Are you from Dakota, kid?" Dickey's implication, from John's perspective, was that John was a little laid back, or perhaps mentally slow.

Dickey would be inducted into the Hall of Fame in 1954. A year later in the spring of 1955, he would appear with a business-like demeanor as he posed with John and a smiling Mickey Cochrane (another Hall of Famer) for a possible promotion photo with the Yankee club. The look on Dickey's face in the picture did not appear to be an enthusiastic endorsement of the young protégé squatting next to him...

Dickey's impressions during this time period did not dampen John's baseball reputation, and it did not dampen his behavior on or off the field. Fellow ballplayers usually considered John likable and funny, always into something or other. One player recalled the story of a Central Park visitor, minding his own business and flying an airplane on a string. He became alarmed and agitated by the presence of a baseball player standing nearby, threatening to shoot down the plane. Wandering away from a nearby baseball game, John pretended to shoot a small rifle, while actually holding a bat. Malangone, ever grinning, was simply having fun, albeit at the stranger's expense and rattled nerves.

Then there is the story of the blind manager of an opposing team, the Hudson Guild, and his daughter, who worked as a communicator between the team's players. John's reputation as a fearsome hitter was already established with his rivals. During one at bat, as John stepped to the plate, the daughter announced his name to her father. Upon hearing the name Malangone, he immediately reacted by demanding that John be intentionally passed. Someone politely explained to the manager that this was maybe not a good idea because the bases were already loaded, with nowhere to put John. The response was the same. "I don't care, walk him. Are you crazy?" If John wasn't laughing then, he surely must have later in the same game when the situation repeated itself.

It was during the 1951 season that John would find a mental comfort zone playing in the New York City Baseball Federation League under manager Sam Susser and a ball club known as the New York Sultans. The Sultans were one of the premier semi-pro teams in the greater New York Metropolitan area and its players prospered under Susser's leadership. Susser realized that something was going on with John's wild personality, but (unlike Dickey) he took the time to nurture John's baseball potential. Susser was patient with John's antics and constantly encouraged the youngster's play on the diamond.

The Sultans had a 34-2 record that season when Susser led the club to Johnstown, Pennsylvania, home of the famous 1887 flood and the now highly regarded Johnstown Tournament. The city gave birth to the All American Amateur Baseball Association (AAABA). The group's founder was the late Glenn L. Martin, whose technology company preceded the Lockheed-Martin Corporation. Martin bequeathed money to support the tournament's growth after his death in 1955. The weeklong tournament began actual play with a limited field of teams in 1945, and by 1951 it had rapidly grown in popularity. The Sultan players, having played on crowded, hardscrabble fields in New York City, regarded Johnstown's beautiful fields as pure baseball heaven. The New Yorkers caught the attention of the local media not only with box score results, but also with their personal reflections on the ball fields in the area. *The Johnstown Tribune*, a local paper, quoted Sam Susser as saying, "Give us one of those fields for an entire summer and we would even take on the Yankees." Further emphasizing the point, the team wished it was closer to the area so that it "could play in Johnstown every day."

With a sensational winning summer season and Johnstown as a backdrop, the Sultans went charging into the tournament, pounding Wilkes-Barre 17-7 and Buffalo 14-7 on successive days. Despite yielding six runs early to Wilkes-Barre, the Sultans, led by John's clutch hitting, pounded away at opposition pitchers for nineteen hits. John hit a two run triple in the first inning and followed up in the fourth inning with one of the longest homeruns ever hit at Roxbury Park, good for three more RBIs. John recalled the game being interrupted after the homer so the distance could be measured. When asked what the distance was, Malangone could only recall that "the first number was a five, like Joe DiMaggio." The offensive juggernaut continued the next day as John and teammates Frank Savia and Lou Forino each collected three hits against Buffalo. John hit his second homer in two days, this one going over a fifty-foot-high screen in left field.

However, the team's fortunes took an abrupt turn during the remaining two games in the tournament. A low-scoring affair ensued against the eventual champion Brooklyn Cadets, who won a 5-3 decision. The Cadets were managed by Jim McElroy, who knew his opponents very well. McElroy helped to build the Brooklyn Cadets into one of the most successful amateur baseball programs anywhere. Still active and on the Cadets Board of Directors, McElroy, recollecting his memories of John, described him as follows:

A tough, hardnosed player, who came to play, and we respected that. He was always smiling, whether he threw a ball from the catching position into centerfield or threw the guy out. He was a happy-go-lucky guy… he could be over exuberant, but he never meant any harm to anyone.

After playing left field in the two previous games, John became a catcher, not always remembering to wear a chest protector. John converted a wild infield throw into a double play by backing up first base and tossing out a Cadet base runner, taking his time returning to first base after the infield overthrow. The loss to the Cadets would take its toll on the Sultans' pitching staff. Down after the first four Cadet base runners crossed the plate, the New Yorkers never caught up. The Sultan pitcher, Al Bowen, even added a two-run homer of his own to make the score close in the ninth inning, but the Cadet pitching prevailed. John managed to get only one hit; he also found himself ejected from the game in the eighth inning after arguing a force out call at second base.

The Sultan pitching staff was now depleted by a lack of rest, and it showed in the final game. The team would lose to Baltimore in a high-scoring affair, 16-13.

The attractive surroundings and the electricity surrounding the Johnstown Tournament helped to provide some mental relief from the recurring sickness plaguing John; however, youthful indiscretions nearly put it back in the forefront on several occasions. John struck up a conversation with a beautiful girl in the hotel where members of the Sultans were staying. While the conversation went well, the resulting infatuation with the young lady led John to get off of the elevator on the girl's floor instead of his own floor. Sensing that John was following her to her room, the woman warned John that she would call the police if he didn't leave her alone. Panic and apology set in simultaneously, with John returning to the elevator immediately. Despite his fear of an impending panic attack, John was able to return to his room without further incident and his anxiety slowly subsided.

Filling in free time, John, Paulie, and Frank Salvia watched a movie at a local theater, but were disappointed with the show and complained to the ticket seller about how the film was simply awful. Carrying on, they didn't stop there; they not only demanded a refund for themselves, but everyone else's money back as well. It didn't help matters when John kept pointing a finger at the cashier in such a manner that the woman told police that Malangone had a gun. The cashier's phone call to the local police brought sirens and flashing lights, followed by a typical "We were just kidding, sir…" response and the usual look of youthful innocence intended to help smooth any tensions.

The summer of 1951 provided the young slugger with a prestigious hometown showcase for batting prowess. That year, the *New York Journal-American* newspaper ran an all-star game in the Polo Grounds. The game pitted teenaged all-stars from the five boroughs of New York City against nationally recognized all-stars. The players were selected by knowledgeable representatives from the *Journal-American*. A photo taken after the game shows John standing near Al Kaline, a future Hall of Famer with the Detroit Tigers. Kaline received the Most Valuable Player Award for the game. Included in the picture was John, wearing an all-star game jacket, no doubt happy he slugged a ball, although foul, over the left field roof. John recalled watching the ball drop down to the street below through an opening behind the left field stands.

Malangone's success also began generating questions from baseball people wondering how old John really was. He looked older than his age and his physical skills were far superior to that of his peers at the time. The happy moments at the *Journal-American* game and the Johnstown Tournament were still overshadowed by one important factor in John's mind: he was "under contract" to the New York Yankees. Krichell sent John an invitation to work out with the Yankees whenever the team was scheduled to play at the stadium.

The glory years of semi-pro baseball in New York and elsewhere were rapidly coming to an end in the early 1950s; the departure of black players to the major leagues, declining attendance and revenue, air-conditioned rooms with televised baseball games, automobiles and the ability to drive to major league parks, plus other forms of entertainment, such as golf and auto racing, all contributed to the demise of various semi-pro leagues. Nowhere was this more evident than at Dexter Park, home of the Brooklyn Bushwicks, where the team played to large crowds for decades. By the time John went to the Yankee spring training in 1955, both the Bushwick team and Dexter Park had vanished into fading nostalgic memories.

Chapter 13
I Need a Church

East Harlem, NY
Maracaibo, Venezuela
Quebec, Canada
1950-1952

During the early years of its relationship with John Malangone, Yankee management had endeavored, as much as possible, to keep the kid occupied and away from East Harlem. The team was well aware of the dark temptations and dangers that were present on the mean streets of the neighborhood, and they encouraged John to be busy in any way possible, especially with baseball. There were a number of East Harlem Mafia social clubs, and John, now a baseball celebrity, was welcomed in them. There were a number of club photos of wise guys posing with the newest Yankee, who was wearing his 1951 *Journal-American* All-Star jacket, and looking awkward as well. This was precisely why the Yankees had reasons to be concerned, although such photos were never made public.

The mob controlled the neighborhood, but there were other antisocial elements as well, particularly in the form of gangs. The Harlem Red Wings were the most notorious, vicious, and difficult to control. The group used Shep's Candy Store on the corner of 115th and Pleasant Avenue as a hangout. The meeting place was located right across the street from Benjamin Franklin High School. The gang constantly tried to entice John to join, but he managed to avoid them whenever he could. Brother Sal was persuaded to join, but he dropped out after meeting the future love of his life, Dolores Scalone. The gang's leader, who went by the nickname Pepsi, was killed by an FBI agent on 110th Street in 1951.

Despite a previous suicidal attempt off of the Triborough Bridge when he was younger, John, along with Paulie Tine and others, was caught diving off of the Willis Avenue Bridge, between Harlem and the Bronx. John did not sustain any injuries, but the Yankees found out about the incident and questioned him about possible motives for the bridge-diving attempts. His answer was simply, "I always do that [laughing]."

There was a notable and positive exception to the Yankee perception of the neighborhood's image. A local gentleman nicknamed "Lefty Mike" Sacino served as an unpretentious role model for East Harlem youngsters. Sacino organized baseball games and practices in Jefferson Park for all of the kids, including John and Paulie. Sacino grew up loving the game of baseball and at the age of twenty was offered a contract by the Jersey City Giants. Told by his mother that "baseball is for bums," Lefty Mike gave up the baseball opportunity and found a job with New York City instead. He continued sharing his sports passion with kids of all ages, including his son, Gary. Lefty Mike, Gary, John, Paulie, and neighborhood friend Dan Benedetto eventually played together on various semi-pro teams after high school. The Sacino family, including daughter Evelyn, who had a teenage crush on John, proved to be a positive influence on John and other East Harlem youth.

Despite the organization's proactive stance, trouble would always find John, even when the demon was momentarily quiet. One evening John had escorted a date to an RKO movie theater in the neighborhood. During the visit to the theater, he entered a men's restroom, forgetting his father's advice:

My father told me to never walk into any place where the door opens in... because otherwise going out, you won't have the strength to crash that door fast enough [frowning]. Not thinking, I opened the door. One guy is by the sink, one guy is hiding in the toilet, and one guy is behind the door. The door shuts, and I am trapped. These guys planned this, waiting for the first asshole to come in there. I happened to be it, ya know? They asked me for my money. I had eleven dollars on me. The guys by the sink and toilet start moving toward me and the guy behind the door had a carpet knife, saying, "Give me your money."

I put the money in the sink, but the guy with the carpet knife said, "Take off your clothes." I thought they just wanted to rob me, but now it is do or die. He never finished the words, because the other two went down "Ba Boom!"... a left, then a right... they didn't know my tremendous strength and both of them went down, knocked out. The guy with the knife was drugged up. I put my left arm out and he sliced it four times, got me good. I could hear the rip on the front and back of my forearm, and my finger was almost cut off. There was blood all over the place and he starts coming at me. I put my arms together and ran forty miles an hour at him. He never expected that and I pushed backward on the door and

his neck caught on a clothes hook. I was screaming my brains out.
The cops came, saw the bodies on the floor, and wanted to know
what weapon I hit them with...

John was rushed to the hospital. The cops at the scene, seeing the futility of dealing with drug addicts, had told John to say he "got cut on broken glass." The early prognosis included doubts that he would play ball again, but surgery proved successful, and the Yankees never found out about the incident. Over thirteen years had passed since the kid was first labeled a killer, and it seemed violence and trouble in one form or another would always be present in his life. John would leave East Harlem as his teenage years drew to a close, but the neighborhood circumstances that shaped his character would never leave him.

The Yankees, through Paul Krichell's invitation letters, continued to welcome John to work out in the stadium whenever the team was playing home games. Malangone ended up participating in workouts with the team in the summer and fall of 1951, when not playing for Sam Susser, the Nebells, or anyone else. John had also spent two years playing third base for money with the Harlem Outlaws. Generally speaking, the Malangone kid possessed a broad, affable smile that attracted "best wishes" handshakes and "lotsa luck" greetings from most of the Yankee personnel. John even got along with Ralph Houk and Mickey Mantle, two people who would sour on him years later. The same could not be said of Bill Dickey, mentioned previously, or Yogi Berra, who, in John's opinion, was "very cold" to him.

John often mixed up names of Yankee players, including the famous Joe DiMaggio. It took John a while to associate DiMaggio's name with number five on the back of his uniform. When not referring to the Yankee Clipper as Charlie Keller (the team's right fielder), he took to imitating the Yankee star by following DiMaggio everywhere in the dugout and locker room. If Joe put his jersey on first, so did John. If Joe tied his right shoe first, so did John. DiMaggio, while never acknowledging any previous encounters with John, finally sat the kid down and gave him timeless advice: "Don't be a follower, be a leader." Although John did not smoke, he was so enamored with DiMaggio's presence that he requested a smoke from the star player. DiMaggio responded by offering John use of a personal cigarette lighter with his initials on it; John has always cherished that special moment as a reminder of the short time spent sharing the Yankee experience with DiMaggio.

Perhaps more than anyone else was a special bond that

developed between John and the Yankee skipper, Casey Stengel. "Casey loved me..." was a familiar refrain of John throughout the years long after his Yankee days came to an end. Any mention of Stengel would always bring a smile to John's face and laughter because Casey was "just like me."

The skipper had his own reputation, earned in part because of his temperament, nicknames, aggressive play, and clownish behavior. Leonard Koppett, a respected twentieth century sportswriter, once described Stengel's behavior as that of "an overage juvenile delinquent."

A young Charles Dillon Stengel was schooled in "small ball" by a pro ballplayer named Kid Elberfeld during Major League Baseball's Dead Ball Era. Elberfeld's hot temper and fierce, combative attitude toward opponents earned him the nickname "Tabasco Kid." Elberfeld's tenure in baseball even included a short stint as manager of the New York Highlanders, the forerunners of the Yankees. Under Elberfeld's tutelage, Stengel eventually made it to the majors with the Brooklyn Dodgers, and later by playing for the New York Giants in the World Series from 1921-1923 against the New York Yankees. Despite his reputation, Stengel was beloved by Giants manager John McGraw for his hustle and aggressive play.

Mike Kahoe, scout for the Washington Senators, once commented, "He's [Casey] a dandy ballplayer, but it's all from the neck down." It wasn't long before Casey (K.C., as Kansas City was his place of origin) or Dutch (for his German ancestry) developed his eccentric reputation, and baseball stories about Casey quickly sprouted like summer crabgrass. Some tales seemingly belonged in *Ripley's Believe It or Not!* files. While in spring training with a Montgomery, Alabama farm club, Casey discovered a manhole cover in the outfield. Realizing he could fit in the small space below the ground, Casey hid himself from view while lifting the cover just enough to watch any activity elsewhere on the field. Stengel's mysterious disappearance got everyone else wondering what happened, until a fly ball hit in his direction prompted him to pop out of the hole and catch the ball.

Perhaps the story with the most zaniness involved an incident where Stengel, then with Pittsburgh, was playing right field one afternoon in Ebbets Field in 1918. He noticed a bird hit the outfield wall and drop to the playing field, completely stunned. Picking up the bird, Casey placed it on his head and covered it with his cap. He then trotted towards the dugout and grabbed a bat for hitting. The Brooklyn crowd unleashed a chorus of catcalls at the former Brooklyn Robins player. Casey tipped his cap to the fans just as the bird came to its senses and flew off the ballplayer's head. The stunned onlookers switched from their catcalls and jeers to cheers and applause for Casey's vaudeville act.

Stengel arrived in 1949 as the new manager of the Yankees, much to the consternation of the veteran ballplayers, who had little respect for the man. Joe DiMaggio declared, "They've hired a clown." Phil Rizzuto, Yankee shortstop, wasn't happy either, having remembered Stengel's shoeshine remarks. Despite the team's deep reservations, Stengel was supported by George Weiss, Yankee general manager, who believed the clownish character was actually a very shrewd baseball aficionado.

By the time Krichell invited John to practice sessions in 1951, things had dramatically changed for Stengel's Yankees. Despite all of the less than flattering initial reactions to Casey's arrival, the club had won World Series titles in 1949 and 1950, and they would eventually win three more titles between 1951 and 1953. Three of those championships were at the expense of the "Bums" from Brooklyn. Casey had changed the coaching staff, adding Bill Dickey, among others, to work with Yogi Berra and other prospects. Stengel also introduced the platoon system to the Yankee lineup; this involved using one player alternately with another player in the same position, producing dramatic results. The manager learned well from the tutoring of Elberfeld and John McGraw. Winning five consecutive titles would not be a bad start for a "clown" running the showcase franchise of Major League Baseball. Stengel became beloved by the New York media, which would call him the "ol' perfessor" and which would enjoy his verbal ramblings and "Stengelese" sayings.

Pressure was building inside of John's mind over participation in team workouts. Yes, there was a natural nervousness when he had played in an intrasquad game at the time of the signing with Krichell, but this was different now. This was serious business—the Yankee way. The intrasquad game before the contract signing was fun because he did not realize the gravity of the situation.

Reflecting back on the early years with the Yankees, John acknowledged the anxiety that consumed him:

Most of the Yankees were nice to me, but I spent more time hiding from everybody and I didn't hang around and socialize. I didn't look at talents or appreciate what these guys could do. One guy became very close to me, Charlie Silvera, a catcher. He said "Hey

*kid, come here. I want you to have these two catchers' mitts." I
didn't help myself by confusing him with Berra.*

However, other Yankees jokingly confused Malangone with
Berra and good-naturedly called John "Yogi." The moniker stuck
with John throughout his years with the Yankees and their minor
league teams. Malangone sayings included substituting phrases
like "IBMs" for RBIs.

While not recognizing John's panic attacks, the Yankees
did begin noticing that John exhibited some odd behavior. The kid
dressed shabbily, with the stirrups placed on backwards and his
uniform shirt not tucked neatly in his pants. John also couldn't tie
bows in the laced spikes, and made knots instead that had to be
cut before removing any footwear. The first cracks were beginning
to appear in the relationship between the rifle arm from Little
Italy and the New York Yankee management. The ripple effects of
Lou Haneles's warning not to sign would be felt much later in the
decade.

One Yankee took note of John's demeanor almost
immediately after meeting him. That player was Billy Martin, an
intense infielder who never held back his opinions about anybody.
This was the same Billy Martin who would later become a Yankee
World Series hero in 1952 and MVP in 1953. This was the same
Billy Martin whose feistiness would eventually make him a
baseball legend throughout his professional baseball career. At
one point Martin approached John, observed him carefully, and
merely stated the obvious, "I heard you are a boxer. I am not afraid
of anybody. But if I get in a fight, you gonna back me up?" John
answered, "If you're a Yankee, I'll back you up."

Despite the professional courtesies, Martin saw John for
who he was long before other Yankees and management caught
on to the Malangone persona and the never-ending antics. Martin
realized that the new kid had emotional baggage and was troubled.
The advice he gave John was routine, saying, "You need to calm
down. Have a drink." But Martin, in a more serious mood later
on, declared, "We will never win the pennant with you." It was a
statement that would haunt John for decades.

The distinction between the two men was quite clear. One
played to win, in spite of his temperament, and the other played to
play, in spite of his talent.

Temporary relief came in the form of a trip to Maracaibo,
Venezuela for a month during the winter of 1951-1952. East Harlem

and Jefferson Park may have been baseball crazy, but they paled in comparison to Maracaibo. The second largest city in the country, after Caracas, the capital, Maracaibo is home to many baseball leagues, with American players often participating during the off season of Major League Baseball. The city and the rest of the baseball-crazed nation recently celebrated one of their own stars in Miguel Cabrera, third baseman for the Detroit Tigers, who became an MLB Triple Crown winner. Cabrera won the award in 2012, leading the American League in batting average, homeruns, and RBIs. Numerous other professional ballplayers from Venezuela have played in the major leagues, and baseball is a source of national pride.

Author Rob Ruck, writing for the Society of American Baseball Research (SABR), in an article entitled "Chicos and Gringos of Beisbol Venezolana" stated, "If baseball has a frontier, Venezuela is its southernmost boundary. And there each winter, from the Maracaibo oil basin to the Andean highlands, Venezuelans play and watch the game with a zeal that goes beyond mere passion." Ruck further commented, "Fans in the sport's southernmost frontier are knowledgeable, enthusiastic and intense."

For John, traveling anywhere, never mind to another country, was overwhelming. He lasted a month in Maracaibo, homesick for his mother and Grandma Panarese. He did not take baseball seriously, and there was clowning around during the games. The antics spilled over to the Granada Hotel where John was staying. A panic attack prompted him to seek some form of escape. Reminiscent of the bridge jumping into the swirling waters of the East River back home, John jumped off a second story ledge straight into one of the hotel's pools.

After I jumped, I remembered that there was a diving pool and a shallow pool. On my way down I thought about making a U-turn, but thank God, there was a diving board, so I had the right pool. I hit the bottom of the pool like a jet. Everybody was screaming. I got in tremendous trouble for that. My manager said, "What the fuck did you do that for?? What are you doing with your life?? You coulda gotten yourself killed!!!"

Even when John had good intentions, they often backfired. Feeling sorry for local youngsters playing ball barefoot on a barren, rock-strewn lot, John treated everyone to sneakers at minimal expense.

I took the kids to the store and bought thirty-five or forty pairs of sneakers. They were cheap. I got in trouble for that. Something where you were not supposed to do anything with the children, I dunno exactly why. Everything was off limits. Wasn't allowed to take food outta the hotel or feed sandwiches to the kids. Everything was a no-no. The little things I did... [voice trailing off, shaking his head]

There was also a social adjustment for local women:

They came to me... good looking women, you know, dating gringos. I took somebody out and I turn around and see twenty women. I said, "Tell those people to go home." She said, "They're coming with us." They were all chaperones!

About gifts leaving the country:

Somebody gave me two gallons of Chanel #5 perfume but I got stopped at "customer service" [customs]. You were only allowed two little bottles. I was told no, no, no two gallons, no Maracaibo, no Venezuela, no nothin'. I didn't know, I couldn't read any signs.

Despite the homesickness, John did not feel the pressure in Maracaibo as he did in New York. Because most people spoke Spanish instead of English, no one could know his secret or anything else about him, nor would they care.

The spring of 1952 brought a change to John's relationship with the Yankees. Sam Susser, the Nebells, and local money games were permanently replaced by entry level into the Yankees' minor league system. Malangone left Harlem to play in Quebec, Canada, in the Class C level Provincial League. The changes agitated the demon in the back of John's mind once again.

We played an exhibition game at West Point and then we went to Montreal. I asked other players, "Where are we?" Nobody knew because all the signs were in French. Nobody could read them. So now I am sitting in the back of the bus, feelin' ok and relaxed. But then Skipper [Frank Novosel] stands up and says, "Congratulations, you guys are now professional ball players. Your contracts are now in effect, and there's no turning back. Let's go win the pennant."

These words, no turning back... that was a BIG thing. I started to panic right away. I felt trapped and nowhere to go. The fog and panic escalated to cold sweats and I stood up hearing sounds in my head like a wounded animal. I staggered up to the front of the bus, holding onto the seats, all confused and told the driver,

"I need a church." The driver said, "Are we here to play or pray?" With dem words, I didn't know what to do. If a window had been open, I woulda dove right out, know what I mean? The skipper said, "What does he want?" Another player said, "I dunno, a church or something." Skipper said, "When you can pitch like him and hit like him, we'll do what you want." With that, the driver turned a coupola corners and there it was [grinning]... St. Joseph's Cathedral.

Officially known as Saint Joseph's Oratory of Mount Royal, the basilica is the third largest of its kind, and the largest church in Canada. Its founder was Brother André Bessette, who was canonized by the Roman Catholic Pope Benedict XVI in 2010.

The edifice is the reputed source of a number of miracle cures that occurred over decades, beginning with the church's construction in 1904. Bessette had attributed the miracles to faith in the Roman Catholic Saint Joseph, hence the origin of the basilica's title. Examining the incident in retrospect, it would appear that once again, there was some sort of divine intervention that gave John the mental peace he desperately needed to survive. The team bus was halted; John entered the church and prayed. No one understood what was going on in John's mind, but the results of that season would make everyone around Malangone take notice.

John eventually felt comfortable in Canada, feeling equal with everyone else, and with the demon subdued, if only temporarily. Like Maracaibo, Quebec was another region with a non-English speaking populace. In the midst of a French-speaking population, there was little concern for people to know any secrets. He still clowned around on various occasions and managed to have difficulty calling and understanding signals behind the plate, but his offensive skills made up for it.

John played catcher for the Three Rivers Yankees (Trois-Rivières). Playing 123 games in the Quebec League, John batted .302 with 144 hits, 17 homers and a .484 slugging percentage. More significantly, he topped off the season by winning the Most Valuable Player Award.

The Provincial League, or La Provinciale, consisted of six teams that reflected the integration changes in professional baseball. After Jackie Robinson joined the Brooklyn Dodger roster in 1947, numerous black ball players sought professional baseball opportunities in the minor and major leagues. Many left Negro League teams and transitioned to Canada, where there was much less racial discrimination than in the United States; many American minor league franchises were established in the Deep South, and black players were subjected to rampant segregation and hostile crowds.

John drew on his racial experiences from back home and enjoyed social relationships with everybody he met. He had total admiration for the black players in the league, always saying that they made the league as competitive as it could be. One of those players was Ed Charles, a member of the Quebec Braves. During a game between Quebec and Three Rivers, Charles, attempting to score, slid into John at home plate, unintentionally spiking the catcher's index finger. The collision nearly turned into a confrontation because of protests from some of Malangone's teammates, but cooler heads prevailed; John would say later that he had the plate blocked and that Charles's slide was clean. Malangone and Charles went on to mutually respect each other's talents. Years later, Charles recalled in an interview:

There was a presence there that you had to pay attention to. He had all the tools, the power, the consistency, so... you figure, like everybody else, this guy can't miss, he's going to be a professional in no time. He impressed me as a little Yogi Berra. We used to call him "Little Yogi."

It was Charles that John had to beat out for MVP honors during the 1952 season. Charles collected 151 hits and maintained a .317 batting average. Ed Charles continued on to the major leagues, playing with the Kansas City Athletics and finishing his career as a third baseman with the New York Mets in 1969, when the team became World Champions over the Baltimore Orioles.

John received the Lord Calvert Trophy, given to a member of the team each year as "the player of distinction," through voting by the local fans. Commenting in a local Quebec newspaper, Malangone declared, "I'm truly honored to receive the trophy. I want to thank [everyone] who also contributed to this great moment of joy."

The *Sporting News*, in an article entitled "38 Yank Farmhands Named on All Star Lineups for '52" included John's statistics from the Provincial League. The text of the article concerned itself with special accomplishments of some of the other players, but not John's. There was mention of Bill Dickey working with another catching prospect, John Blanchard, who would become close to Malangone in subsequent years. Dickey had recommended Blanchard be converted from outfielder to catcher. Blanchard was becoming a rising star, much to Dickey's satisfaction. John would continue crossing paths with both men in the years ahead, but not in the best imagined ways possible.

The temporary joy that John experienced away in Canada was about to be replaced by the growing anxiety and dread of returning to East Harlem.

Chapter 14

You're a Killer, Soldier

Fort Dix, New Jersey
1952-1954

With the outbreak of the Korean War in 1950, it was only a matter of time before the United States Army enlistment officers would be looking for John and others his age. Josephine Malangone would tell John that the army was looking for him, but she wouldn't divulge his location to local army recruiters. John's response to her was simply, "Look, I'm busy playin' ball. I am having a good year. Tell them to go fuck themselves." When he arrived back in Harlem, Josephine reminded her son that the U.S. Army was still looking for him. John asked his mother what she said to any officers inquiring as to her son's whereabouts. Her reply was simply, "I told them you said to go fuck themselves."

Concerned about possible arrest and court martial for John, Dom Bepp expedited matters to get John formally enlisted and out of any serious trouble. It wasn't long afterwards that John found himself being driven by Jerry, Dom Bepp's chauffer, down to Whitehall Street to report for duty. John was read the Articles of War before induction. He recalled that the enlistment officer then declared, "You are now in the Army... there is no I in team. We're a team."

The conversation between the army recruitment office and John Malangone was anything but a normal one when it was time for a physical examination. The panic attack began to surface.

John: *I never told anyone before... you guys don't know this, but I can't read, I can't write.*

Army: *Where you're going, you won't need to read English, anyway.*

John [serious]: *That's great. When I get sick, I get headaches and stomach aches.*

Army: *You got no guts, that's all.*

John: *I can't hear too good sometimes.*

Army*: Yeah? Don't worry, with all your problems, we'll put you up front. Sergeant McCarthy, the dummy goes with your company.*

John nearly aced all of the initial physical and strength tests, except for a bayonet stabbing procedure that he simply refused to do, walking away. The nervousness and panic attacks began to surface once more. To cope with the increasing anxieties, he tried an obvious, if not successful, angle with his superiors. When asked for his occupation, he explained that he was a Yankee and a professional baseball player. The reply from his company commander was clear: "You are not a Yankee, you are not a baseball player. You're a soldier and I tell you what to do!"

This chain of command and structure did not last long. United States Army, meet Private John Malangone. Authority and discipline versus chaos and erratic behavior.

John initially wanted to go to Korea, as part of a death wish from the first moment he arrived in Fort Dix. "I wanted to meet God without a gun," he would later say. The drills involving target practice and bayonet stabbing merely reinforced the nearly lifelong feeling that "he deserved it." The words "You are a killer, soldier!" repeatedly ringing in his ears only heightened tensions and anxiety. Fort Dix records did indicate that John had experienced dizziness, throbbing headaches, nail biting, panic attacks, and excessive nervousness, but no one could figure out what was bothering him. Injured soldiers returning to the base often told stories of horrible atrocities on the battlefront, adding to the anxieties of John and others. John couldn't handle the news and didn't want to hear any of it. He stayed away from the base hospital, catching flak from fellow soldiers who felt he should help the wounded by listening and feeling their pain. To cope with the stress, John attended chapel every day while at Fort Dix, like he had done at Our Lady of Mount Carmel and other churches in civilian life.

Then there was a break and another spell of relief from his mental anguish. A general appeared one day near the end of basic training. The officer was in charge of Special Services, which included athletics and recreation. Soldiers were being recruited for this unit:

Johnny Kucks [Yankee pitcher] lifted my helmet and said to the commander, "Here he is... over here!" This commander had a bug for trophies in A&R-Athletics and Recreation. He comes over and says, "We have been waiting for you. We pulled your papers; you're staying here for two years. After sixteen weeks of special training, we will assign you to special service. You will box, you will play baseball, you will play football, and you will entertain the first wave of soldiers returning from Korea. Many are wounded and hurting. They need entertainment while they are in Fort Dix... they gonna cheer for you. You'll be one of the top autograph guys." Word got around that I boxed before and the commander said, "You got your first fight in two weeks. We're putting you in the heavyweight division."

Memories of East Harlem, Father Joseph, and panic attacks came back to haunt John.

I said, "Oh no, my fighting days are over and I am under contract to the New York Yankees. I am not allowed to fight." This officer repeated words I had heard before... "You're not a fighter, not a boxer, you're a soldier, and I tell you what to do!" But then he took me into his office and said, "Look, you don't have to fight, but soldiers coming back from Korea are in bad shape and it is our job to take care of them. This is a single elimination tournament. Win and you keep going." I said, "I gotta call my mother." Since I couldn't read the numbers, I asked the general to dial the phone for me. I told him the number was Win(dot)1111. He looked at me. "My God, you gotta be an idiot. I never saw a number like this before. Why a number like this? You gotta be in a retarded building."

John explained the situation to his mother and Josephine gave her permission, especially after John told her about the use of sixteen-ounce gloves, which landed softer blows.

John's entire company was shipped out to Korea, while he was chosen to stay behind and entertain returning veterans. His death wish was not to be granted. He also had no qualifications for being a medic, a chaplain, or a conscientious objector, so special service was the only option left. Although guilt crept into the back of his mind, knowing that he would not face combat like the rest of his company helped the panic attacks subside. What also helped John cope with army life was the continued presence of Paulie Tine. Despite being classified 4-F because of his facial skin condition, Paulie hung around Fort Dix most of the time and no one seemed to be concerned.

John went on to fight in Fort Carson, Colorado and Fort Monmouth, New Jersey and at other posts. He possessed the same mindset that he had years earlier, suffering anxiety before and after every fight, while blocking it out during the actual fights. The antics that normally surrounded Malangone's activities disappeared because "there was no time. The Army kept you constantly busy." The first round knockout streak continued unabated. His first fight, against a Tommy Boyle, lasted thirty-two seconds. He became adored and respected by everyone. On one occasion, during a sparring practice in the gym, one California heavyweight champ kept mocking John, who was standing outside of the ring. Guy "Ozzie" Grasso, a promising Yankee rookie pitcher who was inducted into the army at Fort Dix at the same time as John, remembered what happened next:

The boxer in the ring said to John, "What are you staring at? If you climb into this ring, I'll give you a beating." John said to him, "That's the biggest mistake you ever made." John was sweeping the floor at the time, but climbed into the ring with his work boots on and everything. John hit him so hard, that guy's probably just waking up now...[laughing].

John didn't stop there. He wanted to fight every Friday night. He wanted to fight five or six heavyweights a night. He said, "I'll knock this guy out in the first round. Drag him out. Gimme another guy and I'll knock him out. Bring me another guy and I'll knock him out. I'll fight six, seven guys. Pile 'em up and bring them in... I'll knock them all out.

However, John's anger over the boxer's boastful challenge quickly subsided, as it had after the two altercations with mob associates years before in East Harlem. His inner fears still governed his outward behavior where matters of fighting were concerned.

Grasso remembered something else that John had said to him:

"Ya know... I never killed anybody." He was proud of that. I didn't realize at the time what he meant by that.

Several official bouts later, he was fighting for the army's heavyweight division championship, which was held in Fort Dix. His opponent was an undefeated, fearsome fighter who hailed from nearby Philadelphia. Successful as Tom Peoples was, he had never experienced the powerful punches that characterized Malangone's fighting style. A captioned photo in the local Fort Dix newspaper summed up the result:

Tom Peoples is shown hitting the canvas for the third time in round one of his heavyweight title fight with John Malangone of the 60ᵗʰ. Malangone's smashing right hand decked Peoples for two counts of nine, before another right finished him off in 2:30 of the first round.

John recalled the fight and its aftermath:

Tom Peoples was a great fighter, phenomenal. I think he was a Golden Glove Champion before entering the army. When I hit him, it was over. I'll never forget the look in his eyes before he went down. They rolled upward in his head. I thought I killed him... that was my last fight. I was done. I couldn't do it no more. But once I finished the boxing, the post was mine... everybody loved me. All I heard was "Hey, champ" every day after that.

Done with the boxing, John participated in an all-army baseball tournament in Fort Carson, in Colorado Springs. Despite two homers from John, Fort Dix finished as a runner-up in the finals. In another episode of Malangone antics following the tournament, John, egged on by teammates, drove an Indian chief's daughter from the ballpark back to her home.

John asked the daughter, a beautiful woman, where he was taking her. The woman pointed to a nearby mountain and said, "Up there..." John looked up in disbelief at the mountain, not knowing it was labeled Pike's Peak, which rose approximately 8,400 feet above Colorado Springs. The resulting ride up and back resembled a 1920's silent flick with Charlie Chaplin at the wheel. While delivering the woman safely to her father, John felt like he had bounced over every rock driving up the mountain and back down. He passed warning signposts for falling rocks; they were totally useless to John, who couldn't read the signs and had no idea what they meant.

John used Paulie's car. Tine had driven all the way from New York to Denver and back, just to be near his friend as much as possible. Paulie was simply everywhere.

Malangone began to get too casual with army rules and regulations, even going so far as to leave the base for a trip to Florida. Somehow, John did not feel or think of immediate repercussions. This was a habit formed in his childhood years back in East Harlem. He couldn't seem to distinguish right from wrong. John passed word back to the company commander via other privates, stating, "Tell Lieutenant Gracie [Special Services commander] I'll be back in a week or two." East Harlem natives Paulie, Gary Sacino,

Carmine Caridi, some guy nicknamed "The Babe," and John drove to Florida so they could work out at a Lou Haneles baseball school. John went along for the company, hanging out with neighborhood buddies. Total time skipped actually amounted to thirty days, but John seemed oblivious to any consequences for leaving the base.

To say that John was in a lot of trouble afterward would be an understatement. He was confined to the barracks as a form of house arrest for two weeks. John's inexplicable statement to command was that "I thought I was overdue for a vacation." He also informed command that "I would have come back earlier if you had called and asked me." John was serious, and his explanation befuddled the officers, who did not know what to make of him.

Just when things couldn't get any worse, or any more out of control, John and some buddies, including Paulie, decided to slip off of the base and take a car ride.

As usual, John drove without license and registration, and waved goodbye to the guard at the gate. Ironically, the men in the car were assigned to guard duty and were not supposed to leave the barracks. Before serious repercussions and possible court martial and punishments could materialize, along came another divine intervention in John Malangone's young life. This time it would be Corporal James Parker's near-tragic boating mishap.

Parker, a military policeman, was boating in a nearby body of water known as Brown's Mills Lake. His boat capsized, and Parker, suffering severe leg cramps, was unable to stay afloat in the fresh water lake. Malangone, driving by, quickly realized Parker was in trouble...

Everybody is in the car, maybe seven or eight guys. We drove to the lake and saw this crowd. People are screaming and yelling. A boat had capsized. I saw a hand sticking out of the water, so I dove into the lake. I took off. They said I looked like a motorboat going through the water. I didn't realize this was fresh water, and there was no buoyancy. I couldn't swim in fresh water and I was going up and down. I musta swallowed half the lake. I grabbed the guy and used my right arm like a propeller to bring him in, but I was getting tired ten yards from the boat. Suddenly, I look up and see this beautiful girl in the sunlight. She said to me, "Need help?" Next thing you know my feet were touching the bottom of the lake. We were safe, but I couldn't go no more. Other people took over right away and helped revive the guy.

Parker later attributed his life being saved to Malangone's

"prompt and courageous action." Malangone was eventually recommended by upper echelon command for the Soldier's Medal, but not before a reality check. After the rescue, military police asked,

MP: *Soldier, what's your name?*

Paulie: *John we haven't got a pass...*

John: *Oh shit, don't give him my name.*

Other soldiers: *Let's get outta here!*

Safely back at the barracks, everyone in the car thought the incident was over, until Malangone was summoned over the loudspeakers. Captain Gardner commented, "You are the biggest fuckup in the army. What did you do now?" Sensing the worst when he noticed the MPs, Colonel Parker, and a general in the orderly room, John was ready to run out again. Captain Gardner, also present at the meeting, was told, "We are recommending this man for the Soldier's Medal." Parker hugged John while Gardner nearly fainted. John, smiling, told Gardner, "We forgot to sign out." Gardner replied, "You are lucky you weren't court martialed."

According to John, the entire slate of Malangone antics was wiped out, and he couldn't do anything wrong after that. The fact that Parker's rescue involved a white soldier and a black one didn't hurt the army's public relations staff when it came time to promote racial integration and harmony in the service in the early 1950s. Malangone and Parker became poster boys and newspaper profiles.

No one knows with certainty what John experienced that day with the mysterious woman, but he sensed the episode was completely real. John even asked Paulie to get the girl's number as they were escaping to the car. John searched everywhere for the mysterious woman, even returning to the lake several times in the hope of making some contact. No one ever saw anything, and nothing ever materialized.

Ron Weiss was right. You can't make this stuff up...

The aura around John never diminished. No matter what he did in the ring or on the ball field, he was admired and respected by everyone. Years later, Sal Malangone bumped into a New York police lieutenant who presided over the arrest of the Malangone brothers' father, Sylvester, who was accused of shoplifting in the

Bronx Sears store. He got into a physical confrontation with two cops and was brought to the local stationhouse. Sal and Paulie went to the stationhouse to support Sylvester. Recognizing the Malangone name, the lieutenant, a former soldier, asked Sal about any connection to the Malangone who fought in Fort Dix. His curiosity was typical of anyone who followed John's success.

The guy was like Superman in the ring! We followed him. My God what a fighter he was. He was built like Rocky Marciano. He could have been heavyweight champ. What happened to him?

Following the conversation, Sylvester Malangone was driven downtown for processing in a squad car, instead of, as Sal put it, "the paddy wagon." The family's renowned Uncle Harry showed up to represent Sylvester in the usual proceedings. His presence meant some heavyweight clout for the defendant; it wasn't long before the charges against Sylvester were dropped, with apologies also extended to John's father over what was termed "a misunderstanding."

John continued to play baseball throughout his enlistment at Fort Dix. In August of 1954, he contributed some timely hits that enabled the Fort Dix baseball squad to defeat rival Fort Monmouth and win the team's fifth consecutive First Army championship.

During the winter of 1954, John was given an honorable discharge from the army and briefly returned to East Harlem before flying back to Maracaibo for winter baseball. John played catcher for a team called Espadon in the newly formed Occidental League. Although the team finished its season with a 14-19 record, John led the league with seven homers. He was then called up to the Yankee farmhand camp scheduled in St. Petersburg, Florida in mid-February of 1955. Having cleared "customer service" in Venezuela without incident, John was headed back to the business of professional baseball and the New York Yankees with no further interruptions. Maracaibo would continue to provide some solace for John and his issues, but that was only temporary. His talent permitted him to continue to play to play, rather than play to win, while being an "entertainer." The preferential treatment given to John in the army had revived the undisciplined wild side of the young man once more. The cultural clash during the summer of 1946 was nothing compared to the clash that was coming in 1955. This time, the persona of an undisciplined boy and the corporate Yankee image were about to collide on center stage, in the glare of the media spotlight. For John Malangone and his issues, there would be no place to hide.

Chapter 15

Whaddya Doin'?

Miller Huggins Field
St. Petersburg, Florida
Spring 1955

Sal Malangone recalled a radio broadcast:

We used to listen to the radio for the Yankee games. One day, Casey was on the radio and he announced, "We [Yankees] have an up-and-coming ball player, John Malangone. He will be up soon." I remember that like it was yesterday...

The anticipation and excitement of the 1955 Major League Baseball season was in the February air at the New York Yankees spring training facility in Saint Petersburg, Florida. Led once again by Casey Stengel, the Yankees focused on recapturing the American League Pennant; the Cleveland Indians ended Stengel's streak of five straight World Series titles in 1954. When the 1954 season ended, speculation arose over whether Casey would continue to manage. When asked by reporters if he would manage in 1955, the "Ol' Perfessor" replied, "I won't talk about that because I don't have to talk about that." One hour later, still entertaining the press, Stengel was chatting about the team and its needs, occasionally using the word "we" in discussing solutions.

In mid-February, the Yanks opened the Miller Huggins facility with a rookie camp. The camp preceded normal spring training drills required for veteran players prior to the start of the official major league season and opening day. Stengel saw the rookie school as an opportunity for Yankee coaches to instruct new players on any weaknesses they were known to possess. The skipper was armed with profiles on thirty-three players, which included fourteen pitchers, four catchers, nine infielders, and six outfielders. Some of the more notable names in future Yankee history included Bobby Richardson, Tony Kubek, and John Blanchard. Rod Kanehl, an outfielder, would be part of the fledgling New York Mets franchise in the early 1960s. Also receiving a lot of initial media attention were Roy and Ray Mantle, younger twin brothers of

Mickey Mantle, star outfielder for the Bronx Bombers. A February 14, 1955 *Sporting News* report on the Yankee camp observed,

No time is wasted on things the boys can do best. They are coached almost entirely in the points they cannot do well enough. The payoff of this system is tremendous. The youngsters themselves find the three weeks an incredible experience, never to be forgotten.

In John Malangone's case, coaching instruction and practice time involved learning how to effectively block home plate from advancing base runners, as well as preventing passed balls and wild pitches.

The *Sporting News* also mentioned a new lifestyle for the rookies, who were housed in the Yankee hotel (Soreno) in Yankee style. The hotel was one of a number of elegant hotels built in the 1920s that defined St. Petersburg as a winter tourist attraction. The hotel had seven floors and three hundred rooms. For most young baseball players, the hotel represented an opulent lifestyle to which they were not accustomed. That was certainly true for John, considering the cramped quarters that he and his family shared back in East Harlem. John described the Soreno Hotel as "elite, like a castle." For the rifle arm from Little Italy, the luxurious building was a reward for his talent and abilities; for the demon, or "the guy in the back" as John would say, it was to become a wonderful staging ground. Flashbacks became routine again.

Please God, not this one! No more!

One thing Casey made clear to reporters prior to camp was that the Yankee catching department was loaded with talent. This group included Yogi Berra, who led the American League in 1954 with 115 RBIs, Elston Howard, the most valuable player in the International League, and Charlie Silvera, Gus Triandos, Lou Berberet, and Hal Smith. Casey noted that if necessary, he could trade some of the catchers to improve other departments on the Yankees. John Malangone was still in the army at that point in time, but he would emerge on the Yankee radar during the winter of 1954-1955. There would be other potential catchers as well, who would arrive in St. Petersburg competing for a Yankee roster spot in early 1955.

John had a reputation as a slugging catcher with a strong arm who could challenge Yogi Berra for a starting job. Given Berra's major league accomplishments by the spring of 1955, it was amazing that John, as a rookie with one official season of pro ball

(Three Rivers), was being taken seriously by Casey and the Yankee management.

For this rookie kid, the camp presented a golden opportunity to be a professional ball player. He was not just another newcomer, as he had been playing on various levels for the Yankees since being signed in 1949. He was deemed special by everybody. He was "the kid with the rifle arm from Little Italy," having been clocked at 100 mph for throwing fastballs. He was the powerful slugger who smashed a homerun during a tryout game, in his first at bat and first pitch, into the left field upper deck at the old Yankee Stadium. That priceless moment resulted in a contract.

The kid made a big splash with the media and Yankee management, with his boyish grin and the Yogi nickname like his counterpart. Members of the organization had high expectations of success with the young catcher. He was constantly surrounded by Yankee personnel, all eager to hear stories about the Mafia in New York. The players never tired of asking John for details about various gangsters. Even Casey himself was fascinated with the subject, occasionally calling Malangone on his room phone. Relying on his East Harlem street roots, Malangone never resorted to diplomacy when answering innocent questions.

Casey: *Tell me more about the mob.*

John: *Who's dis?*

Casey: *This is skipper. Casey.*

John: *This is skipper? Get outta here, [laughing] if you're skipper, then I am a fuckin' motorboat.*

The kid had posed for a picture with two Baseball Hall of Fame catchers, Bill Dickey and Mickey Cochrane. A legendary competitive catcher with the Philadelphia Athletics and Detroit Tigers, Cochrane was hired as a training camp coach. He was quoted as saying, "It's funny when you think of it. I used to hate the Yankees." Cochrane warmed up to Malangone immediately and offered to help the kid at the catching position. The picture of Dickey, Cochrane, and Malangone made sports sections of newspapers across America. Standing behind the photographer at the photo session were two supporters of John, Casey and another promising young catcher named John Blanchard.

Newspaper articles across the country ran that photo and

chronicled a brief (and false) story of John Malangone showing up at Yankee headquarters and demanding a contract when he was only fourteen years of age.

He was, for the most part, well-liked at the start of rookie camp. He sported a Charles Atlas physique that awed fellow ballplayers and enhanced his boxing reputation. John Blanchard commented, "I wouldn't want to meet you in a dark alley, John." In typical Malangone fashion, John responded, "Why would you meet me in a dark alley? Whaddya doin' there?"

Unbeknownst to management, the kid also had a motorcycle, courtesy of Paulie Tine, who drove from New York with the bike in the back of a Chrysler station wagon. Paulie and John would hang out after daily Yankee practices. If that wasn't enough, Paulie brought spending money from the shoebox accounts hidden in the East Harlem wine cellars, along with a cash bonus from Dom Bepp for good luck.

Malangone's skills were on display, but the flip side of the young slugger was also on full view for everyone to see. For the demon, the media-saturated environment of the Yankee camp and the Soreno Hotel was the perfect forum for displaying bizarre and inexplicable behavior. For starters, there was the highly publicized picture of three Yankee catchers.

Photographer: *How do you spell your name? One L or two?*

John [hesitant and scared]: *Uh... two Ls... yeah... two Ls... Is it ok if you don't put the picture in the paper?*

Photographer: *Are you nuts? You are going to be famous. Everybody is gonna know who you are tomorrow!*

John: [becoming annoyed, saying to himself]: *Hurry up and take the damn picture!!*

Despite the initial camp welcomes, John was beginning to feel uncomfortable with the people in camp and the surroundings. He began slowly withdrawing from social contacts with teammates. He experienced the same anxieties he had in previous workouts with the club at the stadium in past years. There was no escaping to a foreign country where English was not spoken. In the back of his mind a great fear loomed about the neighborhood wise guys.

What if the mobsters got box seats at Yankee Stadium near the

dugout and start yelling, "You are a killer, kid!" from the stands?
Everybody's gonna know... I need to get outta here.

Although Paulie was a source of friendly relief after daily
workouts, he eventually returned to New York. While he pledged
to come back as soon as possible, his absence made matters worse
for John. The turmoil inside Malangone was brewing and growing.

It didn't take long for John to start self-destructing and
burning bridges with the people around him. Ralph Houk, a
former Yankee backup catcher, was assisting Stengel as a coach in
the camp. Houk was nicknamed "the Major" after receiving a Silver
Star in combat during World War II. He was discharged from the
army with Major status, and he had a commanding presence about
him. He had a knack for getting others to follow him and employed
a positive approach in handling the morale of other ballplayers.
John Malangone would prove different. One day during camp,
there were puddles of water on the fields from a recent rain.
Placing and lighting gasoline on the puddles would dry them up
and make the fields playable; Houk asked John to retrieve two
five-gallon gasoline cans for that purpose. Instead of cooperating,
Malangone refused, and even told Houk "to go get it yourself."
Given that the Major was stunned by the disrespect, John lost one
of his supporters at that very moment, and soon there would be
other personnel turning against him. Malangone, drawing on rude
Harlem neighborhood etiquette, was oblivious to the consequences
of his actions. When asked recently about the incident, he looked
away regretfully, saying, "I should have gotten it [gasoline]. I didn't
know what I was doing..."

Soon it became apparent that Casey would act like a
high school dean of discipline, monitoring a wayward student's
troublesome behavior. Casey was informed about a boating
accident involving several players, with "problem child" Malangone
in the center of the commotion. The players helped themselves to
a motorboat sitting at a pier. John thought nothing of hopping in
the boat; his old neighborhood mindset of "What's the big deal,
anyway?" did not involve any second thoughts. John had started
the motor unintentionally, with the boat still tied to the dock. With
nowhere to go, the boat fishtailed and crashed back into the dock,
with both objects sustaining damages. No one was hurt, but the
Yankees ultimately were responsible for the repairs. A familiar
behavior pattern evolved, with Stengel always asking, "Who did
this?" and a smiling Malangone always volunteering, "I did it,
skip."

The well-decorated Soreno Hotel lobby was supplied with baskets of oranges and other fruits for the players to take up to their rooms. But soon after camp started, pillowcases of golf balls started appearing in the lobby for players to take for golfing outings. The usual "who did it?" question led to the usual suspect, John Malangone, and the usual "I did it, skip..." Casey learned that John, during after-hours, grabbed pillowcases and proceeded to round up stray balls lying all over the grounds of the nearby golf course, including those submerged in water spots. While Yankee players didn't mind the antics, team and hotel management were infuriated over the breach of protocol.

What no one understood was the therapeutic value that John derived from fishing golf balls out of the small ponds on or near the course. He retrieved the balls while fully clothed, getting soaking wet. While growing up in Harlem, he had sought relief from flashbacks and panic attacks by diving into the cold waters of the East River. Wading through cold freshwater lakes and ponds near rookie camp provided him with the same relief.

The lobby would not be the only source of antics in the hotel, not with so much room to roam in a seven-story building...

One night I stayed in my room because I didn't want to get in trouble. These guys come into the room with pails. I thought it was water. I said, "Don't fool around, I don't wanna get in more trouble." They threw paper, and came back and threw paper again. They came a third time and threw water. I grabbed a bunch of oranges out of a bucket in the room, went out in the hallway and started firing back. I hit one guy in the head and broke an exit sign. In the commotion, my door closed behind me and I got locked out of my room with no clothes on. So I broke the little glass door in the hallway wall and pull out a fire hose and wrap it around me, with the nozzle hanging out... the next morning ten guys are sitting around the breakfast table and Casey comes over and says, "Anybody know about the oranges being thrown last night?" Blanchard and Kucks were involved, but they didn't say anything. I said, "I did it, skip." He says, "Whaddya doin'?" I said, "I was warming up, skip." He walked away, turned around and came back and says, with a wink, "Who was the catcher?"

Standing next to Casey was scout Johnny Neun, of unassisted triple play fame, who shook his head and commented, *"The lights are on and nobody's home..."*

Guy "Ozzie" Grasso, fellow soldier with John at Fort Dix

and then a pitching prospect invited to the Yankee rookie camp, remembers Malangone's antics:

John was a great hitter and great catching prospect. He was strong as an ox. But he was always in trouble. He broke a headboard in the Soreno Hotel and then got some nails and hammered the headboard back together before anybody found out.

The shenanigans began having repercussions of a personal nature. John, for all his wildness, actually began to sense hurt feelings from his teammates, beginning with Mickey Mantle and his twin brothers.

If somebody hurt me, or I thought somebody was gonna hurt me, then I would listen. These guys just loved me. We [John and the twins] went to miniature golf, the driving range, the batting cage... while I am eating with these two guys, I realize they were twins. Mickey comes over to me and says, "I want you to stay away from my brothers. You are prone to trouble. You are always in trouble." I was confused and I looked at Mickey. "Whaddya talkin' about?" He answered back, "These are my brothers, Roy and Ray, and I want you to stay away from them."

I looked at them and said, "My God, your name is Mantle? I didn't know. [Pointing] That's your brother, Mickey?"

I never said another word to them. They listened to their older brother. Mantle was the first guy to hurt me in 1955. I never did anything to those guys. Whatever happened, I was only doing to myself, although I didn't realize it at the time. I did more damage to myself by letting others punish me.

The initial media fanfare of John soon turned to an embarrassing one because of the signature John was required to give to Louisville Slugger, a company known for manufacturing wooden baseball bats. The company representative asked John to sign papers with his signature, creating another source of instant panic within the kid's mind. Paulie was not present to bail John out and write his name for him. He was trapped in New York because of a snowstorm and John was left to figure out what to do. Blanchard, astutely aware of John's illiteracy, understood the situation and coached John in scripting his name. Despite the writing practice, the name was misspelled "Jhon" on the form, and subsequently appeared on a group of bats. Other players derisively commented on the spelling, having jokes at John's expense. John explained to anyone who would listen that the misspelling was part of a deliberate Malangone clown act at Louisville's expense. In any event, the embarrassing episode simply added to a rapidly deteriorating situation.

Then there was the motorcycle accident, where John's bike was damaged beyond repair. John, while turning a sharp corner and speeding uphill, waved at people on a sidewalk who were waving back, "Hey catcher!" He smashed into a double-parked car. Fortunately for John, the smashup did not produce a career-threatening injury or disability, and it did not cost him lost playing time or opportunities. However, the accident did discourage him about staying in camp.

I went to the clubhouse to get my stuff. I was packing up to go home. Pete Sheehy (clubhouse manager), he loved me. He saw me and said, "John, where are you going?" I told him, "Pete, I had a bike accident. They don't know I have a bike. I gotta go home." Pete said, "Jesus Christ! Look at you, all those raspberries on your back and ass! Johnny, you're gonna lose your career. Come here, let me see what I can do. We'll put you in the tub with saltwater; it's gonna burn."

Despite everyone's inability to understand the reasons behind John Malangone's antics, several players, including Elston Howard, Moose Skowron, John Blanchard, Johnny Kucks, and Charlie Silvera, remained friendly with John. Before the bat-signing episode, Blanchard had realized John couldn't read when he noticed that every time he ordered food from a menu, John would follow him and simply say, "I'll have what he is having." Aside from illiteracy, Malangone had trouble even distinguishing the front and back of stirrups. When dressing and putting on the socks in the locker room, John would hold up the sock to Blanchard; he would oblige and turn it around for John.

Even the best intentions that Malangone possessed went awry. John Blanchard had informed John that he had heard about Coach Phil Page's involvement in a tragic accident. Page had accidentally shot a dear friend during a hunting accident. Malangone sensed a feeling of kinship with Page and his troubles, and for the first time in his life, felt an opportunity to open up about a tragic episode that occurred when he was only five years old. John went to Page's room, armed with the best intentions of communicating honestly with the coach. He wanted to confide to the coach that he needed help, too. He felt anxiety welling up inside of him as he knocked on Page's door. Before he could compose any thoughts, Page had opened the door and asked him, "Whaddya want?"

John didn't answer at first, unable to get any words out of his mouth. Finally, he managed to say, "I could help…"

Page answered, "You can't help yourself! You will never play for me!"

John had on many occasions described that 1955 spring training season as "make it or break it." He continued heading towards the breaking point, this time with his roommate at the center of a new incident. It started with a seemingly innocuous comment made near midnight one evening in the Soreno Hotel. John Blanchard entered Malangone's room and said, "Hey John, it's almost midnight and you didn't get in any trouble yet. One more hour and you're gonna make it through a whole day." Malangone playfully flopped backward and fell on roommate Bob Bonebrake's bed. And as fate would have it, this was no ordinary flop; John's weight cracked a slat beneath the bed, which in turn punctured Bonebrake's suitcase. It was no ordinary suitcase, as Bonebrake pointed out, because it was supposedly "made of alligator skin." Bonebrake protested loudly, and headed downstairs to complain to management about the damage done to an expensive piece of luggage. John offered to buy his roommate "a new alligator," but to no avail.

Unfortunately, the matter didn't end there. Casey informed John the next morning that he would have to pay for the suitcase (but not an alligator). Bonebrake was also gone from the room, having been reassigned elsewhere. Bonebrake was a pitcher in rookie camp and the suitcase accident would lead to further repercussions that could have been easily avoided by Malangone. That same day, near the conclusion of camp, Casey and the Yankee hierarchy were gathered to witness a Yankee intrasquad game and evaluate any potential talent that would make the team's roster for the 1955 season. There had been a number of intrasquad games previously played during camp, where rookies were divided into two opposing teams. However, this particular scrimmage attracted all significant Yankee management personnel, including the coaching staff and a number of returning veteran players, who were eager to observe future Yankee players. Some of the players included Mickey Mantle, Whitey Ford, Phil Rizzuto, and Yogi Berra. According to John, the contest also accommodated numerous fans who paid admission for the privilege of watching future Yankee stars. For newcomers trying to prove themselves to management and their peers, this definitely was a "holy cow" moment, as Phil

Rizzuto often exclaimed in later years as a Yankee broadcaster.

For John, and everyone watching that day, it was a "holy cow" moment of a different sort, and not a positive one. During his turn to bat, John stepped up to the plate only to notice that Bonebrake was on the mound, pitching. Anger welled up inside Malangone over the sight of Bonebrake; he imagined the pitcher running and complaining to Casey the previous night.

That whiny sonuva bitch...

Dropping his bat, John walked near the backstop, retrieved an iron rake and returned to the batter's box. Swinging the rake by the handle, Malangone angrily yelled at a nervous Bonebrake, "Go ahead... put it on the third tooth and I'll give it back to you [ball impaled on the rake]."

All the onlookers were stunned by Malangone's remarks, and both Dickey and Houk came over to John and told him to return to the bench. John later recalled one of them muttering to him to go take a shower. An angry Casey stepped up and asked, "Why you clowning around?" No one else said anything, except an uncomprehending Blanchard, who was aware that the Yankee brass was watching. He punctured the awkward and eerie silence by quietly asking John, "Whaddya doin'?"

But even Casey had had enough, no matter how much he liked John. The manager's mentor, Kid Elberfeld, made sure a young Stengel understood his personal advice: "If you are a big leaguer, act like a big leaguer." Casey never forgot that advice, and realized the need to draw the line with the rambunctious rifle arm from Little Italy. After all, these were the NEW YORK YANKEES, with a reputation to uphold and with zero tolerance for outrageous behavior. Even catcher Charlie Silvera, who liked John, knew the Yankees would not tolerate "monkey business." Malangone's days in camp were now nearly over, despite newspaper coverage that described John as "the interesting kid in the school."

Guy Grasso remembers a batting practice after the Bonebrake incident:

We were taking batting practice and there was a tower behind home plate. Yankee coaches in the tower were giving the batting practice pitcher signals. When John was batting, the pitcher threw him everything but fastballs. Frustrated, John turned to the tower and said, "Give me a fastball and I'll go home."

For John, there was a slow realization that he let a lot of people down, especially Paul Krichell. Nearing the end of his scouting career and acting in a fatherly role, the chief scout had occasionally approached the troubled Malangone and repeatedly asked, "Anything you would like to talk to me about, John?" The response was always a no, or silence. At times, John felt he deserved punishment akin to "ten thousand volts in the electric chair. Ninety-five percent of whatever I did, I didn't mean it... It was impulse. Everybody would say, 'John did it, John did it...'"

Fortunately for John, Billy Martin was in military service and not available to play until the start of the season. Given his disposition, Martin probably would have confronted Malangone head-on and repeated his declaration that, "We'll never win the pennant with you."

Thinking back on his disconnect with reality in the Soreno Hotel, John commented,

I had a number of bad things go against me... the golf balls, the oranges, the suitcase, the boat accident, the motorcycle accident, the pillowcases. They charged me for the cases. I mean those golf balls were heavy, how was I gonna carry the balls anyway? That's a lotta work... and I put them on tables where the oranges were, everybody came down and took the balls! All these great ballplayers in one swoop, the balls are gone! They left the oranges there, I couldn't believe it! Everything was gone! And I got in trouble, but they all said, "Hey! Thanks for the golf balls! Thanks for the golf balls!" Even the coaches! I didn't know a guy made money finding those golf balls out there. The Yankees had to pay for that, but they kept it quiet.

But Malangone also felt a sense of relief that he could go play elsewhere, out of the glaring media spotlight that he had been subjected to during rookie camp.

The question arose as to his uncertain future—what was the next destination? For the kid, it was to be the geographical equivalent of bouncing around in a pinball machine. The Denver Bears? Triple A? With Ralph Houk as manager and John's antics? That was a brick wall. No way, no how. John was going to have a tough time getting placed on any ball club.

Then there was the Double A option, with the Birmingham Barons and manager Phil Page. The manager did not want him at all, but he started the team's spring training in Florida with John anyway. Phil Page objected to John's presence; the spillover of incidents from spring training was still fresh in Page's mind. The manager's patience was exhausted following a restroom incident where John, unable to read, mistakenly entered a ladies' room. John noticed restrooms on both flanks of a refreshment stand, and figured one was a men's room. He guessed wrong, as both were restrooms were for women. The resulting pandemonium pushed the skipper over the edge, despite Malangone's claim of an honest mistake. It didn't matter, for John's credibility was shot and the unknown demon was now raging about unchecked. For the record, John never recorded an official at bat under Page.

He was eventually assigned to Binghamton, New York, Class A, via the team's training camp in Statesville, North Carolina. There is a photo showing John riding a Statesville dime store pony, surrounded by Binghamton teammates who were enjoying John's company. Based on the picture, no one would ever guess John Malangone went through a horrible spring training session with the most famous franchise in professional sports.

John's friends, including Howard, Silvera, Kucks, and Skowron, stayed with the Yankees after spring training. John Blanchard eventually stayed in the minors in Binghamton, but it would be partly at Malangone's expense. Matters weren't helped by a March 2 *Sporting News* report that mentioned Bill Dickey as touting Blanchard to be Yogi Berra's likely successor. While the Yanks headed north to recapture the American League pennant, Malangone headed south, eventually ending up with the Norfolk, Virginia Tars in Class B. He started a four-year journey, playing with various minor league teams from Norfolk to Amarillo, Texas. Never again would a golden opportunity to play with the biggest team name in professional sports present itself to the highly touted rifle arm from Little Italy.

East Harlem resident Mike Lentini recalled a story that John told him about the rookie camp. Lentini summed up John's last moments before leaving:

He told Casey Stengel in so many words he was the better catcher than whoever they had at the time, and I think the next day Johnny had his suitcase packing... [laughing]

Chapter 16

The Long Decline

Minor League Parks
Southern United States
1955-1959

In analyzing the countless, inexplicable episodes of bizarre behavior, John Malangone recalled four levels of trauma that would affect his thinking during periods of stress. Level one was the onset of a panic attack, triggered by a memory of a tragedy or a fear that some personal matter was about to get worse. A panic attack was manageable, especially if John was able to avoid whatever situation triggered it.

Level two was the "fog," where the panic attack took on another dimension; Malangone was unable to focus on anything in front of him, leading onlookers to wonder exactly what was the matter with him. The fog was a frequent ball field experience.

Level three meant cold sweats, in which the panic attack and resulting "fog" led John to lose control of himself. Nervous about taking an elevator to the top of the Empire State Building on one occasion, John broke out in cold sweats. If John had cold sweats, he knew he had to run away immediately and go someplace, like "The Wolfman" of celluloid fame, in order to avoid level four.

Level four was the "volcano" and the worst stage of all. John explained that "If that erupted, either I sat down, or I would fall." Level four meant total helplessness. One such episode was experienced on the bus trip to Quebec and St. Joseph's Cathedral with the Three Rivers club.

Surprisingly enough, holding an iron rake in rookie camp during the Bonebrake incident did not involve levels of trauma. While baffling to onlookers, Malangone's behavior was an immature, kneejerk reaction to Bonebrake's whining about the suitcase. John lost his temper and "did something stupid."

George "Snuffy" Stirnweiss knew what he was getting into with the arrival in Binghamton, New York, of a catcher with an off the wall reputation. The turmoil surrounding John Malangone did not subside with his departure from St. Petersburg. If anything, the negative behavior intensified, morphing the troubled slugger into a human tornado, sucking up anything or anybody that happened to cross his path. So, was it surprising that the guy climbed thirty feet up a large tree on Courthouse Square in the center of town (in a "fog"), just for the hell of it? Or went running alone out into heavy rainstorms (due to a panic attack)? Or a level three where he spent more time lurching wildly on a dime store rocket ship and "bucking bronco" rides than on baseball diamond fundamentals?

Stirnweiss managed the Binghamton Triplets club. He acquired Yankee credentials, having played second base for the team between 1943 and 1950. In 1945 he was the American League batting champion with a .309 average and led the league in stolen bases in 1944 and 1945. He was a member of the 1946 All-Star team and played in three World Series with the Yanks. In 1948 he set a new record at the time with a .993 fielding percentage, committing only five errors that season. Stirnweiss was a consummate baseball professional.

The manager became exasperated by what he witnessed at times with John. "Yogi," true to form, only reinforced his image by just playing to play, as he had done so often in the past when donning a uniform. During one game, he was immediately benched after hitting what he thought was a sure homerun over the fence. The ball was blown back by a strong wind and bounced off the top of the fence, onto the field of play. The outfield relay to second base resulted in a putout of a grinning Malangone, who was not hustling. Stirnweiss naturally exploded at the nonchalant attitude of his rookie.

A comical highlight of John's brief stay on the team came with an overthrow to home plate that stuck in netting behind home plate. John, playing catcher, managed to climb up the netting and retrieve the ball, only to find himself entangled in the netting and stuck, hovering above the plate area and sporting his trademark grin. Stirnweiss, not seeing any humor in the incident, blasted him as being a fool for climbing up the netting in the first place.

Stirnweiss had witnessed the kid's shenanigans in St. Petersburg during rookie camp. He was not welcoming of John's arrival and barely tolerated his presence. He did not hesitate to berate Malangone when it was deemed necessary. Word was that Malangone was "wacko" anyway. In Stirnweiss's opinion, John had not proven himself behind the plate, and was having trouble hitting curveballs. The skipper also had no faith in John's base running skills. After reaching base one game, Stirnweiss replaced

Malangone with a pinch runner. John protested, and Snuffy replied, "You would get picked off in a lunchroom." It didn't help Stirnweiss when an ex-Three Rivers teammate of John, pitcher Marco Mainini, arrived in Binghamton. Mainini's profile matched Malangone's, prompting *The Binghamton Press* to print a headline entitled "Mainini and Malangone: Trips' Dizziest Battery." The article described John as being seventeen pounds overweight and "a human talking machine." John was also referred to in the article as "El Malaprop" for his nonsensical comments.

Stirnweiss adhered to Casey Stengel's platoon philosophy, so right-handed hitting John only batted against the occasional left-handed pitcher. Left-handed hitter John Blanchard had arrived in Binghamton after a brief stay in Denver, and he had the lion's share of starts as the team's catcher. He proceeded to have an outstanding season in Binghamton, setting a club record with thirty-four homers. John, on the other hand, had only eight at bats with one hit in five games; lefty pitchers were scarce. John Fox, a local sportswriter, saw John play an entire game at third base "admirably" for one game, and even Stirnweiss admitted that "John had quieted down to a whisper off the field." However, it would not be good enough; Malangone had to pack his suitcase once more.

As for that photo of the happy kid on the pony, John would later say that it wasn't the real Malangone. He was masquerading his panic attacks that could erupt with a flashback at any moment without warning.

Zi! Zi! Let's go play ball!!

Before "Yogi" Malangone left the Triplets, he left John Fox with comments that made no sense and typically befuddled anyone attempting to understand the enigmatic catcher. John had played in a Scrabble game with Triplet teammates, finishing seventy points behind the next-to-last contestant despite being unable to read. He commented, in "Malangonese," that the score was not the half of it. "I got seventy-nine points and my kibitzer got eighty of them. All I got was the other nineteen." Nobody understood what John was trying to say; the remarks were foolish, but fellow teammates simply laughed it off. If there was ever an example of how dysfunctional John was at the time, these statements clearly depicted it.

John ended up going from Binghamton Class A ball to Class B minor league ball, playing only five games for the Winston Salem

Twins, also part of the Yankee organization. Manager Ken Silvestri thought something was "seriously wrong" with the Malangone kid, and ran out of patience when John hit two doubles in a game and managed to get himself picked off base on both occasions. The first pickoff was the result of a hidden ball trick, while the second could only be attributed to an unseen fog that enveloped the runner wandering off second base. Silvestri told John, "You stay here and I'll have a nervous breakdown."

Relieved to be moving again, John ended up with the Norfolk Tars and Portsmouth Merrimacs in the Piedmont League. Bill Herring was manager of the Tars, and according to John, "He loved me. I couldn't do anything wrong." The Tars folded as a franchise, so John played under Merrimacs Manager Ken Guettler, who gave John playing time every day. John was respected for being a clutch two-strike hitter and a solid "IBM" (RBI) man. This was Class B baseball, and John was more relaxed the further away he was from the majors. He finished the season with a .326 combined batting average for the two clubs. Perhaps more importantly, level three and four moments of trauma were reduced to a bare minimum, although teammates became accustomed to the inexplicable fog flashes.

As for the Yankees, the team would win the pennant that 1955 season, beating out the second place Cleveland Indians by three games. The World Series was another matter, however. The Brooklyn Dodgers team, playing against the Yankees in a World Series for the sixth time since 1941, was determined to win a world championship. The team had never won a World Series, dating back to 1890, when the Brooklyn franchise was founded and nicknamed the Bridegrooms. Jackie Robinson, in one of the most memorable World Series moments ever, stole home plate under catcher Yogi Berra's tag in game one. The series was tied at three games apiece with the seventh and final game being played at Yankee Stadium. A fly ball off Yogi Berra's bat in a critical sixth inning situation resulted in a sensational catch by Brooklyn outfielder Sandy Amoros. The catch ended the Yanks' best offensive hope of the game. Brooklyn pitcher Johnny Podres got rookie Elston Howard to make the last out, which shut out the Yanks 2-0. The Brooklyn victory unleashed an emotional tsunami among the loyal fans, sending shockwaves of euphoria all the way back to Flatbush, Brooklyn. Dodger fans of every persuasion had their prayers answered once and for all that early October afternoon. Both John and Paulie were at the game, but with different reactions. Paulie was upset by how potential situations didn't work out for the Yanks, while John was indifferent to the outcome. Playing to win was still an elusive concept to the rifle arm from Little Italy.

Nothing would change over the next three years in the minors because John was unwilling to change from within. Life was in transition in East Harlem, with the Malangone and Panarese families pulling up stakes and migrating with other Italian families to the Bronx. However, the change of scenery did not change John, and the cause of his affliction remained a secret. The various stress levels continued to flare up and the Malangone emotional tornado continued to suck up others in its path.

Returning to the "A" level in the minors in 1956, John played for the Montgomery Rebels. Montgomery was part of the nicknamed "Sally League," officially known then as the South Atlantic League. The team was managed by former major leaguer Dick Bartell. Bartell spent eighteen seasons in the big leagues, playing mostly shortstop for the Pittsburgh Pirates, Philadelphia Phillies, New York Giants, Chicago Cubs, and Detroit Tigers. Bartell was a fiery competitor in his time, appearing in All-Star games in 1933 and 1937. He was loathed by Brooklyn Dodger fans for two spiking incidents and was targeted by Dodger pitchers in retaliation. He appeared in three World Series, in 1936, 1937, and 1940. The Society for American Baseball Research (SABR) mentions in a biography on Bartell that he was ranked 38th out of the top fifty shortstops in baseball history. According to John, Bartell continued to display his defensive skills in team practices, although he did not play in any games. The Montgomery franchise did not have a winning record during the 1956 season, and the team moved to Knoxville, Tennessee late in the season after being deserted by its local fan base. The losing team was the end of the line for Bartell, who was dismissed as manager, but not before being affected by Malangone's chaotic influences.

Dick Bartell, he loved me. They say I hurt him bad. The club didn't wanna talk to me. We were going through a bad, bad streak, maybe ten in a row, something like that. We were making errors like crazy even though we hit good. I made a statement, "If we had nine Bartells on the field we would win all our games." They [reporters] twisted it and put it in the papers that I said he [Bartell] wanted nine Bartells in the field. The club ignored me for a week... the press said to me, "How do you feel now that Bartell got fired?" I didn't even know what getting fired really meant. I thought it meant that he quit. These are the little things that always got me in trouble.

Bartell left, angry at John over the misquote. His career in organized baseball was over. He spent his last day with the team sitting in the stands and glaring at Malangone. However, Bartell's departure opened the door for a player manager who arrived from Double A ball in New Orleans. John wouldn't have enough time to ponder the loss of Bartell; the new arrival had a fiery temper and, anxious to make an impression in his managerial debut, wasted no time telling John he would be benched if he went 0 for anything in any game. The new skipper's name was Earl Sidney Weaver.

Whether Weaver was aware of Malangone's prior history or reputation is not known. This was Weaver's first managing job at any level, and he was not shy about asserting his authority. The personalities of the two men immediately clashed and the tension exacerbated the slugger's panic attacks. It wasn't long before the manager resorted to labeling John "a clown." In one game, in typical Malangone fashion, personal success was erased by personal blunders. John hit "a rope, like a clothesline," and wound up on second with a double. Employing the hidden ball trick, the second baseman attempted to tag John wandering off base. Malangone, in a playful mood and aware of the trick, grinned and started quickstepping and dancing off of the bag, teasing the infielder ("One and two and one and two...") and goading him to keep tagging. The resulting antics infuriated an impatient umpire, who had had enough and screamed, "You're OUT!" If that wasn't bad enough, the entire episode was repeated, step for step, several innings later.

Weaver would occasionally use John as a pitcher in certain situations. During one game, John entered the game as a relief pitcher and walked four consecutive batters. Weaver promptly removed Malangone from the mound. John complained to fellow teammates that he didn't understand why he had come out of the game, especially since he "...was pitching a no hitter..."

During another game, John was ordered by the manager to knock down an opposing batter in retaliation for a Knoxville batter being hit by the opposing pitcher. This directive brought on the beginning of a panic attack.

He [Weaver] signaled to the catcher to have me throw a knockdown pitch at the batter. I brushed off the signal from the catcher. Why am I gonna throw a 99-100 mile an hour pitch at his head? I didn't do it. The catcher came out to talk to me. I told him no, I'm not doing it, I didn't wanna knockdown the batter. I was afraid of a panic attack. I started getting nervous, but Weaver came out of the dugout and took me out of the game. He accused me of insubordination.

His experiences with the manager left John with painful memories:

He [Weaver] let everybody know he wasn't afraid of anybody. He had a complex, being four feet eleven. He didn't like me. He would always say, "Nothing, nothing ever bothers you!" He was a real SOB. One game I got picked off second base. I just wasn't paying attention. I was getting sick and didn't play for four days. I couldn't explain it to Weaver. I didn't know myself what was happening.

It was common for John to look disheveled at times, with missing socks, untied shoes, or his uniform shirt not tucked in properly, but Weaver would have another reason to be upset with Malangone. When the team transitioned from Montgomery to Knoxville, the players were issued new uniforms. John took his jersey to the tailor, who asked Malangone what number was to be placed on his shirt. Remembering how he played the daily numbers racket back in East Harlem, and how twice he picked the winning daily number, 319, John told the tailor his number was 319. Sporting three digits on the back of a baseball uniform drew immediate attention, including chuckles from teammates and a stern reprimand from the manager.

During one game, while at bat, John missed or disregarded two suicide squeeze signs, prompting Weaver to explode and launch a verbal tirade at John. Missing signs was one thing, but the safety of the base runner on third was an even bigger issue. Fortunately for John's sanity, Paulie Tine, always around, heard the tongue-lashing and provided some sympathetic words for his buddy afterward.

Paulie always followed the bus. He had a tremendous memory and saw things from the outside. When he heard Weaver yelling, he helped me out. We needed each other.

Weaver finally told John, "You're not going to do to me what you did to the other managers. You're not gonna drive me crazy."

The season couldn't have ended fast enough for John, who reacted on all four levels of trauma under duress in Weaver's clubhouse. He would finish the season with a .262 batting average, a .461 slugging percentage and fifteen homers. The round trippers tied John with a young upstart named Harmon Killebrew for the league's best homerun total. But the summer of 1956 cost John the respect of one manager and a denial of respect from another. At the end of that summer, Casey's Yankees won another World Series from the Dodgers and Don Larsen pitched the only perfect game in Series history. John's former roommate in St. Petersburg, Johnny Kucks, pitched the final game of the series, a 9-0 shutout.

The season of 1957 saw more setbacks and trauma and was probably John's worst year in any level of professional ball. He started out in Hattiesburg, Mississippi, working out with the Binghamton Triplets again. Sports writer John Fox, covering the team, described Malangone as "a model of deportment in his first day in camp, an achievement even more breathtaking than his first five line drives off of Jim Bronstad in his first five swings in the batting cage." Playing role model, if such a thing was possible, John took an eighteen-year-old rookie named Deron Johnson under his wing. Johnson had, in John's words, an attitude problem and a "chip on his shoulder." Malangone was quoted by Fox as saying Deron "has a woise attitude than I yusta had." Johnson even inquired of John, "Why are you so fucked up?" John counseled Deron, telling him, "Don't make the same mistake I did." When Johnson inquired what the mistake was, John replied, "I dunno." In any event, Malangone remembered that Johnson actually heeded his advice, staying out of trouble and enjoying a major league career.

A new trouble spot arose in John's ongoing baseball situation; he was newly married to a beautiful East Harlem native named Rosemary Cinque, who had been dating John for several years. The couple had married in March of 1957, prior to the start of the baseball season.

Prior to the marriage, John's parents had arranged for John to marry a woman named Mafalda, who hailed from the Italian countryside town of Avellino. A "country girl" was thought by the Malangones to be a perfect solution for John's emotional troubles. John refused this idea and married the woman of his choice. The new bride was not happy with her in-laws' thoughts on arranged marriages; the issue continually boiled up among all parties involved, with in-laws not getting along with one another.

This became a tremendous source of complications for John, as club policy frowned upon having spouses or girlfriends in spring training or traveling with the team. Rosemary did not accompany John to the Binghamton club, but she refused to stay in New York and followed John to Texas.

After Binghamton, Malangone had been assigned to the Class A Amarillo, Texas team under the stewardship of Eddie Bockman. The skipper liked John and appreciated John's efforts on the ball field. He recalled John's obsession to hit balls with a fungo bat and to catch the resulting pop flies himself. Unfortunately, the presence of John's spouse made matters so distracting and uncomfortable that he could not continue playing ball. John was often late for meetings and practices because his wife didn't want to be alone. On other occasions, John would bring Rosemary to practices, in violation of team rules. Malangone lasted seven games and three hits in twelve at bats, and then he decided to quit, pack up, and drive back to New York.

Despite misgivings about John's behavior, the Yankee organization had not given up on him, and they contacted him in his Bronx home. John recalled someone calling to ask, "Who died?" The club persuaded John to go to Charlotte, North Carolina and play with the Hornets club, managed by Gene Verble. Arriving in Charlotte, John quickly discovered that Verble, who was serious about competing, was similar to Billy Martin in character, and that meant friction. Verble was furious that John had brought his wife and was two days late. Despite being married to John, Rosemary was not aware of John's illiteracy and his inability to read traffic signs. Upon arrival in Charlotte, Malangone skipped a scheduled game and took his wife out to eat.

Despite earning a game-winning hit in his first official contest the next day with the Hornets, matters took a turn for the worse. Rosemary was banned from the road trips, creating a strain between John and her. Verble, meanwhile, in John's words, "crucified me." Similar to past situations, John would seemingly smack balls out of the park that would actually remain in play, and fail to hustle when rounding the bases. Verble, like other skippers before him, would scream and remove the troubled player from the game. John was so miserable that he batted .216 in fifty-four games and wanted out again. He was unable to concentrate on anything, even dressing like a "rag doll" when team personnel, dressed up in sport jackets, were being publicly honored at a dinner in a nearby local hotel. It seemed at times that the fog was everywhere.

A flashback during one game led to John having a panic attack during a strikeout call by umpire Henry Morgan. Malangone and Morgan had always gotten along, but on this occasion, Morgan ruled a strike on a missed swing, while John argued that it was a foul tip that "hit the floor." John, suddenly nervous, let his imagination go wild. Speaking resentfully to the "guy behind his back" (his invisible demon), John muttered, apparently loud enough for Morgan and Verble to hear:

John: *Go fuck yourself, scumbag...*

Morgan [visibly agitated and tossing John out of the game]: *You're outta here! You fucking clown!*

John [refocusing on Morgan]: *Whaddya crazy? Why? I wasn't talking to you! You are a bum!!*

Verble [screaming]: *You're gettin' fined! What the fuck did you do now?*

The bad news kept coming, as John was informed that Paul Krichell had passed away in June of 1957. Aware of Krichell's passing, a fellow player had sarcastically commented to John, "Your rabbi is gone, and [referring to John's presence on the team] it won't be long before you're gone, too."

The next stop for John in midseason after Charlotte was the Wilson Tobs team in Wilson, North Carolina. Notwithstanding a newspaper photo displaying John holding a bat while wearing his stirrups backward, matters for the slugger improved considerably. Rosemary returned to New York, removing the social distraction from the club, and John was embraced by his new skipper, Pete Suder. With less pressure and a friendly manager, "bad apple" John finished the summer of 1957 with a .354 batting average in twenty-six games and no level four volcanoes.

Malangone's journey through the minor leagues could not be evaluated on the basis of statistics alone, as he was either loved by players, fans, and reporters for his zaniness and hidden and underutilized talent, or loathed by serious-minded managers and coaches for the same reasons.

"Yogi" Malangone's talent at bat was often overshadowed by his notoriously bad base running skills. Managers would resort to using pinch runners for him, when they had the opportunity to do so. John was often a defensive liability as well. Despite having a powerful throwing arm for a catcher, John drove both pitchers and managers crazy at times with signal calling. His outlook for his battery mates was very basic: throw the ball over the plate. John would flash signals behind the plate that could not be interpreted by pitchers. Managers would scream, "I don't want three fastballs in a row, I don't want three curveballs in a row, I don't want..." His response to all the orders and suggestions was an innocent one. He would simply say, "Look, want me to go pitch instead?"

While catching during one game, John became surrounded by one of his fogs. Turning to "blue" standing behind the plate, John inquired, "Do you know what I called for?" The ump responded, "Don't be a fucking wise guy." Malangone made the situation worse by incorrectly looking for a slider on the next pitch, when an incoming fastball sailed past his shoulder and nailed the umpire. Believing that John deliberately set up the pitch, the umpire, now in pain, ejected the catcher, leaving other players to wonder what happened.

Yet no one could understand the reasons for his behavior. In his later years, he would reflect on how the further down he was in the farm system, the more relaxed he became; he would always fear the glare of media publicity and East Harlem neighborhood stories at the Major League level. But no matter where he played, the flashbacks he experienced continually from childhood would resurface at any time.

The different socks... The pain in the temple... I can feel it...

During one game, an attack prompted a volcano—a total meltdown. Getting a single, John kept running down the first base line past the bag, into the outfield, and then scaled over the fence. Malangone circled around the entire outfield fence and reentered the ballpark from the left field foul line. The subsequent ejection prompted other players to pile on the wisecracks:

Hey John! Pay it no mind... Hey John, I know why you climbed the fence. You had a ball in your pocket and you wanted a homer instead of a single... Hey John! If you stopped at third on the way back, you coulda had a triple... Hey John...

Anxious moments could creep into his mind while simply leading off bases.

The javelin flying through the air... I am running ahead of it to catch it... it will be OK now, it never happened... There it goes again, am I gonna catch it again?

Sometimes John was simply a magnet for trouble. He was popular with the local fans, but during one game, John had to confront a huge, drunken sailor sitting in the stands in Norfolk. The sailor taunted John while he knelt in the on deck circle, slurring

Malangone's Italian ancestry, and the place where he grew up.

He said, "How come you're not like those guys [Mafia] that shoot up the city [New York]? Yeah, I said it. Hey catch... Hey, did your mother have any children that lived?"

Not content with just verbalizing, the sailor stepped over the low railing, intending to use fisticuffs with John, but he never had the chance. The drunkard was unaware of the fearsome Malangone left hook, which rendered him unconscious. In John's words, "He went down like a tree." In a display of foolish second-guessing by the club, John was fined and suspended, and he was told he should have walked away from a confrontation. No one realized that a fight was the last thing on Malangone's mind.

With panic attacks and the fog phases, John would lose focus and awareness of the circumstances surrounding him. Being a loose cannon on and off of the field was good therapy, because he wouldn't have to dwell on guilt, tragic mistakes, or haunting childhood memories. On the *Long Road Home* documentary, John described his new identity following Yankee rookie camp as, "I am a clown, don't fool around, clown. Now I played the part." The minor leagues were a perfect forum for "Yogi" Malangone antics because oftentimes club owners, in an effort to improve sagging attendance, resorted to zaniness themselves by using entertaining stunts or tricks. They employed professionals like Jackie Price, a well-known ex-baseball player who entertained the fans with skilled baseball performances. His more renowned stunts included taking batting practice while suspended upside down from a pole or backstop. He also employed an air gun, which fired a baseball into the outfield, and Price would jump into a jeep and catch the ball on the fly.

Malangone tried to replicate the stunt in Norfolk using the Mercury that Paulie Tine brought from New York. The Mercury's brakes, unfortunately, did not stop the car, which skidded along the wet grass and crashed headlong into the outfield fence and scoreboard. In John's words, "People were jumpin' outta the o's and ones." John was not hurt, and he gained more popularity with the amused fans. They turned out the next day in droves to survey the damage scene. The objective of increased attendance was accomplished.

John wisecracked about some headline the next day that read something to the effect of, "If you don't give Malangone a hit, then he'll go right through the scoreboard."

Malangone also participated in other promotional stunts, including cow milking contests in Charlotte and Norfolk. In both cases John, dressed and promoted as the "city slicker," filled his buckets with more milk than the local farmers, who were supposed to show their strength and quickness in handling the cows. Instead, embarrassed by Malangone's unexpected success, the local farmers became upset about losing in front of the home fans. In one of the contests, an angry farmer ended up chasing a grinning, laughing Malangone all over the ballpark after the contest was decided in John's favor. For John, this was pure fun and a relief from everything else around him.

We'll never win the pennant with you…

When not clowning around, John was withdrawn, by his own admission. When not sharing the company of Paulie Tine, he stayed alone, away from other people. One significant exception was the empathy he had with the local African American population. His minor league career, from 1955 to 1958, was spent in the South; from Amarillo to Norfolk, the region was blanketed by overt, legal racial segregation that severely discriminated against its black citizens.

Despite the integration of Jackie Robinson into baseball with the Brooklyn Dodgers in 1947, many areas of the country were just beginning to experience social changes being forged by Martin Luther King and the civil rights movement. Black players in the South were either not welcomed or were jeered by white fans, and these athletes were often not sufficiently supported by the clubs that employed them. Baseball parks were routinely segregated, with African American fans forced to sit in poor viewing areas, usually behind outfield fences. Road games were especially tough on black players, who were refused accommodations at segregated hotels or service at rest stops. John always got along with his black teammates, and he would speak up against local food merchants not willing to sell sandwiches or "chicken in the baskets" to anyone because of black players on the bus. He would criticize his white teammates if they were not willing to take a stand on certain matters that involved the well-being of everyone on the team. His childhood racial experiences, good and bad, in East Harlem and Canada proved to be a continuing asset for John in the growing turmoil of the fifties era. His feelings on the subject were deep and emotional, having witnessed firsthand the overt discrimination that black people were facing at the time.

This was something very close to me, ya know. These guys had two strikes against them. I could relate to that. Some of these guys couldn't read, either... that was right up my alley. I was suffering and they were suffering. It was for different reasons, but when someone is hurting, I feel they are a part of me, ya know?

Despite the ability to relate to others who were hurting, John had a tough time co-existing with "roomies." His personal worries about panic attacks made him uncomfortable around others in close quarters.

When I went to Norfolk I had a tough time. They wanted all players to live in groups of three or four. I didn't like that. Norfolk never knew about Paulie, who stayed nearby in Virginia Beach. Paulie and I shared living quarters whenever we could. We hung out together all the time. We always needed each other. He never interfered, never said anything, but he would follow the team bus everywhere.

When not playing ball, John preferred staying away from his teammates, choosing to spend weeks sleeping in his car, especially during his tenure with the Norfolk Tars. John told teammates that he was staying at the "Hotel Mercury." Tommy Venditelli, infielder at Norfolk, got along well with John. His fellow players put him in charge of locating the phantom hotel. He later told John,

They told me to follow you. We spent weeks looking for this Hotel Mercury and never found it. We realized there was no such thing... I followed you all over the place, but I couldn't keep up with you. You drove like somebody was following you. You'd make a U-turn on the railroad tracks.

Venditelli recalled finally locating John:

He would take his car to Virginia Beach and sleep there all night. He would do this for weeks.

The Mercury eventually met its fate in the famous scoreboard crash. When John was asked what happened to the car, he simply grinned and said, "Me and Paulie just left it there, just like with the Cadillac at the Willis Avenue Bridge."

John resumed playing in 1958, again in the Carolina League, this time for the Greensboro Yankees. Greensboro catcher Glenn Steve Crihfield provided this assessment on the team:

Every year, the Yankees put all the crazy players on one team so only one manager has to mess with them, and this year it's Greensboro... [laughing] oooookayyy...

Greensboro's "crazy players," including John, played well as a team that year, finishing five games off the front-runner, the Danville Leafs. Malangone played the entire season for just the Yankees, and he batted .256 with seventeen homers in one hundred twenty two games.

Vern Hoscheit was the manager, with a disposition similar to Gene Verble of the Charlotte Hornets. He didn't make things any easier for "Yogi" Malangone. He once remarked to John, "If I had your fucking talent..."

The Yankees never officially released John from any professional obligations or his baseball contract. In the spring of 1959, another motorcycle accident ended John Malangone's professional baseball career, once and for all.

I was in spring training in Florida for Knoxville. I had a bike accident and I cut my hand. I was lucky to still be alive... the Yankees didn't know I had another bike. I was racing downhill on a narrow road and the turn was too tight. My leg was broken. The bike was demolished. I went to a hospital and never told anybody, and I called Paulie in New York to come get me. I had a secret wish to end everything and quit anyway. I knew in my heart that 1955 was my big chance and that it was now too late.

The Yankees did look for John, and contacted the family, but Josephine Malangone informed the organization that her son was finished and he was not coming back. John was left only with the memories, and they would haunt him the rest of his life. He would frequently think back by saying, "If only I had done it the way I was supposed to..."

John finished his minor league career, including Three Rivers, with a .276 average and sixty-eight homeruns.

There was a stark contrast between John and the other players by the end of Malangone's time in the minors. Johnny Kucks and John Blanchard made it to the Yankees and helped the organization's winning ways as the team transitioned from the Stengel years to the Ralph Houk era in the early sixties. Yogi Berra continued burnishing his eventual Hall of Fame credentials and even managed the Yanks to a pennant in 1964. Elston Howard spent most of his fourteen-year career with the team while taking over catching duties. Deron Johnson went on to have a solid professional career for seventeen years, beginning with the Yankees. Earl Weaver would eventually rise to the major league level and guide the Baltimore Orioles to the World Series on three occasions, one of them a loss to Ed Charles and the Miracle Mets in 1969. Harmon Killebrew would go on to be a Hall of Famer with the Minnesota Twins club. Killebrew, regarded as a prolific homerun hitter and modest man, was affectionately nicknamed "Killer," something that Malangone, with matching power, wanted to avoid having to think about at all costs.

Although his professional baseball career had ended, the suffering that plagued John Malangone most of his young life would continue. There was no relief in sight.

"The guy looking over my shoulder" would remain invisible to everyone who came in contact with John. Failing in an effort to talk with Phil Page, John considered reaching out to a neighborhood character back home nicknamed "Moose." A street peddler by trade, Moose was no laughing matter when he accidentally killed someone in a street fight over accusations of philandering with another man's wife. Despite relating his own experiences to that of Moose, John never followed through with the idea of taking Moose into his confidence. The truth about John Malangone's dark secret, one that kept him from becoming a potential superstar with the Yankees, would remain hidden for decades to come.

Zi! Zi! Wake up! Zi...

PART II
Penance

"You never forgot, did you?"

Sylvester Malangone, on his deathbed, to his son, John, in 1980

"I don't know how I survived..."

John Malangone, reflecting on his life

"John, we hardly knew you."

Cousin John Panarese, reflecting on family
views of John Malangone

"Everybody forgives you, Johnny..."

John's brother, Sal, commenting during a family gathering

Chapter 17
Bronx Tales

The end of a career with the Yankee organization did not stop John Malangone from continuing to play baseball; his permanent return to New York City was characterized by playing more baseball at the semi-pro level. In fact, a transition occurred in the fall of 1957 following John's worst season in the minors. In September of that year, John and Paulie played some games for a Bronx team called the Mel Greene Cubs, a semi-pro club originally managed by a pitcher named Moe Resner. East Harlem natives on the roster who grew up with John included Paulie's brother Mike, and the father and son tandem of Lefty Mike Sacino and Gary Sacino. Jefferson Park in the old neighborhood spawned quite a few talented aspiring baseball players during that era, and many continued to play together after high school and minor league careers were over.

During breaks from minor league ball, and in the years immediately afterward in the sixties, John frequently returned to his old stomping grounds in East Harlem and Jefferson Park. Tony Belli, a local resident and ballplayer who was part of the generation behind John, summed up the neighborhood's universal feelings about John:

One thing you knew... one thing you always heard, like echoes, that there was this guy, this legend, John Malangone. The legend was that he did everything with a baseball better than everybody else. We had some pretty good athletes, ballplayers, but they used to say to each other, "You're good, but John is a level or two above." That was kind of the gold standard for our baseball players.

Brother Sal recalled how neighborhood reactions were always enthusiastic:

We would be playing in the pool hall and someone would come in and say, "John Malangone is playing over in Jefferson Park. They gonna hafta move the fences back." People would get excited and rush over to the park to watch him play. Everybody looked up to him and wanted to be like him. I usta get up on top of the pool table and proudly remind everybody, "Hey, that's my brother!"

The talent of the man, as always, was accompanied by the usual antics. One neighborhood resident, Joe Santarpia, remembers standing near a backstop in Jefferson Park and watching John.

John was taking some batting practice swings and missing. I started teasing him about missing the pitches, not realizing I was clinging to the chain link fence with my fingers inside the fence. Next thing ya know, he swings and the bat goes flying outta his hands right at me. I was lucky I got my fingers outta the fence in time. He just stood there, good naturedly smiling, saying, "Oops, sorry about that..." He smiled and I knew better about what he was doing.

The loss of opportunities with the Yankees was supplanted by a homegrown resurgence of interest in playing on local metropolitan New York teams. He was welcomed by old neighborhood friends back into local competition and proceeded to play for various teams in different leagues and tournaments, always for money. With the pressure of proving himself as a ball player for the Yankees gone, John's performance in the local leagues dramatically improved. His reputation as a power hitter grew in leaps and bounds. Players in defensive positions always took a step or two back whenever John Malangone stepped up to the plate.

Milton Wadler, who played with the Bronx-based Arthur Avenue Red Wings, declared, "He was a hitter. Always a hitter... always!" Red Wings manager Sal Florio would always warn his players, "Do not mess with John Malangone. He doesn't play. Keep your mouths shut and play baseball."

However, along with the big bat and powerful arm came the same flaky behavior that marked Malangone's tenure in the minor leagues.

Bob Goldsholl, a former broadcaster with WPIX and CBS in the New York area, was also a former minor league pitcher in the Giants organization. He ended up playing amateur ball in the New York metro area. Goldsholl remembers John Malangone well. Regarding John as "sort of a legend" in the New York baseball community, Bob finally got an opportunity to pitch against John and the Bronx Yankees. Goldsholl was confident in his pitching abilities, possessed a great slider, and was not intimidated by Malangone's presence in the batter's box. However, he did find John to be a distraction; Goldsholl observed that John was constantly grinning as he stepped to the plate. He was annoyed, wondering "what John was smiling at." He soon came to realize, like other players, that John was cocky in a nice way.

I told him later that he was "at home in the batter's box. He looked happy when swinging a bat at home plate. Hitting was so easy for him." I also told him, "I guess you are not intimidated by anyone."

The following season, both of them ended up playing together, with John catching "a great game" for his pitcher.

Despite John's popularity and the respect he earned from other ballplayers, even Bob Goldsholl would notice something awry in John's demeanor. He phrased his observation in a manner similar to the comments made by others through the years, saying, "Not all the tools are in the shed." John's pain was to continue eating at him all through his baseball career; the secret would remain intact for nearly three more decades.

During this time, John occasionally played for an amateur club known as the New Rochelle Robins, managed by the genteel Dick Caswell. A native of St. Louis, Missouri, Caswell moved to New York after leaving the Air Force. He got involved at the inception of the Robins club in 1956, and he played in the field, managed in the dugout, or acted as the team's general manager ever since. In the early years of its existence, the team was a member of the old Colonial Baseball League and the Sound Shore League. The Robins won tournaments in Maryland, Michigan, and Pennsylvania, and they participated in international competitions against Canada, China, Japan, and British Columbia. In the home county of Westchester, New York, the Robins won the Westchester Baseball Association Championships five times. Going into the 2013 season, the club had an overall record of 2,167 wins and 1,142 losses for a .655 winning percentage.

Dick Caswell, awed by John Malangone's power, never knew or understood the real John Malangone or his issues. He first noticed John while he was playing for the Bronx Union Y at Macombs Dam field. In later years, he would get a glimpse of the commotion that always surrounded the slugger in an AABC (American Amateur Baseball Congress) Tournament held one summer in Albany, New York. In a semifinal game, John, leaving second base, attempted to avoid being struck by a ball hit to the shortstop position. Twisting awkwardly, he suffered a sharp pain in his left leg and had to leave the game. The diagnosis from a subsequent hospital visit revealed a hairline fracture. Anxious to play in the championship final against the Brooklyn Eagles the next day, John publicly declared the injury a sprain in order to avoid packing up with his wife for a return ride home. Only Caswell and Paulie, who followed John to the tournament, knew what was going on. Due to the injury, John did not start the championship game, but in the late innings he was approached by Caswell, who asked, "John, do ya think you can pinch hit?" Overhearing the conversation, John's wife angrily declared, "You will get hurt. If you go out there, I am leaving and getting divorced." A strong impulse to play overrode any fear of getting divorced, and John stepped to the plate and belted a hit that could have been a triple. Despite excruciating pain, he managed to go ninety feet to first base, trotting, walking, hobbling, and finally crawling on all fours onto the bag.

The Robins eventually lost the game, but Paulie and John couldn't wait around for the outcome. They were too busy chasing after Rosemary, already in the couple's car and long gone from the field. For John, his priorities quickly changed from playing baseball to restoring marital harmony.

Dick Caswell, in a recent conversation with John, had forgotten the incident. John smiled and said, "You had to remember that, you paid the hospital bill."

The games in which John and Paulie participated also had excellent competition from public institutions, including prisons and mental hospitals. John recalled one game against Creedmoor Psychiatric Center in nearby Queens, New York, which fielded very good employee-based teams.

I got hit in the head by a fastball. They [Creedmoor staffers] said, "We want you to come with us for observation." I said I am alright. They said "No, please come with us." So, I went in there, maybe for about half an hour. They asked me some questions, like, how do you spell your name? I couldn't read and I misspelled it with two l s instead of one. Paulie is there, getting impatient and waitin' and waitin'. They said, "We going have to keep him for more observation." Paulie said, "What? Wait a minute... why? What happened?" They said, "He's not talkin' right." Paulie went bananas. He goes, "What? Wait a minute, he always talks like that... with him you never know what the fuck he's talking about.

[Motioning to John] Let's get the hell outta here, I gotta go."

An upstate penitentiary in Ossining, New York, known as Sing Sing, provided John with a ready-made audience of admirers. During one game, John hit a homer that soared over a guard watchtower, prompting one inmate spectator to remark, "Do that again and I'll ride it right on outta here."

Following the 1964 season, John and Paulie joined a team called the Bronx Yankees, a dominant sandlot team that played many games in Van Cortlandt Park and at Babe Ruth Field, situated next to the old Yankee Stadium. The Bronx Yankee roster included East Harlem athletes Malangone, Paulie, Dan Benedetto, Carmine Caridi (future actor in the *Godfather* movie trilogy), Gary Sacino, Mike DeRosa (a Bronx baseball legend and ex-minor leaguer in his own right), and Floyd Layne. Floyd's stature as an outstanding athlete in basketball in the early 1950s also included a prowess for baseball. A lefty fireballer in baseball, Floyd was followed by big league scouts when he was only thirteen years of age.

Mike DeRosa, as a teenager growing up in the Bronx, had heard about John:

I heard about him in the fifties. He was a legend in East Harlem. Everybody knew about the "big hitter." He kept us laughing all the time. One day we had a doubleheader at Macombs Dam Park and John showed up in street clothes. He told us he went out to get a dozen eggs for his wife, but somehow wound up at the ball field. He got a wrinkled uniform out of his car trunk and played two games. The wife never got the eggs.

DeRosa also recognized Paulie Tine as a very good player, but perhaps more significantly viewed Paulie as John's "guardian angel." He knew Paulie followed John everywhere, "even into the army."

Malangone's reputation as a power hitter was so established that Bronx native Burt Beagle once wrote, "Malangone, a former New York Yankee farmhand, is respected as the most dangerous hitter on the Bronx sandlots." Beagle further stated that John "hates to take a walk. And he is not afraid to let a pitcher know his feelings after an intentional walk."

One of John's career highlights included belting three homeruns, while narrowly missing a fourth, and driving in nine runs in the final game of the 1965 Bronx Sandlotters Tournament. John was presented with the Most Valuable Player award for the occasion, but he suggested the award go to another player, saying, "Give it to the kid." That other player was a teenage phenomenon named Ken Singleton, who according to John batted six for six in the game. Singleton went on to play Major League Baseball with the Mets, Expos, and Baltimore Orioles.

On occasion, while playing in Macombs Dam Park near Yankee Stadium, John would say hello to his former Yankee roommate John Blanchard, then on the big league club's roster, whenever Blanchard was arriving at the stadium for a Yankee home game. However, Blanchard was traded from the Yankees to Kansas City in 1965 and was devastated by the news. He contacted John for support. "Yogi" Malangone offered Blanchard another perspective on the trade:

You are not going there to be a janitor are you? You are gonna play professional ball, right? It can't be that bad. Want me to take your place [laughing]?

For all of the wonderful memories that John had playing for the Bronx Yankees, one in particular would stand out and ultimately impact the ballplayer's damaged psyche. It involved playing a doubleheader for big money against a tough opponent, which was commonplace in that era. Reinforced by a gambling habit learned back in East Harlem, John placed a large sum of money on the games. John pitched 1-0 shutout in the first game and played the entire second game as a catcher calling signals behind the plate. The Yankees, ahead 2-1 in the bottom of the ninth, faced a precarious situation. The bases were loaded with one out, and their opponent's best hitter, an excellent spray hitter and slugger, stood at the plate, ready to hit.

John called timeout and offered to come in to relieve the starter. John's offer was rejected, so he told the pitcher to throw an inside pitch, but it didn't matter. The Yanks' worse fear was realized when the slugger smashed a one hopper past the pitcher and up the middle, past second base. But from out of nowhere, the flashy second baseman for the Yanks, in one motion, backhanded the ground ball and flipped the ball to shortstop Mike DeRosa, who stepped on second base. DeRosa then threw to the renowned Floyd Lane at first base, capping a sensational double play and ending the game in a breathtaking fashion. This was a Bronx Yankee version of the Tinkers to Evers to Chance double play combination of Chicago Cub fame.

While the victors celebrated, John reflected on the

sensational play and the fielder responsible for saving the win. The play became a lasting memory for Malangone, not only for the hefty winning bets, but also for the guy with the sure-handed glove playing second base. During the postgame celebration, John asked around, "Who is that guy? Get his name. I'll share my money with him." That guy's name was Ron Weiss, and the game would mark the beginning of a lifelong friendship between Ron and John, one that would endure through good times and bad right up to the present day. While both men still never tire of talking about the game's outcome, both men will stress that Weiss's presence more importantly initiated a change in John. John's suffering would continue for years after meeting Ron Weiss, but that special moment nevertheless marked the beginning of movement for John in a positive direction.

Chapter 18

The Game Changer

New York Metro Area
1960s-1992

Ronnie Weiss first walked into John Malangone's life in 1964, when he joined the minor league Bronx Yankees and initially competed against John in metro area amateur and semi-pro games.

Ronnie, twenty-seven years of age at the time, brought his own impressive credentials when he joined the team. A typical New York City kid who grew up in Yorkville in Upper Manhattan, Weiss played stickball, boxball, and other street games. He recalled childhood memories in the busy city streets:

All my waking hours were spent on the street in front of my house. I reluctantly went in to eat, but came right back out and played until we lost the ball or I was dragged away by my family. The proving grounds for my life were developed on the asphalt streets of Yorkville. Baseball helped me develop a sense of belonging in my neighborhood.

He persuaded his dad to supply Spaldeens to keep stickball games going. Ron was eventually introduced to sandlot baseball in Central Park, joining a team called the Pirates and playing third base at the age of ten. When a teammate remarked that baseball was just a game and no big deal, Ron decided otherwise; he believed from an early age that wanting to win would never be a mistake. With his passion for the game ignited, his fierce competitiveness in baseball would serve him well wherever he played, and at any level. In time, his spirited character would also gain the respect and admiration of "the great John Malangone," as he so often referred to John later in life.

At the age of twelve, Ron developed a friendship with Jerry Umano, a neighborhood boy who encouraged him to join the Harlem Police Athletic League. The two boys continued playing baseball together, including games in nearby African American neighborhoods, believing that the competition would eventually sharpen their baseball skills. Ron would always speak fondly about this phase of life as being a cultural experience that lasted throughout his entire life; as a teenager, he developed a deep love and appreciation for jazz music. Ron and Jerry joined the American Baseball Academy, a program held in the National Guard Armory on 34th Street in Manhattan. Professional ballplayers, including Phil Rizzuto, Yogi Berra, Gil Hodges, Monte Irvin, Gene Hermanski, and Gil McDougald all taught baseball skills at one time or another at the Academy.

As a youngster, in the years following World War II, Ron grew up in a neighborhood that was Hungarian, Irish, and heavily German. Although his father owned a candy store in the neighborhood, there were few Jewish residents in the area; Ron would complain to his parents about neighborhood kids picking on him because of his Jewish background. He would always be told to go deal with these issues on his own. This situation prompted Ron to attend Seward High School in lower Manhattan, where his background was accepted and he was more comfortable with the student body. Taking accelerated courses, he graduated at the age of fifteen. He became captain of the baseball team during his high school years. During this time he worked in his father's candy store and got another job installing typewriter keys. After high school, he attended CCNY in upper Manhattan, not far from Yorkville. While majoring as a teacher in physical education, he made the CCNY baseball team as a sophomore and started every game for three years. In 2007, he would be inducted into the CCNY Hall of Fame for his baseball accomplishments. He would credit baseball scouting legend Lou Haneles for mentoring him on the game of baseball.

In 1959, Ron joined the army and continued to play sports, managing his own baseball and basketball teams. Leaving the army and joining the reserves, he got a job with the 7UP Soda Company driving a soda delivery truck and "muscle building" in the process. During all this time, he and Jerry Umano continued their friendship, playing ball and joining a semi-pro team called the Phillies. They played in the Tri-County League, which covered the New York metro area. The Phillies were an independent team, paying their rostered players small sums for compensation. Unfortunately for Ron and Jerry, the league folded a short time later, and at the age of twenty-two, Ron Weiss stopped playing baseball. Embracing a new vocation in life, he started a teaching and coaching career at Knox High School in East Harlem.

It wasn't long before Weiss' inner desire to play baseball resurfaced. In 1964, the thrill of playing with the semi-pro Bronx

Yankees proved to be just "what the doctor ordered," in Ron's words. The team proved to be very competitive and successful. In 1965, John and Paulie Tine joined the team. Weiss had previously heard of many Malangone legendary baseball feats, and now he had a chance to play with John for the first time. The Bronx Yankees provided the beginning of a lifelong friendship for Weiss and "the great John Malangone."

Mr. "play to win" complemented Mr. "play to play" and the two began respecting each other's talent and abilities. There was one game where both players hit a pair of home runs. Ron became accustomed to John's antics during games, and he recalled one game where John, who was pitching at the time, attempted seventeen pickoff attempts on a first base runner during just one at bat. The hitter, and the rest of the opposing team, complained loudly to the plate umpire about moving the game along and how John's pickoff attempts were totally ridiculous and sacrilegious from a baseball standpoint. John, grinning from ear to ear as always, obliged the complaints by occasionally interrupting the pickoff moves and quick pitching the emotionally distraught batter. The umpire raised his right hand twice to call strikes, not noticing that John was a few steps in front of the pitching rubber and getting away with the calls. This raised more howls of protests from the other team, whose players were so beside themselves that they failed to pay attention to any other details. On the seventeenth throw, while sporting his trademark grin, John picked off the base runner, which put an end to the controversy and also resulted in John laughing in satisfaction. Ronnie, accustomed to John at that point, enjoyed the rhubarb as well. If John acted like he was "playing to play" during the game, that was okay with Ronnie for two reasons. One, he always gravitated to the best player on the team (in this case John Malangone), and two, in Ronnie's words, "Hey, he got the guy out."

Malangone and Weiss parted ways after the 1965 season, shortly after playing the aforementioned big moneyed doubleheader, which included Ron Weiss's memorable game-saving defensive play.

In 1970, Weiss's teaching and coaching jobs produced playing dividends for the young instructor. Ron had coached a student, Sabah Mendez, who graduated and was signed by the Yankees as a prospect. Released by the Yankees because of a sore arm, the former student joined a widely respected Hispanic baseball league that was based in Central Park. The kid asked Ron if he wanted to play, and shortly thereafter Ron accepted the offer to play third base for a team in the league that was sponsored by Pepsi-Cola. Ron played one season with the team. He felt nostalgic about his playing days with John Malangone, and kept calling the team's catcher, Willie Vega, "John."

Weiss was finished with baseball for the second time in his life, and he decided to play softball to ease the transition out of the hardball game. Ron competed in fast pitch softball leagues over the next twenty-five years, only to be slowed down by a variety of injuries. His marriage to Patricia Suarez in 1972 produced a son named ARon, in 1976, and Weiss would spend his time parenting and coaching the boy in the game of baseball. In 1991, Ron finally retired from teaching and coaching in the New York City public school system. He began to spend more time at home writing about his life experiences. Little did Weiss realize that his writing would eventually include the experiences of John Malangone, with whom he had lost contact over twenty-five years ago. Fate would reunite the two men and rejuvenate a friendship that lasts to the present day.

Photos

Orlando A. Panarese, born 1929, died 1937. Orlando was the son of Sylvia and John Panarese, and John Malangone's uncle. John always affectionately called Orlando "Zi."

Our Lady of Mount Carmel Church is an iconic fixture in East Harlem. The church houses a bell tower that John frequented in the years immediately following Orlando's death. John sought emotional relief in Mount Carmel for nearly his entire life.

John and Sylvia Panarese, circa 1910 in Italy. The couple were John's maternal grandparents and parents of the deceased Orlando A. Panarese.

A 1931 wedding photo of John's parents, Josephine and Sylvester Malangone, on the right. On the left is John's Uncle, Enrico Malangone, nicknamed "Demo" by the mob. Enrico is joined by his wife Fannie, also known as "Aunt Faye."

John, at 3½ years old, on a pony ride in front of the Malangone residence on 114th Street in East Harlem, in the winter of 1936.

John's childhood friend and uncle, Orlando, on a pony, in the spring of 1937, shortly before his death.

John's building and alleyway on 114th Street in East Harlem was torn down in the 1950s. The photo shows an identical alleyway, still standing, several blocks away in the same neighborhood. John would practice throwing baseballs sixty feet to hit low targets on the back wall, without breaking any overhead lights. The alleyway is where John developed his "rifle arm."

John's ninth grade class at Benjamin Franklin High School in 1947. John is in the third row from the bottom, third from the left. John's tutor, Mr. Locke, is pictured in the second row from the bottom on the far left.

John and others at a typical East Harlem social club. John is wearing the All-Star jacket from the *New York Journal-American*'s 1951 All-Star game at the Polo Grounds. The neighborhood's social clubs and organized crime reputation were a source of concern to the Yankee organization.

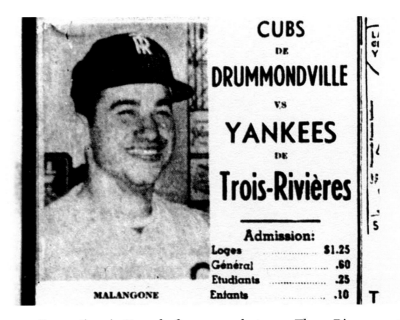

Promotion, in French, for a game between Three Rivers (John's club) and the rival Drummondville Cubs in 1952 in the Provincial League in Canada. Three Rivers was a Yankee farm club at the time.

This most valuable player award, the Lord Calvert trophy, was given to John following the 1952 season in Quebec, Canada. The trophy survived the personal destruction of some of John's baseball accomplishments during the 1980s.

John joined the U.S. Army in 1952. He was not sent to the Korean War front. His role was to provide sports entertainment for troops returning from combat.

In his final boxing match, in 1953, John knocked out Tom Peoples at a U.S. Army heavyweight boxing championship in Fort Dix, New Jersey.

CPL. JAMES D. PARKER (left), 9th MP Co. motorcycle patrolman thanks Pfc. John Malangone of the 60th Inf. Regt., who saved him from drowning in Browns Mills Lake last Friday when he was stricken with leg cramps. Malangone dived into the lake, pulled him to safety and quickly revived him by applying artificial respiration. (Signal Photo by Harper)

Rescuer of Drowning MP Recommended for Medal

Pfc. John Malangone of Hq. and Hq. Co., 60th Inf. Regt., who rescued a Military Police corporal from drowning in Brown's Mills Lake last Friday night, has been recommended for the Soldier's Medal by his CO, Capt. William C. Gardner.

The hero, post heavyweight boxing champion and member of his regiment's baseball team, dived into the lake to save Cpl. James D. Parker, a motorcycle patrolman with the 9th MP Co., stricken with leg cramps some distance from shore.

The MP was barely conscious when his rescuer reached him and pulled him to safety. Malangone quickly revived Parker by applying artificial respiration.

The patrolman claims he owes his life to Malangone's "prompt and courageous action."

Malangone, whose home is in New York City, played at the Polo Grounds in 1951 as a member of the New York Journal-American All-Star baseball team. Before his induction, he played with the Three Rivers team of the Canadian Provincial League, part of the New York Yankee chain. He is now Yankee property.

While stationed at Fort Dix, John rescued Corporal James Parker from drowning in a lake in Browns Mills, New Jersey in 1953.

John posing with a bat in his NY Yankees uniform in rookie
camp in 1955. The photo was never published because of the
conspicuous hole in his stirrup and the shoe polish rubbed in
the white sock, to cover the opening. The photo is emblematic of
John's behavioral issues in the camp.

John riding a dimestore pony during the 1955 Binghamton
Triplets spring training camp in Statesville, North Carolina.
The picture was taken prior to the start of the season and after
John was released from the Yankee rookie camp.
Photo by John Fox, Binghamton Press.

A Louisville Slugger® bat signed by John in Yankee rookie camp
in 1955. He was ridiculed by teammates for the misspelling
"Jhon" before the company attempted to correct the mistake.

John posing with a baseball in spring training, 1957, in
Hattiesburg, MS. Despite being in a Binghamton uniform for the
picture, John was reassigned elsewhere for the season.
Photo by John Fox, Binghamton Press.

John (center) and Wilson Tobs teammates, 1957. John's shirt sleeves were cut so he could wear the uniform shirt.

John during spring training of 1957.

Three buddies playing for the Mel Greene Cubs in the Bronx, N.Y. in the fall of 1957. From left to right: Paulie Tine, John Malangone, Mike Tine (Paulie's brother). The trio were often called "the three musketeers."

John's former Yankee teammates, catcher John Blanchard and pitcher Johnny Kucks, remained lifelong friends with John. Kucks once remarked, "I'll take John on my team any day. He will bring in more runs than he will give up." Photos by Bruce Spiegel.

John and Mark Van Overloop, founder of A League Of Our Own
(ALOOO). John has spent over twenty years playing and being
involved in the league.

John is shown here entertaining former New Rochelle Robins
teammates with stories. John has attended Robins reunions for
the past twenty years and is a favorite among veteran players.

ARon Weiss, John, and Ronnie Weiss in the summer of 1998.
John volunteered to coach ARon, who was sixteen at the time.
ARon eventually made his high school varsity squad.

Ed Charles, Provincial League rival and former major leaguer,
reunited with John at the film debut of *Long Road Home* at CBS
studios in 2006. Photo by Bruce Spiegel.

Chapter 19

Your Friend Was Calling Your Name

New Jersey, New York Metro Area
1965-1992

John Malangone's career path had diverged considerably following the end of his minor league career in the Yankee farm system. In 1959, following the motorcycle accident, John returned to New York City and acquired a position with the New York City Municipal Water Department. Although unable to read, John was hired anyway by higher-ups within the department who knew his background. A few years later, he also had an auto mechanic's job in the Sears Roebuck store on Fordham Road in the Bronx, across the street from Fordham University. Aware that John could not read, an admirer took care of the job application, and John began working for commissions prior to joining the semi-pro Bronx Yankees. He toiled in the automotive repair business for three decades. By 1969, he had been promoted to night manager at the urging of his coworkers.

His engaging smile, his ability to read people, and his barrel-chested physique, stuffed in tight-fitting work overalls, gave Malangone an unmistakable aura and presence in the garage. His New York Yankee status and his local reputation for ball playing enhanced his popularity among everyone who worked with him. The sixties in the Bronx saw tremendous demographic changes, and this combined with the prevailing social issues and unrest of the times brought tension to the Sears workplace. Malangone's presence, his urban background, and his experiences with various ethnic groups proved to be major assets when serving the diverse customer base that patronized the garage. He was able to assess situations and give advice to college kids who were employed in the garage...

Too much theft. Associates, wise guys... and demonstrators from different groups, demanding minority hiring. People were stealing the place blind. That's why I told management to hire college kids. They could be trusted and they were willing to work and to listen. You don't know everything just because you are book smart and you can read. But you gotta know how to talk to people and respect them. There are certain things you just can't say sometimes, so keep your mouth shut.

John would not discuss the Yankees to fellow workers, nor would he talk about anything that was troubling him. Oftentimes, there would be silence instead of conversation; he would appear moody or despondent, accompanied by a faraway look in his eyes. Instead of engaging in a conversation, he would merely shake his head or mumble something or simply not respond at all. No one ever knew about his personal secret or what might be bothering the guy, just that it was better to leave him alone.

The dark moods would be replaced at times by happier moments and congenial comments about everything. John would discuss Grandma Panarese saving the family money during the Great Depression (by reversing worn out shoe heels), sing a Tony Orlando song about knocking three times on the ceiling, and give personal advice about everything in life. Nearly everyone in the garage was unaware of Malangone's inability to read, and his dark childhood secret was never shared with anyone. He would also frequent mob social clubs after hours in the nearby Bronx Italian neighborhood of Arthur Avenue. Earning a paycheck from Sears was not always sufficient, for anyone needing to feed a family, especially when starting out "at a dollar an hour." However, by mingling with wise guys in the clubs, opportunities for low-level money making scams, such as sports betting, presented themselves to John; old habits learned back in East Harlem still remained with him.

By the late 1960s, John nearly lost all interest in playing baseball on any level and left the Bronx Yankees. Meanwhile, the major league Yankee dynasty had collapsed by the end of the decade. In 1969, Mickey Mantle announced his retirement from baseball. The man who told John to stay away from his brothers in Yankee rookie camp would be destined for entry into the Baseball Hall of Fame. In the view of many Yankee fans, Mantle is considered among the top five players who ever played for the organization.

John lost total awareness of anything occurring in Major League ball, including the widely publicized 1969 World Series between the Miracle New York Mets and the heavily favored AL Champion Baltimore Orioles. While the matchup featured many marquee players, two had been prominent in John's minor league career: Ed Charles, third baseman for the Mets, and Earl Weaver, manager for the Orioles. Malangone, sinking deeper into his moods and flashbacks, remained oblivious to the dramatic outcome of the Mets' victories that enthralled and captivated the hometown New York fans.

During this era in John's life, the Malangones and Panareses had migrated out of East Harlem to an area of the Bronx known as Country Club. Many Italians had left the Little Italy neighborhood and were settling in the east Bronx, due to demographic changes that saw an influx of new immigrants from Puerto Rico. The arrival of newcomers in East Harlem led to ethnic tensions between the Italians and Puerto Ricans. Perceived racial bias led to strained relations between the extended Malangone family and John's wife, Rosemary, who was part Venezuelan and part French. The friction caused John and Rosemary to move from the Bronx and settle into a home in Little Ferry, New Jersey in the early seventies. Networking with former buddies from his days in Fort Dix, John was able to locate a home to his liking, with Paulie Tine assisting and signing John's name on the required paperwork.

The Malangones began raising a family that included five children, Anthony, Mary, Christina, Gregory, and Elizabeth. John began commuting daily from Little Ferry to Sears in the Bronx, and also to the New York City Water Department in downtown Manhattan.

The years proved difficult for John, due to the strain of working two jobs to make ends meet and support his wife and five children. Oftentimes, John did not see or interact with the kids because of the long hours. Harboring the inner fears associated with panic attacks, he often avoided touching or hugging or squeezing his children too hard, for fear of accidentally harming them. He often remarked, "I was an absentee father. I wasn't there, but even when I was there, I was out of it." The stress from working long hours, the guilt associated with neglecting his family's emotional needs, and the panic attacks led to alcohol abuse by John, something he had avoided even in his most difficult moments with the Yankee organization.

Just when things couldn't seem to get any worse, several emotional earthquakes rocked John's fragile psyche. In the spring of 1980, Paulie Tine, while employed as a security guard at Saint Elizabeth's Hospital in upper Manhattan, was shot and killed. Two men had approached him while he was transferring packages between vehicles one evening. The assailants escaped, leaving Paulie to crawl towards the main entrance, begging for help. Despite emergency care, he died a short time later on the operating table. Summoned by the hospital officials, John and Paulie's brother, Mike, rushed to the scene but were too late to say anything to the dying man. The surgeon present at the scene approached a distraught Malangone and asked, "Are you John? Your friend was calling your name on the operating table before he died."

Immediately following the shooting, people began to question why it even happened in the first place. News blurbs indicated robbery as a motive, but nothing was taken. Sal Malangone would reflect later that Paulie, with his nice guy reputation, would not have resisted or made matters worse. If anything, he might have said, "Are you kidding me or what?" The shooter ended up being prosecuted and sent to prison. Despite the personal beliefs of family members that there were suspicious motives behind Paulie's death, nothing beyond attempted robbery was ever proven.

Seeing Paulie's name on a headstone in St. Raymond's Cemetery in the Bronx was too much for John to handle. John described his best friend's death as "one of the worst days of my life. I felt it should have been me." Paulie Tine had been everything to John Malangone; they played ball together as youngsters night and day, and they remained inseparable during John's playing days in the minors and semi-pro leagues, as well as the army years at Fort Dix. Paulie was present for John at the Yankee contract signing and the closing papers on his new home. On John's wedding day, he remarked with tears in his eyes, "There goes my best friend." Paulie was a guy who everyone loved and respected as being one of the nicest people to be around.

Happy as John was with Paulie during the years they hung out together, he never mentioned Orlando and the accident. Paulie's tragic death would ensure that the secret would never be shared between the two friends. If anyone would have understood and sympathized with John Malangone's agony over Orlando's death, it would have been Paulie Tine.

Paulie's passing sent a grieving friend into a deeper depression and revived in John long-dormant suicidal thoughts of jumping off the Triborough Bridge. John simply disappeared from everyone's sight for months. The withdrawal nearly cost John his job at Sears. That John survived this setback can be regarded as a miracle in itself, since he had still not shared his secret or fears with anyone after four decades.

During this time, John's firstborn child, Anthony, became involved with a malevolent teenage clique of wannabe gangsters. Members of this group turned on Anthony during a car ride in Manhattan and shot the boy five times at pointblank range in the back seat. Anthony escaped out of an open car window and miraculously survived. John dubbed the assailants, who were later sentenced to prison, as "the gang that couldn't shoot straight." Anthony, upon recovery, wanted revenge and asked John to help him. The answer was no, the police were handling it. The teenager's reaction was predictably angry, and even created a sense of paternal betrayal. The two did not communicate well for years. Once again, strong feelings of guilt resurrected themselves in John's mind, and he blamed himself for being absent from the lives of his children.

A year later, in 1981, John's father Sylvester, who was suffering from lung cancer, passed away. Despite childhood abuse and violence that John endured at the hands of his father, the two had gradually reconciled over the years to the point where they frequently played pinochle together. Sylvester's diagnosis also brought father and son closer to each other. Paulie's death ended the games because John was unable to cope and simply disappeared from the family's gatherings. John eventually did bring his father home from the hospital, aware that Sylvester was nearing the end. On his deathbed, referring to John's secret, Sylvester uttered these final words to his son, "You never forgot, did you?"

John broke down and sobbed openly over Sylvester's death that day, but his secret had still remained intact. Nothing had changed after nearly forty-five years. John's mental anguish and suffering continued unabated into the eighties, and he finally sought help from the Veteran's Administration. Several referrals led to John meeting a psychologist. John talked about his panic attacks, his emotional upheavals, and his baseball career; never once did he reveal his inner secret or the roots of his mental anguish. The psychologist reacted by telling John he was reminiscing too much about baseball and that he should get rid of all his trophies, newspaper clippings, and memorabilia. Following the meeting, John destroyed and burned much of the collection. The Lord Calvert trophy earned during the 1952 season in Quebec miraculously survived, if only because John was disorganized in securing his prized accomplishments. The psychologist's recommendations proved disastrous because they removed the one source of pride in John's life while doing nothing to relieve his emotional distress.

The suffering continued when the venerable Grandmother Sylvia Panarese passed away in November of 1987. While the matriarch's passing affected everyone in the extended Panarese and Malangone families, it hit John the hardest.

I wanted her to bury me... I never thought she would die. I was shocked. Then, I died with her a thousand times. I was back to five years old, living my worst nightmare all over again. I cried like a baby.

Unknown to everyone associated with John was that Sylvia Panarese was responsible for maintaining a shroud over the origin of her grandson's personal troubles. Her death did not change John at all. Fifty years later, John's torment and secret had remained just that.

The iconic image of John Malangone, baseball slugger and rifle arm from Little Italy, had now faded into a distant memory. In the mid-eighties, John had transferred to the Sears store in Paramus, New Jersey, and most co-workers at Sears and members of the New York City Water Department never knew that Malangone had flirted with big-time success as a baseball player with the New York Yankees. Following Sylvia's death, John retired from Sears and the New York City Water Department as a full time employee. He did remain in a part-time teaching capacity at Sears, setting the stage for an unexpected friendship renewal a few years later.

The years passed into the nineties, and things remained unchanged until a "stranger" showed up at the Paramus store looking for John. The visitor at first appeared to be a stranger only because initially John failed to recognize a once-familiar face. It was that of Ronnie Weiss.

Chapter 20

I Did It

New Jersey, New York Metro Area
1965-1992

In the early nineties, following retirement, Ron Weiss began facing emptiness in his life which eventually led to professional help for depression. A year later, in 1992, his son ARon, then a sixteen-year-old at Stuyvesant High School, was cut from the varsity baseball team.

Ron decided the boy needed some additional coaching for any future tryouts for the high school program, and he knew exactly who to turn to for help. Who other than the rifle arm himself?

Weiss's occasional friendly visits to the Sears automotive garage in the sixties always resulted in reminiscing about past glories with the Bronx Yankees. The friendship between the two men slowly developed while sharing tuna sandwiches and ice cream at Jahn's Restaurant, a popular eatery in the neighborhood. Despite the good times, the two did not keep in touch, going separate ways over the next two decades.

In 1992, Weiss's search for John led to the discovery that Malangone had transferred to the Sears store in Paramus, New Jersey. Ron, fixated on the need to talk with John, wasted no time crossing the George Washington Bridge in pursuit of his old teammate. He made an offer of a tuna fish sandwich lunch to discuss old times and to ask for coaching assistance with ARon.

John initially did not recognize his old teammate from the Bronx Yankee days. When Ronnie recalled the memorable double play, John suddenly realized who he was talking to and said with a smile, "I remember you. You're Ronnie Weiss."

After saying hello, Ron discussed the nature of his visit. Ron soon discovered that talking with his old teammate was not going to be that easy, especially after making a flattering offer.

I would like to do your life story. Every time I hear guys talk about great hitters with two strikes on them, your name always pops up.

John was not having any of it and remained guarded.

It's strange you came out here. It's ironic... another father just asked me to train his kid [Despite his silence, one customer had recognized John and approached him for training help]. I never even played with my own children. I never played with my brother when I was growing up. I am afraid to say yes, because I have a secret I never told anybody about. I need to think about it.

Weiss refused to be discouraged by John's initial reaction. He would not take no for an answer. He became extremely persistent with follow-up lunch visits to the Paramus garage. If nothing else, his tenacity would prove necessary when dealing with John and his changing moods.

Weiss was encouraged because John began to waver about not talking, and Ronnie was also very curious. A secret? About what? He decided to press the issue, but Malangone inexplicably responded with a very puzzling answer:

You can read all about it when my book comes out...

Weiss, undeterred, came back to Paramus again and again. Perseverance was the key to getting John to say yes and to reveal this secret. Malangone, for his part, stubbornly continued to resist the inquiries. When Weiss wouldn't take no for an answer, John inwardly considered contacting local police and having Weiss charged with harassment. John had distanced himself from baseball. His personal secret had continued to be internalized, and after nearly fifty-five years, he felt Weiss's presence to be threatening in nature. John was on the verge of retiring and didn't want his status quo altered in any way. Despite Malangone's pleas to stop bothering him, Ronnie wouldn't give up.

According to John, Weiss told him,

It was an honor to play with you. But with all your talent, why did you do the things you did? I mean, all the antics on the ball field...

Finally John relented, opening up one day, while eating a tuna fish sandwich, during a routine lunch hour break.

John: *I never told anybody, and now I am gonna go against my Grandmother's words. I killed my uncle.*

Ron: *What? You killed your uncle?*

John: *Yeah, I killed my uncle.*

Ron: *How?*

John: *I hit him in the head with a javelin I made wrapping wire around a broken umbrella. We went down to the horse stables on my street. I threw it and hit him in the head.*

Ron: *Killed him, right?*

John: *No. He went to the hospital and came out. He died a few weeks later. I did it.*

John did not display any emotion. He explained in detail everything that occurred. Ron Weiss was shocked but regarded the matter as an accident. He still wondered how a man lives with that knowledge locked away inside his mind. He felt honored that John shared his secret with him; he knew that the friendship was about to grow exponentially.

The conversation did not end there, and after subsequent discussions between the two men, Ron encouraged John to go back and discuss the issue with his mother. John would have to talk about everything openly now because his family, led by his venerable grandmother Sylvia, had never discussed the pain he was experiencing. Yet it would take another two years before John would discuss anything with any member of his family. The secret would only be shared with Ronnie Weiss until then.

The conversations about Orlando's death would prove therapeutic, with John finally cracking under an emotional strain and weeping about all of the mental anguish that he had been suffering since the age of five. However, Weiss realized that his friend needed to be further convinced that Orlando's death was an accident, and he suggested that the two men visit the New York City Department of Records. It was time to discover the official cause of Orlando Panarese's death. John was "shaking like a leaf" when he entered the records department. He expected the worst, but was greatly relieved when he learned that the cause of death was listed as accidental. Still anxious, John asked Ronnie to read the document two more times. He suddenly felt a whole new lease on life.

John later described his reaction as "a tremendous spear coming outta my back." Malangone's personal demon, fed by guilt, would no longer haunt the man's conscience as much as it once did, and the panic attacks would gradually subside. John was a "free" man and happy to be alive. He was changing his outlook, and was willing to discuss openly with Ronnie, and eventually others, the trauma he had experienced in his life. He had a clear mind and possessed a wider range of vision when observing situations around him. He also began to view his failures in a different light, accepting responsibility for his actions over the course of his life, including his time with the Yankees. He was now even in a position to help and inspire other people who were struggling with their own demons.

At the time, Weiss had also become aware of John's inability to read, and began assisting John with a variety of reading materials, including a dictionary. John would describe this activity in typical Malangonese as "symphonics."

I realized I had to learn to read. I was trying to do this before I met Ronnie again. I attended Project Head Start in Hackensack [New Jersey]. I felt stupid and ashamed and dropped out. I was afraid to ask for help. Six months later I tried again, but it was the same thing. While Ronnie was helping me, I decided to go back again, to a class at Bergen Community College. This time I raised my hand and asked for help. I was not gonna be ashamed. The teacher told me, "My God, you have that disease." I said, "What did you say? What are you, a doctor or teacher?"

John was diagnosed with dyslexia. After nearly sixty years, with professional help he was finally able to read with confidence. He was able to confront and overcome a disability that plagued him for years and got him into countless troubles, from misreading ladies' room signs to depending on Paulie to sign legal documents.

This secret about his reading disability would not be publicly revealed for five more years, following the publication of the "Damned Yankee" article about John's life.

Ron Weiss would prove to be the game changer for both John and himself. His willingness to assist John would rejuvenate the lives of both men. Weiss began putting John's story to paper as a writing project. He would gradually learn, as the background details of Malangone's childhood unfolded, that the environment surrounding the accident was very deep and complicated with family issues. The accident and the circumstances related to it, including the reactions of the Malangone and Panarese clans, fed and nourished the demon that had plagued John for decades.

Chapter 21

The Meaning
in a Name

Panarese Households
Harlem, NYC, to Florida
1919-present

Sal Malangone, John's brother, was well versed in the affairs of the Panarese household. He reminisced about the usage and eerie connections of the Orlando name among family members:

My Grandmother's [Sylvia's] fourth-born child was named Orlando, born in 1919. He died in 1925, when he was accidentally hit by a truck and dragged down the street a half a block. He was following his older brother, Grant, and his friend down the block, when he was told by the older boys that "his mother wanted him home." Believing the older boys, this Orlando boy stepped away off the curb and was immediately struck by a truck. Guilt would haunt Grant and his friend for many years for saying something stupid, although my grandmother forgave them. This Orlando was pronounced dead at the Joint Disease Hospital. He was just getting ready to make his first holy communion. He was killed and never made that first communion. Soon after he died, he would come to my grandmother in her dreams and say, "Don't cry Mommy, I am coming back to make my first communion." My grandmother told this story to my Aunt Yolanda. Yolanda knew everything about our family history. Orlando kept coming back to my grandmother's dreams, repeating that he was gonna make that first communion.

Then, the second Orlando, who was given Anthony as a middle name, was born and he was the same age as the first Orlando when he was accidentally hurt by John, and died as a result. But that accident did not take place until two weeks after he made his first communion.

Orlando was buried alongside his older brother, under the same headstone. Twelve years separated the loss of both boys.

Orlando was a popular name choice for boys during the

thirties and forties, but proved to be a curse within the Panarese clan.

Following the funeral, Sylvia Panarese's daughter, named Orlando, decided to have everyone call her Yolanda; this followed an accidental near-drowning episode at Orchard Beach in the Bronx. The girl began to sense negative fates associated with the name. Yolanda became the accepted name for the young lady, who was just eleven years old at the time, although there was never a legal change involved. The woman was always known to John Malangone as "Aunt Yolanda."

However, the Orlando namesake didn't stop there within the larger Panarese family, nor did the bad luck or fate associated with it.

Sylvia's grandson, Orlando Panarese, born in 1939, was the child of "Duffy" and Theresa Panarese and was raised in the Tremont section of the Bronx. This Orlando (a.k.a. Duffy) married Mary Janaskovic and raised a family in Tremont as well. This couple had a son named Orlando Jr., who was Sylvia's great-grandson. This Orlando was born in 1960, and he carried the middle name of Lonny. He married, at a very young age, a girl named Chinsea. The couple had a boy, named Lonny. The boy hardly knew his parents; his father died of a drug overdose and, distraught over the death of her husband, the mother, Chinsea, committed suicide by jumping off the roof of an apartment building. The deaths of both parents left Lonny in the care of the surviving grandparents, Duffy and Mary. Unfortunately, matters were made tragically worse when Grandfather Orlando, a.k.a. Duffy, suffered a fatal heart attack while working on a job for the New York City Parks Department in 1987. Duffy's wife, Mary Panarese, moved to Florida with her grandson Lonny. The great-great-grandson of Sylvia Panarese would grow up without worrying about any future curse of the Orlando name.

Chapter 22

Dark Secrets and Family Turmoil

East Harlem, NYC
Country Club, Bronx, NYC
Little Ferry, New Jersey
1937-present

The ancient Greek historian Polybius once wrote, "There is no witness so dreadful, no accuser so terrible as the conscience that dwells in the heart of every man."

The conscience that dwelled in the heart of the little boy that summer in 1937 morphed into a personal demon that would torment John Malangone for nearly sixty years. That demon would be spiritually fed by the inattention of the Malangone and Panarese families, the ignorance of neighborhood residents, and the implicit validation by local mobsters that the boy was a killer. It would also be fed by the relentless physical abuse that Sylvester Malangone inflicted on his son.

He blamed Josephine for failing to monitor John and Orlando's whereabouts on the evening of the accident. In his mind, the tragedy would always be Josephine's fault.

For Sylvester, physical abuse was his personal trademark. The anger and violence associated with his behavior never stopped. When not fighting with Josephine, he mercilessly beat his son with his tough leather barber strap for any number of reasons.

Sal Malangone reflected on a typical domestic incident that occurred almost on a daily basis:

One day my father was throwing chairs at my mother. Somebody sent word to John at the [Jefferson] park to hurry up and come home. He asked my father what was going on and my father grabbed John by the throat and started choking him, saying, "You little SOB! Don't come in my house and tell me what to do!" I am jumping on my bed, begging my father to please stop. He stopped at the same time I was wetting myself. My mother jumped on my father and he let my brother go and went after my mother again. He picked up a shoe and hit her in the head. There was a bloody gash on her forehead. All the tenants in the hallway were screaming at my father, saying, "She's a woman. What are you doing? Let her go!"

My father yelled back, "Leave me alone! Let me get at her!" The neighbors held him back and my mother ran out of the building across the street to her mother [Sylvia]. She ran up the stairs with blood running down her face. All the neighbors were yelling, "Barbiére! Barbiére! They are at it again!"

It [the fighting] reflected on me and my sister. We were ashamed... always ashamed. Nobody else on the block acted like that. My parents had a terrible reputation.

A number of explanations were offered over the years as to the root of Sylvester's abusive nature. One observation was that the father simply possessed a nasty temper. Another was that he was extremely jealous of Josephine, and that he became very possessive of her. He always wanted her in the house and to have her attention whenever it suited him. Yet another was the possibility of migraine headaches or a brain tumor; Anna recalled that her father was always being tested and having x-rays for pain, real or imagined. The man was even committed to Bellevue Hospital by Josephine for a brief observation following a violent incident, in which Sylvester trapped a rat behind an apartment radiator; he stabbed, killed, and then repeatedly mutilated the creature in a bloody fit of rage.

But as the Malangone children became aware of the family history, another explanation for Sylvester's temperament surfaced. Sal and Anna recounted the story of their grandmother, Anna Ventri, who was their grandfather John (Giovanni) Malangone's first wife. Anna was raising the couple's son, Sylvester, while John was serving a prison sentence for organized crime activity. Sylvester, a young boy at the time, was excited to see his mother Anna returning to the family residence one day and, in an overly exuberant manner, accidently bumped his mother backwards into an ash can. Anna suffered a cut on her leg that did not heal and she was subsequently diagnosed with gangrene. Doctors recommended amputation, but Anna's mother, an Italian immigrant from the old country, would have none of the medical advice. Abiding by her deeply religious faith, she emphatically declared to anyone who would listen, that "we believe in the miracles... she will get better."

Anna did not survive the infection and a short time later, Sylvester, now motherless, was placed with Anna's parents. The Ventri family wanted nothing to do with John (Giovanni)

Malangone when he was released from prison. Making family matters worse, Malangone took a Polish woman, also named Anna, as a second wife.

Looking back in time, Malangone family members now feel that Sylvester, after Orlando's death, was shrouded in personal guilt himself and had begun reliving his mother's accidental death. Whatever the reason might have been, the family was made to suffer for decades afterward.

For the Malangone children, unexpected relief often came from local mobsters. Sal explained,

My father's apartment was a meetinghouse for many of the local mobsters. This clique would come to the apartment and get haircuts from my father on Sundays. During the week, they would visit and bring cakes and sit around the dinner table playing cards. They played all day long instead of going and playing in Brownie's candy store. They were good to us [the children] and would give us a quarter to go get candy. Playing cards wasn't a bad memory for us because we got money and there was never any fighting between my parents when they were there. We heard the foul language all the time, but nobody seemed to mind. My mother would always make coffee for them. I used to look forward to having these people come into my house. There would always be peace and quiet.

Anna Malangone, John's sister, explained that the men hanging around the candy store "were not the best of people." Since Sylvester chose not to have a permanent job, he inevitably gravitated towards this local clique and involved himself in the numbers racket. He would do jobs around the neighborhood involving painting, mechanical repairs, and cutting hair to supplement his income. When not preoccupied with local "business matters" of one sort or another, he expected his wife to be at home and to give him her undivided attention. The arguments were inevitable and often turned physical. While younger sister Anna and little brother Sal were spared actual physical contact, John was relentlessly beaten. Anna summed up the situation for John:

He [Sylvester] always took it out on John. John was the oldest, and always strong and tough. My father took his anger out on John to get back at my mother. Hanging John out the window [after Orlando's funeral] was his way of making my mother suffer more.

John would always say, "I felt that I deserved it..."

The beatings inflicted on John by Sylvester were tolerated by John and despised by Josephine, who could not stop the beatings. Sylvester was the head of the household, and John never complained about the thrashings to his mother. Sylvester always reminded Josephine that it was her negligence that caused Orlando's death. Josephine's feelings of guilt were manifested in constant subservience to her mother, Sylvia Panarese.

Sal and Anna, although mostly spared, were occasionally drawn into the circle of violence meted out to Josephine and John. Anna recalled receiving a bloody gash on her forehead from a thrown cup. Sal suffered a terrible mishap when boiling hot soup, knocked off of a stove during a confrontation between John and his father, poured down inside of his boot. The trapped soup scalded the skin off of the boy's ankle, leaving Sal screaming in agony. Grandfather Panarese heard the cries for help and quickly used a knife to cut open the boot, but the damage was done; Sal has spent the rest of his life with a scarring disfigurement of his ankle.

When Sal became an adolescent, he accidentally knocked over and damaged the family's transistor radio, a valuable household commodity in the 1940s. Sylvester was furious. This time, he decided to target his youngest child with the dreaded barber strap. Having reached for the strap, Sylvester quickly turned and proceeded to bring down the leather over his son, when suddenly his motion was halted in midair. After two more unsuccessful thrusts, he turned and realized that John had grabbed the end of the strap. The older boy's strength, developed from years of throwing in the alleyway and doing those mob chores, was now on display. He was not, under any circumstances, letting go of that strap or allowing his kid brother to be hurt in any way. The boy was becoming a man now, and Sylvester knew it; after a few moments of silence, he released his grip on the strap and yielded it to John. That strap, returned to its nail on the wall, was never again used for hitting John or anyone else. The years of relentless beatings for John Malangone were finally over.

Anna, remembering her brother's pain, often remarked with admiration for John.

I thanked God he survived this. I thank God he didn't do what my father did.

Anna was referring to John's turn at fatherhood and how her brother, against all odds and despite his upbringing, did not repeat the cycle of domestic violence in his own family of five children (two sons and three daughters). The memory of Orlando's fate dwelled deep in John's psyche, so deep that he did everything to avoid a replay in any way of that fateful day in 1937.

I was an absentee father. I chose work to become that way. For thirty-two years I was afraid to speak to my children and most of all I was afraid to play with them for fear of hurting them. The strength I had in my arms... I would grab guys and they would go to their mothers and cry. A child being born, one right after the other, was very hard for me. I was afraid of them. I was always afraid of losing my children. It was hard for me to discipline. It wasn't that I didn't listen. I couldn't understand what they wanted. I was so emotional, so dysfunctional... Why would they want me home with what I did? I always wanted to touch and hug my children, but I always came home late, working two jobs. If I could have done it over, I would have been more talkative, more helpful.

John's approach to his family led to the inevitable marital bickering that nearly ended the marriage in the late nineties. Although he was summoned to a divorce proceeding in front of a judge and had to confront a female attorney who was, in John's words, "a barracuda," the divorce was never finalized. In baseball parlance, for John as a pitcher, this would have been considered a no decision.

John's son Anthony getting shot by his former friends didn't improve relationships within the family. John did not wish to seek vengeance because he feared the worst consequences. It was the same approach that he took when younger brother Sal was bullied in the old neighborhood and asked for his brother's help; John told Sal to go home and then walked away. Whenever Sylvester implored John to stand up to neighborhood toughs, he would turn and walk away. Despite the legitimacy of boxing, watching opponents lying on the floor of the ring also caused him to walk away. Guilt from the accident and the fear of killing someone with his unparalleled strength was always the overriding factor. Notwithstanding the mental turmoil, his family life turned out better than his own childhood. Daughters Christina and Mary recollected their childhood memories about John.

Mary recalled,

Dad left the house at 6:00 am and didn't come home until 9:30 at night, when we had to go to bed. We saw him on weekends and sometimes took family trips, watching him play ball. He didn't talk that much and was always quiet at home. We weren't always that close, but he didn't bring any negative experiences home with him. It wasn't in his nature. He never took out anger or frustration on the kids.

We weren't always hugged by our father, and he wasn't always around, but I never had any doubt that he loved us. He expressed his love in other ways.

Christina noted,

I remember his "unavailability" but I also remember his kindness and the things he did do as a father. He always brought home grab bags of educational toys on weekends and would buy spiced cakes and egg sandwiches on Sundays. Sometimes we would act out plays and sing and dance together.

We were grounded a lot, but we didn't know why. Maybe that was his way of keeping us safe. Maybe it was from bad memories of the environment he grew up in. He was fearful of something bad happening. When we went somewhere in the family car, Dad would drive around the block twice, circling and checking the house. He never told us what he was looking for.

Even if John had been home with his children, he would never have relived his childhood with them. The family would never be subjected to their father's East Harlem neighborhood experiences or the symbolism engendered by the infamous barber strap hanging on a wall. Although John continued to suffer internal anguish and pain, he never wished for anyone else to suffer and managed to break the cycle of domestic violence that had plagued the Malangone family for decades until Sylvester's passing in 1981, over forty years later.

Chapter 23

If I Can't Throw
Over Seventy

Roy Hobbs World Series
Fort Myers, Florida
Fall 1994

Ronnie Weiss's persistence, patience, and understanding of John's situation enabled the two men to converse on any and all subjects, and both quickly revived a strong friendship that had seemingly ended years before in the mid-sixties. Malangone had tremendous respect for Weiss as a teacher and coach and, inspired by Ronnie's confidence, eventually warmed up to the idea of coaching on his own. ARon for his part had remained with his varsity baseball team in his junior year as a volunteer manager. He kept score, handled equipment, hit outfield practices, and continued learning about the game's nuances. The bonus for ARon's efforts was John's willingness to coach the boy's baseball skills. Ron Weiss himself was immensely proud of the results. His son's progress and self-confidence improved with Malangone's assistance, and ARon made the varsity roster as a player the following year.

The tutelage of ARon Weiss was only a small component of the baseball revival that Malangone and Weiss were enjoying in the early part of the nineties. A new phenomenon was beginning to sweep across the country in the form of adult baseball, categorized as "over thirty" and "over forty" leagues. The concept of competition for older men held instant appeal to ex-major and minor leaguers, as well as players who never advanced beyond their youth leagues, but still had the urge to don a baseball uniform and compete in a game. In 1986, a gentleman named Steve Sigler posted an ad in *Newsday*, a Long Island newspaper, looking for people who wanted to play baseball. Sigler was not satisfied playing softball in his middle age, and he appealed to men looking to continue playing competitive baseball in an older age group. Sigler's ad proved to be a smash hit; twenty-five years later, a small group of players developed into an organization that now boasts a membership of 45,000 members nationwide. Older men's baseball is a reality in the form of the Men's Senior Baseball League (MSBL) and Men's Adult Baseball League (MABL).

In New Jersey, the United States Over Thirty Baseball League (USTBL) was formed. Malangone and Weiss, enthused by the idea of playing baseball again, jumped at the opportunities that the new baseball league presented to men their age in the league's over forty division. His panic attacks subsiding, John described himself as "having a clear mind." He and Ronnie joined a team called the Cardinals, managed by Nello Arrighi, and began playing in 1993. During one game, Arrighi had offered to catch for John during warm-ups prior to the start of the game. The manager initially was pumped up, pounding a catcher's glove and exhorting Malangone to "Come on, come on... put it right here." John replied, "Look over your shoulder. It's already behind you, stuck in the backstop screen."

Just when things began looking up in his life, the winter of 1993-1994 proved to be a major step backward for John. Media stories in December of that year were full of details about a car accident involving a Houston Oiler football player. Jeff Alm, the driver of the car and a defensive tackle for the Oilers, survived the accidental car crash unscathed, but his passenger, close friend Sean P. Lynch, was killed after being thrown from the car. Alm, viewing what had just occurred, committed suicide with a shotgun. Police and other sources speculated that Alm was overcome with grief and guilt, and this provided a possible motive for his suicide. John, aware of the story, reacted vehemently and reverted to his old withdrawn way of life, shutting himself down for nearly three months. Any progress that he had previously made coping with his recollections of Orlando's accident was nearly wiped out. Jeff Alm's tragedy had revived painful replays in his mind like a video loop all over again.

John spent much of the winter away from most people he knew, including Ronnie Weiss, who initially brought the news story to John's attention. His time was consumed doing private car repairs and returning, almost daily, to Mount Carmel Church in East Harlem. Just as he had done in childhood, John spent countless hours lighting candles at different prayer stations inside the church, and at times even slept, hidden in the pews. Being a church regular allowed him to befriend the local priests and church officials, who encouraged him to participate in throwing contests for fun on the secluded grounds of Mount Carmel. The daily visits eventually proved therapeutic, and before long, John was tossing baseballs again in various gyms near his home in Little Ferry, New Jersey.

Playing baseball again gave John a new lease on life. He and

Ron participated in a league all-star game in 1994 at Cooperstown, New York, site of the Baseball Hall of Fame. Despite his renewed enthusiasm for playing, John struggled with rotator cuff issues and spent much time in therapy, swimming and weight lifting to strengthen his throwing arm. His arm sufficiently healed by the summer of 1994, John approached Ron about aiming for higher goals in baseball—namely, playing to win for the first time in his life. No more clowning around, no more antics, no more "play to play." John remembered Billy Martin's words about never winning a pennant with him, and this time he was determined to win a championship. John also stated one condition for playing at a higher level: Ronnie was to tell no one that John once played for the Yankees. He considered the news unnecessary and thought it would only serve as a distraction from his goal of winning.

In late 1994, John got the opportunity that he was looking for that would help him atone for his past baseball failures. He and Ron, acting as "free agents," were picked to join a team named the New Jersey Wonderboys, a team headed for a post season tournament in Florida. The Wonderboys consisted of players from New Jersey and Staten Island. The tournament was the Roy Hobbs World Series, named after the fictional character played by actor Robert Redford in a movie entitled *The Natural*. The Wonderboys were entered in the Masters Division, a grouping of teams with players over fifty years of age.

Weiss and Malangone were the last two players selected by manager Tommy Faherty for the team's roster. According to John, a comment was made that both players, the oldest on the roster, were potentially useful as "a couple of waterboys." John was sixty-four, and Ronnie was fifty-seven, so not much was expected from them going into the tournament. Additionally, the age factor had also became a personal issue with Ronnie, who feared John would look foolish playing in Florida and possibly ruin a potentially good story about John overcoming his demon. But John remained focused on his long-term goals, repeatedly telling Weiss, "Ronnie, I am down here to win. I have to win the championship." Despite the age concerns, John prevailed, declaring, "If I can't throw over seventy miles an hour as a pitcher, I am coming back home."

Ronnie acquiesced to John's feelings, realizing this was a different John Malangone who was talking; it was a decision that the two "old men" would never regret.

Faherty, observing John practice pitching, was impressed. He approached John, saying, "I've been watching you throw all week, and you are always on the black." John replied, with his trademark grin, "All I need is the black. You can have the white."

Thanks to the "old men," Malangone and Weiss, the Wonderboys made a big impact at the tournament, which held its first ever Masters Championship. After losing the first game of the tournament, the team claimed six straight wins, with significant contributions from Malangone and Weiss. John pitched two games in the tournament, finishing with a 2-0 won-lost record, fifteen innings pitched, and a 2.33 earned run average. His pitching speed was never in doubt because he continually threw over seventy-five miles an hour. He attributed his pitching success to consistent location. John also batted .333 with three RBIs. Weiss finished with a .381 batting average, knocking in five RBIs along with eight hits and seven runs scored. Both men made huge contributions in the final game when the Wonderboys matched up against the Florida Masters club. Weiss knocked in two runs in the team's 4-3 victory, but it was John Malangone's clutch, two out single in the bottom of the last inning that clinched the game for New Jersey.

For John, it had been the moment he was waiting for, a chance at redemption, and a belief that he could play the game of baseball to win. Billy Martin's haunting words were still on his mind. He only wished Martin had been there to witness the accomplishment (Martin died in an accident in 1989). Nevertheless, the moment was all the more special because he was able to share that moment with Ron Weiss as his teammate.

The joyous occasion would be repeated in future years. Malangone and Weiss reunited with their old buddies Mike DeRosa, Dan Benedetto, and Gary Sacino. Stanley Lewis, formerly a Bronx native who played with the Bronx-based Mohawks, joined the squad as a pitcher. The team was managed by Mike DeRosa, and it participated in the Roy Hobbs Tournament for the rest of the decade. Moe Resner, a member of the squad, wrote a column at the time entitled "Westchester County... Be Proud of our own Yankees" for a local New York area media outlet. Resner referred to the team as a "select group of Westchester County and New York metro area players who still play baseball. The team consists of guys who never made it to the big leagues." DeRosa was a former minor leaguer, while Sacino tried out for the Milwaukee Braves. The Bronx Yankees would reach the finals several times, while winning championships in 1996 and 2000 with Malangone and Weiss on the roster.

In the 1995 tournament, John's tragedy was no longer a secret. By that time, Malangone's story was shared publicly and tournament players became aware of his Yankee background.

Recently, when holding up a ball that was autographed after his first pitching victory in the 1994 Roy Hobbs Series, he exclaimed in a moment of exuberance, "This was my first win after forty-five years."

Chapter 24

The Yankee That Never Was

New York Metropolitan area
1993-1994

Weiss continued to write about the specifics of Orlando's accident and the subsequent repercussions on John. However, many details were revealed slowly by John to Ronnie Weiss and to other writers over a period of years. While the accident itself became well known, anyone discovering additional details of John Malangone's childhood, teenage years, and Yankee career would indulge in a fact-finding process that resembled peeling layers off of an onion. Even John himself was still reluctant to revisit every memory or issue that lay buried in the recesses of his mind. Time, and lots of it, was required for Malangone's healing process.

Ronnie Weiss spent long hours researching and talking to John about his past and his views on everything in life. Weiss wrote a story about John's life and wanted Malangone family members to review it. However, he changed his mind, and in early 1994, Weiss decided someone else needed to write about John Malangone and told John his plan.

How the hell did you ever play ball? With all that pain? This story is too powerful for me. I am going to call the Daily News *and* Sports Illustrated.

John initially resisted this idea because he hadn't consulted with his family about the story and most of its members were still alive. This raised old fears within John about how much the family at large knew about Orlando's death. He worried about his mother Josephine's reaction to such a public airing of personal events.

Deciding to enlist the assistance of reporters in the local New York area, Weiss contacted Wayne Coffey, sportswriter for the *New York Daily News*. Ronnie was aware of Coffey's human interest stories and relayed a message to the writer: "Boy, have I got a story for you." Ronnie went on to explain John's background with the Yankees and how he was supposed to be the next Yogi Berra. Coffey, relying on his journalistic instincts, sensed a potentially interesting story in the making and responded to Weiss's initial inquiry. Wayne met Ronnie and John at the Delightful Coffee Shop, an appropriate setting in East Harlem due to its long local history, on First Avenue and 116th Street. An intriguing conversation was followed by everyone walking over to Jefferson Park. Home to John's meeting with Paul Krichell, the park was also host for many softball games played there by Wayne Coffey himself. Coffey found out firsthand what the "rifle arm" of Little Italy was all about while playing catch with Malangone.

A subsequent interview was held at Josephine's home in the Bronx. Up to this point, John still had not told his mother what was happening. John, now displaying a new emotional courage, decided to break Grandma Sylvia Panarese's sacred rule that "no one is to talk about this." Josephine, who was surprised at the events rapidly unfolding, reacted bluntly by shouting, "Get them the hell outta here! You're gonna make my son sick!" She called Uncles Duffy and Grant to press her case and to ask Wayne to leave. But John prevailed with the last word, saying, "Ma, I been sick..." Josephine was speechless at first, but reflected afterwards on the accident, "There was nothing we coulda did. The yelling, the screaming, waking up everybody."

John had to seek permission for telling his story from all the Panareses, including Duffy and Grant. He also sought approval from his sister Anna and brother Sal.

The December 14th, 1994 Sunday edition of the *New York Daily News* featured a two-page spread in its sports section entitled "The Yankee That Never Was." Coffey's article captured the feelings of an athlete who suffered tragedy but made a comeback as a ballplayer later in life. Successful and well-written, the article would be just the beginning of media coverage on John's life in various forms.

In John's opinion, "It still turned out to be the number one story written. Beautiful."

Recalling the interview process with John, Coffey commented,

It was unbelievable. To this day, I never, ever encountered anything like it, and really anybody like John, who lived with a shame and a secret for so long. You can feel John's goodness and kindness and the weight he had been carrying all these years. I had a sense I was only scratching the surface.

The story gathered much acclaim from readers who either knew John personally, or who identified with his personal struggles. Additionally, John decided to reveal his secret to John Blanchard, one ex-Yankee to whom he was comfortable disclosing the story. Blanchard had read Coffey's article immediately after publication. He appeared at a local baseball card show, allowing Malangone to catch up with him and tell the truth about everything that happened back in the fifties. Blanchard's reaction was sympathetic, although he wondered why John was unable to confide in him back then. The meeting with Blanchard was followed by another meeting with former Yankee Johnny Kucks, who resided in northern New Jersey and had also read the *Daily News* piece. Kucks was also understanding and supportive of John's revelations.

The article opened up an opportunity for Malangone and Weiss to coach together. "The Yankee That Never Was" was also the beginning of media publicity in the form of magazine and newspaper articles, a film, a television show, and a website for a rejuvenated John Malangone. Coffey's article was also reprinted in the 1995 print edition of the Roy Hobbs Tournament. Everyone in the tournament became aware of John's background.

However, the article also revived ghosts and long buried memories from East Harlem.

Chapter 25

I Will Turn You Into a Pastry

New York Metropolitan Area
1994-1995

Shortly after Coffey's article was published, a well-dressed stranger appeared out of nowhere and approached John and Ron Weiss in the Sears Paramus store garage. At first, John did not recognize the man, who possessed a serious, businesslike demeanor. John later recalled the event clearly as if it were yesterday:

This guy comes up to me and says, "Get in the car." I looked at him. "Who the fuck are you?"

The stranger's reply: *You little snot nose!*

John [smiling, waving both hands]: *Whoa, whoa, whoa... back up. You gotta have some respect!*

Stranger: *You don't remember me? I am Jerry, Dom Bepp's bodyguard. Get in the fucking car now! Do as I say and get in the car! Dom Bepp wants to see you right now.*

Not recognizing him right away, John stood there in defiance, but after a few moments, slowly realized that it was really Jerry after all these years. The suit, the Stetson Hat, the voice... it all started coming back. He replied with a tone of innocence,

Is Dom Bepp still alive? How old is he now? I can't believe it! I'll see him when I get the time.

Jerry: *What's the fucking difference? You writing a book? Why do you wanna know his age? Keep your age to yourself! Get in the fucking car now! Do as I say and get in the car!*

After exchanging a few more mild insults, John realized he had no choice and complied with Jerry's demand by getting in the limo. He sought Jerry's approval to bring Ronnie along for the ride. Weiss, nervous about the conversation, asked John, "What did I do?" He climbed in, eventually deciding this encounter would be no big deal, and that everything would be fine. After all, he figured, this couldn't be much different than any other upside down day in the life of John Malangone, right?

The ride was uneventful with little conversation, although Jerry continually stared at John in his rearview mirror. Instead of taking the shortest route to a specified location on the lower East side, Jerry zigzagged all over Manhattan. This gave John an uneasy feeling and made Ronnie unusually nervous, prompting him to ask John, "What's going on?" John replied, "He wants to be sure we're not being followed."

After looping through East Harlem several times, Jerry then drove downtown into the famous Little Italy neighborhood of lower Manhattan and promptly escorted everyone to a meeting room behind a local bakery. Ron suddenly remembered that his own mother had visited this bakery a few weeks before, using John Malangone as a reference and asking for a dozen cannoli at half price. That approach didn't work, especially since the responses from store employees included "Who?" and "Never heard of him." While the two men waited for Dom Bepp to appear, Ron requested coffee; Jerry responded with food and coffee for the visitors. Oblivious to the gravity of the situation, Ron complained to Jerry that his coffee was not "light and sweet." At that point John intervened.

Time out... do you know who that is?

Ronnie, smiling and being smart, responded,

I dunno, maybe he wants to try out for second base.

John: *He's not trying out for second base. He's Dom Bepp's driver and bodyguard. Don't you understand that?*

Jerry pulled John aside.

Tell the guy no more coffee. Dom Bepp is ready to see you.

When an aging Dom Bepp finally entered the room, John quickly moved to embrace the man he recognized from many years ago; Malangone was immediately stopped by two bodyguards who pushed him backwards. Observing the presence of Ronnie Weiss, Dom Bepp quietly asked John who the man was and why he was there; satisfied with John's answer that Ronnie was a writer, Dom

Bepp returned his focus to John. Addressing John in businesslike fashion, he quickly got to the point.

Congratulations on your newspaper article. You are not going to print any word about me in any book or magazine. Do you understand that?

John, his mind suddenly swelling with countless memories from the past, began heaping lavish praise on Dom Bepp.

I want everybody to know what a generous man you were and what you did for me and how you weren't prejudiced towards people and...

Interrupting John, Dom Bepp continued in a louder tone, making sure Ronnie also heard every word of what he was saying,

Ch´ tajja ritt´? I´ ne me voglio repet´re. O si no, t´impast cumme na pasta! Tu vuo´ diventa nu cannuolo o na sfugliatella? Chiur´a vocca e statt zitt´. Ai capit´? Ai capit´ che t´sto ricenne?

What did I say? I don't want to repeat myself. Otherwise, I will turn you into a pastry. Do you wanna become a cannoli or a sfogliatella? Keep your mouth shut and keep quiet. Do you understand? Do you understand what I am saying?

The point was made and John kissed Dom Bepp's ring. Jerry chauffeured Ronnie and John back to Sears. However, that was not the end of it for Jerry, as he asked the two men if he could spend some time with them. Jerry was seriously ill and preferred to spend his precious time reminiscing with John about the old days back in East Harlem.

Publicity from Coffey's article presented John with a new baseball-oriented opportunity. John was offered a baseball coaching job at Manhattan Community College. It was not a plum coaching position as the baseball program had no home field, no practice facility, no scholarships, and only several weeks remaining before the start of a new season. Initially reluctant about the offer, John took the job, and he asked Ron Weiss to be an assistant coach. The coaching bonded Malangone and Weiss into a partnership that neither could have foreseen or imagined. Ronnie was able to help alleviate John's fears of working with youth in a coaching capacity.

Coaching young men at the college level was not without its challenges for John. Several players, aware of John's inability to read, did not respect his knowledge of the game of baseball.

These college kids were very hard to handle. They knew what buttons to push. They did a book report on my life and even mentioned Orlando's death. Some of them were very mean, saying whatever they wanna say, like "You can't read, you can't write, whaddya tellin' us what to do? How could you get a coaching job?"

The lack of respect from these players eventually led John to challenge them to an intrasquad game, where John pitched and Ronnie played third base. John announced to the critics, all placed on the opposing team, "I am gonna pitch against you guys." Malangone followed with a dominant performance that silenced his critics, who were unable to generate a single hit off "the old man." Additionally, John homered off the pitcher, whom he called "snotnose" because of the youngster's brazen remarks. When the game was concluded, several apologies were extended by some players, one of which included the compliment, "I can see now why they made you coach." One student was impressed enough to ask, "Can you teach me how to throw a knuckleball?" Yet, believe it or not, some players complained to college administration that "they were showed up, and that wasn't right."

The negative drawbacks of taking the coaching positions extended to the team's results over the next two years; the team distinguished itself with a 0-39 won-lost record. Malangone later commented, "You can't win 'em all, but it would be nice to win one [laughing]."

Chapter 26
Damned Yankee

New York Metropolitan area
1997

Wayne Coffey's piece in the *New York Daily News* was only the beginning of public recognition for John Malangone's story. In December of 1996, Ronnie Weiss read a story in *Sports Illustrated* entitled "Someone to Lean On." The story, by a sports writer named Gary Smith, detailed a real-life relationship between a mentally disabled man and a local South Carolina high school football team and its coach. The coach, Harold Jones, the football team, and the school personnel permitted the young man at the time (the story began in the 1960s decade) to become part of the sports program and to "attend" Hanna High School as a permanent member of the junior class, so he would not have to graduate and leave the school. The young man was nicknamed "Radio" by locals because he carried a radio everywhere he went. The story inspired a movie, *Radio*, in 2003, starring Cuba Gooding Jr. as James Kennedy, the subject of the story. Amazingly, the story of "Radio" has continued right up to the time of this book's publication. James Kennedy still attends Hanna High School on a daily basis, now accompanied by his nephew who is enrolled at the school.

Smith's piece intrigued Weiss so much that he contacted the author and informed him about his buddy, John. Weiss gave Smith enough details to interest him in pursuing John's life story. In the summer of 1997, Smith contacted John and traveled to New York, despite Malangone's trepidations about opening himself up to a well-known and respected reporter of an established national publication. Old fears had resurfaced in John's mind about the accident with Orlando being publicized. Despite John's initial misgivings, Smith alleviated the old slugger's anxieties.

The writer spent nearly three months interviewing John, his relatives, and other ball players in John's hometown of Little Ferry and the greater New York metro area. Smith toured the old East Harlem neighborhoods and Jefferson Park and visited Rao's and Patsy's landmark restaurants, as well as several mob-owned social clubs. The only word Smith had for the suffering that the ex-Yankee had endured was "unbelievable." Smith's research and writing resulted in "Damned Yankee" being published in *Sports Illustrated* in October of 1997. The article included photos of Orlando Panarese and the 1955 picture of John posing between the Yankee Hall of Fame catchers, Dickey and Cochrane.

Public reaction to a nationally published exposé on John Malangone's story was swift, with many readers identifying with John's suffering. Many drew parallels between John's story and their own personal struggles and setbacks in their lives. There were frequent comments about viewing Malangone through the psychological lens of post-traumatic stress disorder because the ex-Yankee exhibited so many symptoms associated with the disorder. Following Orlando's death, John endured survivor's guilt, repeated flashbacks, recurring nightmares, upsetting memories, and detachment from reality. A letter from one attorney outlined a tragic automobile accident in which he experienced survivor's guilt and felt responsible for the death of family members. He blamed himself for the outcome, despite not having anything to do with the car crash. Enduring his trauma for eleven years, he altered his outlook after reading "Damned Yankee." He finished his letter by saying, "Thank you for providing me with the insight to confront the demon which has been torturing me."

Another individual, in therapy for personal trauma, was given a copy of Smith's article by her minister. Her letter, after outlining her struggles, ended with,

God loves you, dear friend, and so do I. Thank you for being a blessing to me today. Because of you, I think I was a little bit nicer to my passengers today.

Another letter writer commented,

I feel glad that you were able to face down your fears and overcome them. I believe we are born here on earth to learn certain lessons. Your lessons were unspeakably hard. On the whole, your story is uplifting, a tale of triumph of the human spirit.

Still another reader:

Truth is stranger than fiction. Thank you and Gary Smith for bringing to light the touching and amazing story of John Malangone.

The *Sports Illustrated* article was used as a teaching device about life and mental health issues in some educational institutions as well. It wasn't long before middle and high school students were writing letters to John about their views on "Damned Yankee" as part of a health class assignment. Some students not only read the article, but also watched the follow-up interview on John that was aired on Maury Povich's television show. The responses were overwhelmingly positive and included keen insights.

I am impressed with your hard work. To you, destroying your arm and punishing it was supposed to be bad. As a result, you got a rocket for an arm. You never let yourself off the hook. You deprived yourself of a childhood.

If you had talked to your family or a therapist, you may have been able to reach clarity sooner.

God set you on this path to teach others a lesson. To teach people not to be secretive, not to give up.

If it hadn't been for the death of your uncle, don't you think you would not be the great ballplayer you are today? ...all the trouble that you put your arm through to punish it, made it strong enough for the big leagues. If Orlando did not die, you never would have tortured yourself like that, right? Would you give it all up [to have] your uncle back?

You have made me see that I should be happy with what I have.

I think your parents should have talked about the accident with you.

That it was so terrible that you completely disregarded people staring at you or you hurting yourself, simply to get the demon away from you is quite astounding to me. It must have been so terrible. Your story has aroused much sympathy from my class. That you got on with your life is also superb.

The odds that anyone could get to be noticed by a major league scout are so small and the fact that you did without much formal training amazed me.

One young lady, speaking for her classmates, praised John for his courage in continuing to live life, but was not sympathetic to other people in the story.

[About the neighborhood]...*I did want to tell those people to give the poor kid a break.*

[On Phil Page in Yankee camp] *Your coach was like a huge bucket of water and when he said, "You? You can't help yourself." It was as though he had just poured this huge bucket of water all over your last bit of hope, the tiny flame, which made it go out.*

Ending on a happier note, the girl indicated that her class was able to hear John's voice on the show.

...we got to hear your voice, which we all enjoyed, especially how you pronounced beautiful.

That was "bootyful" in Malangonese.

"Damned Yankee" continued to generate interest after its initial publication. The article was republished in two books, *Beyond the Game: the Collected Sports Writing of Gary Smith* (where John Malangone is the leadoff story) and *Sports Illustrated: Going Deep: 20 Classic Sports Stories.*

Gary Smith has worked as a sportswriter for *Inside Sports* and several newspapers, including the *New York Daily News*, before joining *Sports Illustrated* in 1982. His writings have been featured in national publications, such as *Rolling Stone, Esquire*, and *Time Magazine.*

Smith's writing career is studded with award-winning accomplishments, receiving many honors for his work at *Sports Illustrated*. He was nominated nine times for the prestigious National Magazine Award series and won on four occasions. His stories have appeared in *The Best American Sports Writing* a record thirteen times.

New York Times writer Richard Pérez-Peña profiled and complimented Gary Smith in a sports piece entitled, "The Sports Whisperer, Probing Psychic Wounds." The article attributed Smith's writing success to his ability to get inside people's mindsets without judging them. John Malangone proved to be a prime example of Smith's efforts.

In spite of all the recognition that Gary Smith has gained and continues to receive for his numerous writing efforts, the author views the "Damned Yankee" story as one of his most memorable.

Definitely one of the most interesting stories that I have ever written. That story ranks at or near the top. It was one of the most fascinating, individual tales that I have ever heard. John was one of the most loveable and enjoyable characters that I have ever worked with. John possesses a sense of humor and an ability to laugh.

Malangone and Smith continue to communicate with each other. The two men recently conversed about a news item, published in *Sports Illustrated* and in numerous other media sources, about a sports tragedy that occurred in Germany in August 2012. A German high school athlete, tossing his javelin during competition in a track meet, accidently killed a track official. The athlete, grief-stricken over the accident, was reported to have received extensive counseling support to deal with his trauma. Perhaps if John had received such support after Orlando's death, he might have taken a different path through life.

While sending John to Germany to provide support for the teenager was never seriously considered, John commented jokingly about language barriers. Any such possibility would have required translators for German, English, and, yes, Malangonese...

Chapter 27

Tragedy Strikes Again

New York Metro Area
1998

Following the publication of the *Sports Illustrated* article, John Malangone appeared on NBC's *Maury*. During the show, John, along with other guests, recounted personal stories about how one mistake had changed each of their lives. Ron Weiss, sitting in the television audience, was introduced as the man who helped to turn John's life around. Despite a few tense emotional moments under the glare of television lights, John got through the broadcast program without suffering a panic attack.

Media publicity for John's story continued after Gary Smith's article and the television interview; Caroline Brewer wrote a piece for the *Bergen Record* entitled "Victory at Last," which recapped John's life and secret trauma. The front page article featured a large photo of John taken during his early spring workout with the Bergen Rockies, a team in northern Jersey. The article also noted that after the coaching success John had with ARon, he was inspired to coach other teenagers in the local area.

In the midst of all the new publicity surrounding John Malangone, both he and Ronnie Weiss continued playing ball during the spring and summer in New Jersey in 1998. Shortly before the two men joined the Bronx Yankees in the annual Roy Hobbs World Series, tragedy struck both men very deeply when ARon Weiss, at the age of twenty-two, passed away at the Weiss family home in Yorkville, Manhattan on the Jewish holy day of Yom Kippur.

ARon was studying for his Masters at the University of Maryland. He had just graduated from Geneseo College the same year.

Malangone's coaching of ARon in 1992 and 1993 had paid great dividends for the teenager; ARon, after being cut from the varsity team at Stuyvesant High School as a junior, made the squad as a senior and batted .400 in his final season. John worked with ARon on his throwing and hitting in the winter months, and ARon benefited greatly from the ex-Yankee's knowledge of the game. ARon had become well aware of John's lifelong struggles and had appreciated his mentor's comeback in playing senior baseball.

The night before ARon passed away, he, John, and Ronnie were watching the television show *Jeopardy* together at the Weiss residence. At one point, ARon put his arms around John, hugged him and whispered in his ear, saying, "I'm very proud of all you recently accomplished."

ARon's death was a shock to everyone. For John, the flashbacks from childhood surfaced once again.

Weiss went into a deep depression following ARon's passing. He wondered how he would carry on without his son, "feeling pain so great it squeezes the breath from your body." During Shiva, Weiss's wife, Patricia, approached manager Mike DeRosa of the Bronx Yankees with a special request: "Please make sure Ronnie goes to the World Series."

Like John, Ronnie Weiss would turn back to baseball to deal with his grief. Two months later, both men were in Florida for the Roy Hobbs tournament. Stepping to the plate during his first turn at bat, Weiss removed his helmet and viewed a greeting card that he had previously tucked inside the helmet. The card was a birthday greeting from ARon that said, "My father, my strength, my friend." Weiss paused for a moment, then placed the helmet back on his head, stepped to the plate, and lined a base hit to left field. Later, when asked how he was feeling about the hit, he commented, "It felt great, as if ARon was with me, holding me close."

The Bronx Yankees did not win the Masters Division that year, but Weiss batted .333 for the tournament and hustled all over the field on defense. DeRosa would later remark after the games ended, "Playing ball was the healthiest thing he could've done."

Today, Ronnie Weiss still plays in A League Of Our Own. Dressed in his blue jersey, he wears number twenty-two on his back. The number represents ARon's age when he died. Now, as it did then, swinging a baseball bat and getting a hit brings a great feeling of relief. Baseball was, and still is, Ron Weiss's peace.

Chapter 28

Good Therapy
on Sundays

Various Ballparks
Northern New Jersey
1993-2001

Twenty ball fields in northern New Jersey serve as home grounds to a baseball organization known as A League Of Our Own. The league, founded in 1995 with three teams, provided anyone over the age of forty with an opportunity to play baseball. Its popularity grew, expanding to nine teams and a playoff two years later. Further expansion included a night league and a Sunday fall league. The league's prestige grew with hosting tournaments at Doubleday Field in Cooperstown, New York, Hudson Valley Stadium, and even Yogi Berra stadium in nearby Montclair, New Jersey. By 2009, the organization boasted twenty teams on Sundays in the spring and summer, fourteen in the fall season, and seven in the night league.

The founder and president of A League Of Our Own is Mark Van Overloop, a Fordham University graduate who has posted his pitching accomplishments on the league's website. His statistics include 300 career wins and 3,000 career innings in twenty years of adult baseball. Mark has been well acquainted with John and Ronnie Weiss, having the pleasure of watching both men play in the league for years.

Surprisingly, Van Overloop's first encounter with Malangone was not the most memorable experience; it occurred in 1993, the year before John and Ronnie headed for the Roy Hobbs World Series in Florida. Mark recalled the moment with total clarity:

We were playing in an all-star game back in '93. I am forty-two years old, so that makes John about sixty. I was put up to pinch hit. He starts yelling, "Get him outta there, lemme go up and hit for him." That didn't exactly endear me to him, but then five years later in 1998 he came into the fall league and I got to know him. We became good friends and everything else went well. By the way, I struck out in that game anyway.

In 1999, Ronnie and John came to play for me on the Orioles in the night league. In 2000, John played for the New Milford Yankees in the summer league and the Marlins in the fall league and won the League's Cy Young award. He pitched thirty-two innings, won three games, and possessed an ERA of 3.09. He did that as a sixty-nine-year-old and won a championship. Next year, as a seventy-year-old, he pitched for forty-three innings. Still was effective but got hurt after that.

For John, as he entered the new millennium, A League Of Our Own and baseball in general would remain constants in his life. But new setbacks and changes in the decade would challenge his resiliency, as they had dating all the way back to Orlando's death in 1937. John would stumble emotionally again, and would withdraw at times from those people who supported him the most.

In the spring of 2002, John opened the baseball season by helping his team, the Bergen Yankees, defeat the Rockies in a doubleheader. John started and pitched the first game for a win, and followed up by coming into the second game as a relief pitcher to save the win for the Bergen Yankees.

It would be the last time John Malangone would ever pitch in a baseball game.

Later that same day, John tripped over his favorite pet dog, ironically named Lucky, and tumbled down a flight of stairs in his home. He suffered a severe injury to his neck and spinal column. Following weeks of surgery and recuperation, the medical prognosis given to John was that it was too risky to resume throwing a baseball, as this would result in more damage to his spine. With the threat of paralysis, Malangone's playing days were now officially over. A lifetime of throwing, beginning with fruit and taped balls made of string in the tenement alleyway, to passing ships near Jefferson Park, to ball fields from Venezuela to Yankee Stadium to Canada, had come to an end.

Despite not being able to play, John would continue to watch the League's games every Sunday in the summer and the fall. He would always cheer for and support any team that had Ronnie Weiss on their roster. While Ron continued to play ball without his old teammate, John would always be present at every game that involved Weiss. In 2007, Ronnie Weiss was inducted into the 42nd City College of New York Athletic Hall of Fame at a special banquet. During the ceremony, Weiss acknowledged a longtime baseball mentor, Lou Haneles, for his baseball expertise and encouragement. Haneles, a CCNY alumnus ('37) himself and influential in both the lives of Weiss and Malangone, passed away during that same year.

Players and spectators greeting John at games on Sunday mornings always have expectations of hearing John's voice booming from anywhere. John was either on the field or inside the dugout area; players would be listening to either a hearty laugh, a commentary, or wisecrack on anything that happened before, during, and after the game. Even umpires got a kick out of the old timer's standard remarks, including, "Hey blue, get the beer caps outta your eyes..."

Following Sunday morning games, players from the league would have coffee gatherings at the Park Ridge Diner in Park Ridge, New Jersey; this was and still is considered standard fare in Mark's league. The get-togethers provide a forum for players who share a wealth of baseball knowledge and humor. As always, John Malangone takes center stage in these discussions, with priceless and hilarious tales of everything from the mob to the Yankees to boxing matches.

Mark Van Overloop summed up Malangone's value to the League:

John's a goodwill ambassador for us. We are all glad to see him. He's had a few physical issues but we are happy that he is just out there with us, watching us, cheering us on. It seems every time I pitch a game John would ask, "How many wins do you have for your career?" I would always say, "Don't ask 'till the game is over. I don't want to jinx anything."

The good feelings generated between John and the Sunday morning baseball crowd would prove beneficial to Malangone as a support system. This was particularly true in the spring of 2007 when he lost his first-born child Anthony to heart failure. His death rocked John very hard.

My heart was broken when he died. I felt tremendously guilty working two jobs all those years and then turning around and seeing that my son was already a man. It was always in the back of my mind that I would lose my firstborn because of what I did to my mother and grandmother with the lastborn [Orlando]. I always thought I would be punished with that. It almost happened [Anthony's gang-related shooting], but I didn't know it would happen thirty sumpin' years later. I always worried about that. It took me down, all the way down, with no flashbacks, all the way back to Orlando. I almost lost the power to live, to think... I had no good days and started gambling again, but I caught myself when I realized I was punishing myself all over again.

Anthony's passing was followed several months later by the death of John's mother, Josephine Malangone. Josephine had lived nearly a century, and shortly before her death, John mentioned to her that he never told her how much he loved her. Her reply was, "I never told you either."

The two then acknowledged that it wasn't necessary because both had shown generosity, compassion, and love for each other throughout the years. Her passing was, in John's words,

Very mellow ... I lost somebody I could speak to, the older we got. Her last words were about how much she loved me. She never understood sports because she thought I wanted to play with the Knickerbockers [laughing].

Yet, after seventy years, Josephine Malangone, adhering to her mother Sylvia Panarese's dictum of silence about the tragedy, never spoke about Orlando to her son.

A League Of Our Own would provide, in John's words, "good therapy on Sundays" when he needed support coping with the accident that ended his playing career and the deaths of family members.

The new decade also presented another opportunity for John to publicize his story as a follow up to the "Damned Yankee" article. At the beginning of the decade, another man walked into John's life and attempted to document Malangone's story. This gentleman got a chance to see John play baseball for nearly two years before the accident involving his pet dog, Lucky. However, instead of another print portrayal of John, this individual would produce a film about the ex-Yankee's life; the cameraman was Bruce Spiegel, producer and editor of the CBS television program *48 Hours*.

Chapter 29

Long Road Home

Hackensack, New Jersey
New York Metro Area
Winter circa 2000-present

New Jersey resident Bruce Spiegel walked into the Hackensack YMCA building one snowy February weekend morning, looking to shoot hoops with a friend of his.

I went upstairs to the gym to see what was going on, and there was nobody there except this elderly guy [John] throwing baseballs up against the wall. He was wearing a baseball cap and sneakers and was throwing against a padded wall. I had no idea who he was, I had no idea about senior baseball, I had no idea about anything. I just watched the guy for a little while, and I thought hmmm...

I walked over to him and said, "Excuse me, hope you don't mind my asking whaddya doing?" He said to me, "I am getting ready for next season."

At that point I thought maybe something's not quite right with the guy. I didn't think anything more of it and walked out of the gym. Next time I saw the guy was a month or so later, and I remembered what he said to me. I asked him, "How's the season going, John?"

He starts to tell me all these stats, how he pitched the other day and last Sunday, and how he got a hit here and so on. I still had no idea about senior baseball. He sees that I am perplexed, so he says, "Come on out to the truck." Then as we are walking to the truck, he offhandedly says, "I used to play with the Yankee organization." I said to myself, alright, yeah. Even though I am a huge baseball fan, I couldn't process what he was saying. We go to the truck, and he hands me a copy of Gary Smith's article and says, "Read this, you'll understand who I am."

He then told me about senior baseball. I took the article home, read it, and my jaw dropped. Oh my god, this was absolutely true about the Yankees. After that, we got to talking, and he says, "Why don't you come out to a game?"

So, I took a small camera and went out to see a game. At this point I wasn't thinking about making any film. But I thought, "Wow! This is an amazing story." I watched middle-aged and older guys playing baseball for the sheer love of playing. It was incredible. I never saw adults playing hardball before. I met Ronnie Weiss and John's brother Sal that day and we went to a diner after the game. While they were talking, my first thought was, "I gotta shoot some of this stuff." I shot some footage, but not a lot.

John came to me and said, "I am going down to Florida in November and I am going to play for the Bronx Yankees in the Roy Hobbs Tournament." I said to myself, "You gotta be kidding me..."

John said, "If you wanna come down you will meet Mike DeRosa [the manager] and all these other players." I said to myself, "I gotta do this."

Spiegel traveled to Florida with a camera, determined to get as much footage as possible about John and other players. John also told Bruce about St. Petersburg and his experience with the Yankees. The two men drove to the site of the old Yankee training camp and located the old Miller Huggins field where John had played in 1955. The visit opened up a flood of memories for John, who talked to Bruce on film about his recollections. Bruce remembered John's reaction:

We found the field where he practiced with the Yankees. John said, "There it is, home sweet home, right there. I hit one outta this park, right center. That was some shot." I thought, oh my God, he's reliving his past at the field. The scene I filmed was very real.

Following the emotional visit in St. Petersburg, Spiegel filmed action during much of the weeklong Roy Hobbs Tournament in Fort Myers. He interviewed numerous ballplayers, not only on the Bronx Yankees, but also on other teams as well. After returning to New York, Spiegel decided to make a film documentary on the story of John Malangone's life. What followed became a labor of love for Spiegel. For several years, Bruce researched John's life and went wherever John had played baseball. The research included interviews with family members, former baseball personnel, such as

Ed Charles, John Blanchard, Johnny Kucks, Charlie Silvera, Eddie Bockman, and various other minor league players and managers, and of course, Ron Weiss. The result was a fifty-five minute documentary entitled *Long Road Home*. Spiegel summarized the entire process:

It was a great thing for me, absolutely wonderful. It was the best film experience I ever had. John was great and all the people I met were great. Nothing will ever be as important as the time I spent with John. John standing in the midst of Miller Huggins Field reliving his amazing life will always stay with me.

Six long years passed before the film was completed. After making a debut at CBS studios in Manhattan in 2006, the film was also shown at the Yogi Berra Museum in Montclair, New Jersey, in front of an overflowing crowd of baseball celebrities, spectators, current and ex-ballplayers, and friends and family members. The occasion was considered a huge success by everyone in attendance. Some of the special guests included Ed Charles, Floyd Lane, and Bob Goldsholl. Many of John's teammates, from the New Jersey-based A League Of Our Own, were also in attendance. Mark Van Overloop, league president and teammate of John, remembered, "The place was packed, standing room only." Moe Resner, who played with John on the Mel Greene Cubs in 1957 and the Bronx Yankees between 1996 and 2001, attended the showing and wrote a column for *Major League Baseball Scene*. Resner commented, "Bruce's undertaking was unbelievably dynamic." Ed Randall, host of *Ed Randall's Talking Baseball* show on radio station WFAN in New York on Sunday mornings, was also very impressed, saying, "How can I possibly interview John on the air in only twelve minutes?"

The film was then shown at various local film festivals, including the Garden State Festival, the Staten Island Film Festival, the Bronx Film Festival, and the Major League Baseball's Hall of Fame in Cooperstown, New York. In 2007, the Cooperstown Baseball Hall of Fame festival, showcasing ten films, awarded a first place prize to Spiegel's documentary.

Spiegel's DVD continues to be shown to numerous and receptive audiences in the New York and New Jersey metropolitan area homes, libraries, religious institutions, historical societies, and other public gathering places. Jeffrey Lyons, former media critic for WNBC, praised the documentary by saying, "It will touch in a very special way."

In April of 2013, Spiegel posted information about John Malangone and *Long Road Home* on a new website. The site features a two-minute trailer of *Long Road Home*, as well as additional photos and articles on the lives of John Malangone and Ron Weiss.

Following the Cooperstown award, Phil Mushnick, columnist for the *New York Post,* wrote a review of *Long Road Home* in November 2007, and commented on Bruce Spiegel and the film:

He knows a good story when he bumps into one. And when he bumped into John Malangone, six years ago, he knew what he had to do.

And so for now, Long Road Home *stands as the best documentary you've never seen about the incredible life of the best New York Yankee prospect you never heard of. Figures.*

The columnist summarized the contents of the documentary, stressing that it had a "happy, soulful ending" and concluded the column with the statement, "It belongs on TV." Mushnick referred to the fact the Yes Network, run by the Yankees, never showed any interest in broadcasting the documentary. To date, that situation has not changed, and rival programming networks such as ESPN and HBO have not shown any willingness to air the story. Mushnick's column was published in November of 2007, but its message still resonates today.

Over time, a number of film proposals by various groups of people were presented to John; the suggested storylines covered everything from John's trauma and comeback to fictionalized Mafia-based tales. To date, none of them have materialized into actual films, leaving Spiegel's *Long Road Home* as the only film produced on the life of John Malangone.

Chapter 30

Penance and Reconciliation

East Tremont Neighborhood
Bronx, NYC
Summer 2012

The cards stacked on the sign-in table at the chapel inside of the Sisto Funeral Home in East Tremont reflected handsome features of the deceased gentleman who was laid out in the open casket nearby. Besides the customary printed prayer, the card indicated the man's date of birth: July 22, 1931. This made him less than a year older than a lone visitor who was sporting his ancient Yankee cap and sitting before the casket. Before the scheduled visiting hours, John Malangone managed to quietly visit his uncle Antonio "Tony" Bozza, who had married Aunt Yolanda Panarese. The nephew had high regards for this gentle, kind man who was highly respected by the Malangone and Panarese families. Uncle Tony was special to John for another reason; he had saved John's life decades earlier while both men were working on a construction project. Working in a skeleton framework of a building, twenty-two stories high, John had grabbed a sheet of plywood and started to carry it from one area to another, when suddenly Tony jumped off a scaffold, tackling John and wrestling the plywood out of his hands. Bozza understood the risk immediately when he observed John carrying the wood in such a manner that would enable a sudden gust of wind to lift his nephew airborne. This was just another miracle in John Malangone's turbulent life.

Alone with his thoughts, John was able to mourn Tony's passing due to his uncle's age and a long illness. A modest man, Uncle Tony toiled for years in the construction industry. Even though the hard labor was dangerous, Bozza was not known to complain loudly about his struggles and challenges in life. He was dearly loved by all who knew him.

Suddenly, there was movement in the casket, with two hands extending outward and gripping the open side. The hands were those of a young boy, as was the hair and face. Staring and smiling at John with topaz eyes, Orlando Panarese, now upright in the casket, asked, "Giann! Jamme fore a juca! John! Let's go out and play!"

Could this be... no, no, wait... a possible panic attack coming on. The volcano, long dormant, was beginning to rumble... no, no, can't be happening. Get a grip John, this is not real. God, please, not again...

Although the fear and paralysis subsided, John was haunted by the scene and the simple reality that, after all these years, after positive interventions by Edward House, Paulie Tine, Tony Bozza, Paul Krichell, Ronnie Weiss, media people, sympathetic mental health and teaching professionals, after all of that, there was still trouble. A demon, long suppressed but not gone, was still lurking in the background, waiting for an opening, anywhere, to be resurgent.

Amazingly, despite all of the kindness and understanding shown to John by caring people in his later years, there were still a few unsympathetic individuals who would continue to call him a killer, or worse. Whether these attacks were due to fear or jealousy related to Malangone's public attention and accolades can only be speculated. However, it is certain that the verbal cruelties and personal remarks have enabled the demon to remain alive, feeding on residual guilt in the back of the man's mind. It is a battle that will continue for the rest of John's life, although his better days far outnumber any other negative moments.

The wake for Antonio Bozza was well attended, especially by family members, comprised of three generations of Panareses. Despite the heavy attendance, John was easily spotted wearing his old Yankee cap. The conversations that took place with relatives were congenial, but they also brought to the surface in John's mind a realization that some people in the immediate family knew about what happened to Orlando but never discussed anything with him. Seventy-five years after the accident, Grandma Sylvia Panarese's dictum, "no one is to speak of this anymore," was still in effect. Most members of the extended Malangone and Panarese families were not familiar with these particular details of John Malangone's life. The ex-Yankee never talked to anyone in the families about his suffering, and he stayed away from most of his other relatives for decades.

John Panarese, beloved grandnephew of Grandmother Sylvia Panarese, attended Antonio Bozza's funeral. John Panarese was affectionately nicknamed "Father John" by Panarese family members because of a youthful inclination to join the Roman Catholic priesthood. Although he chose another career path, the nickname stuck with him anyway. Following the funeral proceedings, he spoke in a representative way for all extended family members when he commented to John, "John, we hardly knew you."

This was a major part of why John never got past his role in Orlando's death in the first place. Troubled by the awareness of this situation, and sensing that a window of opportunity in his life might be closing, John decided to challenge the silence by calling a family meeting with his siblings, Anna, Sal, and Sal's wife Dolores, a long-cherished member of the family. Most importantly, the meeting also included the two surviving Panarese aunts, Margaret and Yolanda.

The gathering occurred Labor Day weekend at Yolanda's home with everyone in attendance understanding the purpose of the meeting. Margaret, who had a propensity to monopolize other people's conversations, was asked beforehand to restrain herself and let John do the talking. John had nicknamed his aunt "Radio" because he had on one occasion confused a radio broadcast with Margaret's monologue during a dinner conversation. Only after unplugging the radio, then checking the back of it for an on/ off switch, did he realize that Margaret had continued yakking unabated.

After the ground rules for the meeting were established, John kicked off the start of the conversation.

I knew I would never speak to Grandma. I couldn't even look at her. Every holiday I would hide under the dinner table and grab peanuts off the table and eat them underneath. I just wanted to say one thing, without hurtin' anybody. How sorry I was. To the two aunts here who took care of me, I am sorry about what happened. Being five years old, nothing was developed... the mind, the brain, therefore instead of blocking out what happened, I blocked everything else out. You need to know how sorry I was because a lot of people got hurt by my actions. I never realized how hurt you guys were too [Yolanda and Margaret].

Sal interjected to say, "Everybody forgives you, Johnny." At that point, Yolanda hugged John and reassured him that he turned out alright. Anna, in tears from the start, also hugged her brother. Margaret got up and hugged her nephew, reminding him that Sylvia had a dream with "Orlando telling her to leave John alone." However, "Radio" was just warming up. Margaret commented that her nephew was a baby at the time and that he wouldn't even know what happened. John then recalled a similar accident and managed to continue anyway.

Fifteen magazines, four books, twentysumpin' newspapers, the News, the Post... I didn't take any money for the TV show [Maury]. There was a story last week about a teenager in Germany who killed a track official by accident with a javelin. He was very upset. He's in a hospital getting help.

Margaret interjected,

Don't you see? You're gonna become famous... your purpose [in life] now is to help other kids.

The conversation, involving five people, splintered into four mini conversations at that point. They eventually coalesced back into one, with "Radio" prevailing over everyone else.

If you have a choice between being a famous ballplayer and helping kids, which would you choose? Helping kids, people would love you for that. That's more important than baseball.

"Radio" continued.

My mother was always very religious. She said it had to happen. That was the way life goes. She always loved him [John] and forgave him a long time ago. She even forgave that other boy [Grant Panarese] when a truck killed her first son [Orlando].

Family members reminisced about everything after that, from childhood stories to Dom Bepp to more "Goose" tales to Father Joseph to thankful expressions for everyone still living. Suddenly John interrupted everybody.

Now that I broke the ice, we will all go out and eat a nice dinner next time at a nice restaurant. Today's meeting was more important than being famous.

Uncle Tony's passing had helped bring the remaining family members together. John did feel closure after the meeting, having, in his words, "prayed for this meeting for almost eighty years."

He was able to finally say out loud to loved ones, "I am sorry."

They responded with, "We love you."

Penance for sixty years... now forgiveness and redemption... at last.

Chapter 31
Stories Then and Now

Dick Caswell Field
New Rochelle, NY
New York Metropolitan Area
Fall 2012

In the fall of 2012, Dick Caswell and Robins players, dressed in red jerseys, were staging their sixth annual alumni reunion game at a renovated ball field in the City Park athletic complex in New Rochelle, New York. Robins players of all ages were invited to participate in the game and to reminisce about memorable moments from previous years and even previous decades. The Robins roster has included college players, ex-minor leaguers, and a few veterans from the majors. One well-known alumnus is Andrew MacPhail, who held executive positions with the Minnesota Twins, the Chicago Cubs, and the Baltimore Orioles.

The reunion also included some veteran players who never played for Dick Caswell's team, but attended nevertheless to enjoy the festivities. Some players wore Major League Baseball uniforms. Harry Greenfield, longtime Robins veteran, and Moe Resner, formerly of Mike DeRosa's Bronx Yankees, wore cream-colored Major League Giants uniforms. Resner, a lifelong New York/San Francisco Giant fan, is known for filming segments of the last New York Giants baseball game ever played in the Polo Grounds in 1957. Decades later, Resner produced a DVD entitled *End of an Era*. In 2012, the Giants organization celebrated the fifty-fifth anniversary of that game and honored Resner for his memorable and historical footage.

Present was the team's field manager, Willie Mack, a soft-spoken gentleman and a veteran of the old Negro Leagues from the forties and fifties. Mack managed the club from 1978 to 2009.

Regardless of the players' backgrounds and uniform colors, one thing was certain; nearly everyone present recognized John Malangone when he arrived at the park, sporting his weather-beaten Yankee cap. The aging slugger sported an unmistakable aura of pride and his trademark grin as he greeted old teammates and younger Robin players. John was reveling in his baseball element, sharing thoughts on everything from the Bronx Yankees to various individuals. He described his lifelong friend, Floyd Layne, as "one of the best to ever play baseball." He referred, as always, to his closest friend, Paulie Tine, and his brother Mike as outstanding ballplayers. He talked about how the Paul Krichell signing "saved my life." He presented a Joe DiMaggio story to old-timers, many of whom never tire of hearing about the famous "Yankee Clipper." As he always did at any baseball gathering, John demonstrated how he swung his bat at pitches. He emphasized his point by saying "turning your right hand over left" and further explained how "hitting horseflies with a shovel" strengthened his wrists all those years ago.

One prominent guest present at the reunion had never met John Malangone. The gentleman was Bob Wolff, the renowned sports broadcaster. Wolff, whose credentials include calling Don Larsen's 1956 World Series perfect game and the 1958 National Football League title game between the New York Giants and Baltimore Colts, attended the gathering to support longtime friend Dick Caswell. Wolff has two sons, Bob and Rick (drafted by the Detroit Tigers), and a grandson, John (drafted by the Chicago White Sox). They all played ball for Caswell's Robins over the years. Bob Wolff once commented, "After the Dodgers left Brooklyn, there were three teams left in New York: the Yankees, Mets, and Robins."

It wasn't long before John jumped into his fifth gear of storytelling with Mr. Wolff, explaining the story of a tournament in Albany, New York, involving a championship game between the Robins and Brooklyn Eagles. John recalled how he took off his leg cast for a hairline fracture suffered in the previous game, delivered a pinch hit, and crawled to first base in the final game.

Robins players were mesmerized by Malangone's presence and his stories. Various players took turns surrounding John during the course of the Robins exhibition game, and some recalled highlights of playing with him. One player remembered how "John would come down, jump out of his Jeep, get three hits, hop back into his Jeep, and take off." Another player added, "I was scared of him. He was a barrel-chested guy who hit rockets. You didn't wanna mess with him." From a third player, "We were in awe of him." A fourth: "He was the greatest I ever saw."

Generously complimenting Malangone, Harry Greenfield aptly spoke for everyone present when he commented, "John, you were always the legend here." Harry described John as "the greatest I ever played with."

A few players recalled some Malangone antics as well. They remembered inexplicable behavior alongside real baseball talent. One teammate recalled an absentminded Malangone behind the plate.

He was catching behind the plate and suddenly we realized he wasn't wearing his chest protector. But it was too late to tell him because a foul ball hit below his neck and knocked him backwards. Greenfield came over to check on him and a large brown object came out of his [John's] mouth. Harry was horrified, thinking the worst, maybe his tongue was cut off or a broken bone or something. It turned out to be a small cigar stub, stuck in his mouth but knocked loose... he [John] got up smiling after that.

Another story was about loyalty to his teammates.

Nick Furlong [Notre Dame baseball and football star, drafted by the N.Y. Mets], our pitcher, was deliberately spiked one game while covering first base on a putout. The batter and the other team played dirty. Next time that guy came up to bat, John stood up behind the plate and yelled out to Furlong, "That's him, the guy that spiked ya." The pitcher didn't waste time nailing the guy in the back. Before the batter could charge the mound, John yelled, "Here's the ball," and threw it back to Furlong. Nick had the ball in his hand and the batter suddenly realized he would be hit a second time, so he backed off. He wasn't gonna mess with John either. He knew better.

Many of the players had no idea about John's life story, his background, or the childhood tragedy and its consequences. They only knew what they saw when John showed up at games to play, or perhaps what they gathered from small tidbits of information through the baseball grapevine. They had no idea that the man standing before them had taken numerous punches in the game of life, only to continually rise up and survive the worst of them. His trademark grin and laughter always prevailed and masqueraded the personal suffering that he endured over the years.

Non-Robins players also knew some stories about John Malangone. George Preston, who met John in A League Of Our Own, recalled how John "always had great stories to tell—it was not just his skill." Preston cited John's candor, saying John was "open and frank." Preston knew John as a coach in the league and declared, "He was the smartest guy on the ball field." Preston referred to a game in which his team was behind by two runs in the bottom of the ninth inning. With the bases loaded and nobody out, the numbers three, four, and five hitters were scheduled to bat. The three hitters included T.J. Kempton, Preston, and Ron Weiss. Acting on instructions from John, who was managing, all three power hitters laid down successful bunts that scored three runs and won the game. It was a feat that the opposing team never saw coming.

Old-timer baseball fan John Roque was at the reunion. He never played for the Robins, but his son played against the team. Roque knew all about John's career. He recalled fondly how he followed Malangone's promising career back in the 1950s, avidly reading the *New York Daily News* and the *New York Mirror* sports pages. He commented, "He came up with Mantle, Blanchard, and Kucks. John contributed quite a bit; he was into the game. But, he was very boisterous." Roque and Malangone enjoyed meeting each other face-to-face for the first time.

One visitor to the reunion unaware of John's early history was Mike Cordero. A Bronx native, Cordero had recently turned fifty and enthusiastically started playing baseball in A League Of Our Own. Cordero overheard John talking about hitting a ball "outta sight" over the rooftop in the 1951 Journal American All-Star Game in the fabled Polo Grounds, home of the then New York Giants. Malangone described how he watched the ball clear the rooftop and drop to the street below, as an opening between ballpark decks allowed John to follow the flight of the ball. Cordero, listening intently, immediately identified with the story and told John and everyone else present that he did the same thing. This revelation left everyone, including John, scratching their heads because the Polo Grounds stadium was demolished around the time that Cordero was born. After questioning Cordero about his story, the listeners learned that Mike did it on his Xbox game the day before. Only then did Cordero realize that John Malangone was talking of real experiences, not fantasy ones.

In truth, the reunion really belonged to Dick Caswell because the new turf ball field on which everyone was playing was to be named after the Robins manager. After a team meeting with Robins personnel, Caswell proceeded to give away new bright red Robin jerseys to everyone present. John received one with number thirty-seven on the back. Memories of the "Ol Perfessor" Casey Stengel, who wore that number, surfaced in John's mind. His classic grin slowly emerged on his face, as he commented, "Yeah, Casey..." Somewhere Yankee ghosts were smiling on John, and everything was fine now.

Chapter 32

You Can't Make
This Stuff Up

Florida, Virginia
1950s

Baseball stories involving John Malangone are numerous, but so are stories about the rifle arm's antics off the field. Mentioned earlier was the famed "Hotel Mercury" automobile, frequently used by Paulie and John for sojourns everywhere. There were actually two Mercury vehicles owned by John during the 1950s. One such vehicle was a convertible that met its fate in the crash into a minor league scoreboard. The other was the hardtop version, acquired in East Harlem after Paulie cracked up the Cadillac on the Willis Avenue Bridge. John and Paulie drove that particular Mercury everywhere, from St. Petersburg, Florida (baseball camps) to Montreal, Canada (frequent visits to St. Joseph's Cathedral). Before John was drafted and stationed at Fort Dix in 1952, he and Paulie drove south to watch the Yankee spring training during the month of March. The pair drove from New York all the way to Florida with studded snow tires on the Mercury, something John later regretted because "all I heard was thumpa, thumpa, thumpa."

Once in Florida, the pair decided to swap the snow tires with ordinary tires from a parked vehicle on a local roadside. While in the process of jacking up the car and changing the tires, John and Paulie were interrupted by a local policeman who was more than a little inquisitive.

Officer: *Whaddya guys doing here?*

John: *Giving the guy a set of new snows, sir.*

Officer: *Does the owner of the car know that?*

John: *It's gonna be a surprise, sir.*

Officer: *You're under arrest.*

At the local stationhouse, John explained that he was with

the Yankees and that he was going to their spring training camp; the reaction from the cops was laughter and disbelief. "Whaddya Superman, now, too?"

After the stationhouse staff verified the status of the two suspects with Yankee management, John and Paulie were released from custody. John went back to the arresting officer and asked him, "Why did you arrest us?" The cop replied, "Because it don't snow down here, Yankee."

In Abbott and Costello like fashion, John turned to Paulie and said, "How did he know I was a Yankee?" Paulie, blissfully unaware of cultural references, replied with a proud smile, "Because you can hit."

Gary Sacino, a lifelong friend of John from his East Harlem days, recounted a trip he took with John to Florida. While John was stationed at Fort Dix, he decided to leave the base on his own, without permission, and go to Avon, Florida with Gary Sacino, Paulie, and others for a Lou Haneles sponsored baseball camp. Sacino, with a wide grin, described what happened next:

We all drove down to Florida in a teacher's car. John worked out a deal with this woman to deliver her car to Coral Gables. We got the car, went to Fort Dix, picked up John and then had to drive him all the way back to 111th Street in East Harlem just to say goodbye to his mother! Do you believe that? He said, "Hey, I can't leave without saying goodbye to my mother." Apparently he never went anywhere without saying goodbye to his mother.

What happens is there is books in the back of the car... now all six of us guys couldn't squeeze in the car, because those books were killing us. So John waves his hand and says, "Get rid of the books. Throw 'em out the window."

Half the books went out the window. I says, "John, how you gonna face this woman?" John drives all the way down to Coral Gables and confronts the woman, and gives her a story. Then we go to Avon to play ball. Now before we left, each guy had an unemployment check. We go down there, and now we are playing baseball, and now it's time to come home. Everybody says, "How much ya got?" Nobody has any money and now we need money to get home. To make a long story short, I wired home for some money and somebody else did too and we got a total of one hundred thirty-five dollars. Two guys left on their own.

So who is the auto mechanic? John Malangone. John says, "I'll get a car, don't worry about it." He comes up with a 1941 DeSoto limousine. Where did he get it? I dunno. No license plates, no papers, no nothin'. Big car... In the meantime, we're not eating too good. We met a couple of gals who invite us for food, and we're all thinking it's for dinner. They came out with coffee and cookies. Three guys went for the cookies and cleaned off the plate. The gals said, "What's wrong with you guys? Don't you guys eat?" That's how bad it was. We got by that night, and John says, "There's only one thing to do. There is plenty of oranges in Florida. Load up the car with oranges." We loaded up the car with oranges. We got one hundred thirty-five dollars and we start driving. I said, "How we gonna make it all the way to New York?" We go to Georgia and start selling oranges, "Two for a quarter, three for a quarter..."

We get some money and start using it for gas. Going into the Carolinas, we got two blowouts. The tires were shot. We pull up to a junkyard at night, and John says, "Don't worry about it. Who is the oldest guy? I'll handle everything." He goes over the fence, and starts tossing tires over the fence. Then the sheriff come out, with a shotgun. We all lined up against the fence. Caught us good. He says, "Whaddya guys doing, ba, ba, ba, ba..."

John was our spokesman, explaining to the sheriff, "We are all professional baseball players. I'm from the Yankees, this is Gary from the Phillies..." John's talking up a storm and its one o'clock in the morning. He's talking and talking and finally the sheriff puts up his hands and says, "Alright, alright."

He lets us go and we put the tires on the car. Now we are driving with a car still loaded with oranges. We were starving, sick of oranges. I remember it was a Friday, start of a weekend. John says, "Let's stop at this grocery store." We stop and go in. We paid for some bread. Guy gave us a loaf of bread. John said, "How about some baloney? We're really short of money." Guy says "OK, I'll give you a little baloney."

John says to me, "Try and get some pork and beans." I said ok and took some cans of pork and beans off the shelf and stole 'em. Next thing ya know, "Boom" we are back in the car. John's got the Tip Top bread, the baloney and I got the pork and beans. Now we're making the sandwiches. Before this we were eating orange sandwiches. Disgusting! I couldn't stand it no more. The juice dripping out of the bread...

Now we give Paulie Tine a sandwich. All of a sudden, he yells, "I can't eat this!!" I said, "Why, Paulie, why?" He says, "Today is Friday!! It's Friday! I can't eat meat! This is a sin against God!!" He rolls down the window and throws the sandwich outta the car! I said, "Oh my God, whaddya doing, are you crazy?" Paulie kept yelling, "You guys are sinners, you guys are sinners!! Don't you know God is watching you? Ya can't eat that baloney, ya can't eat it!" We yelled back, "Paulie, we're hungry, Paulie! Can you understand that?"

We continue on, and now we're really getting low on gas and money. John says, "Let's stop at a new car dealer and trade this car in for a new one." I said to him, "How are you gonna trade it in?" He says, "Don't worry about it." So we go to a new car dealer and John says to the salesman, "See that Mercury over there? We'll take that." Guy goes, "Whooo, how wonderful, how much you putting down?" John says, "We'll make a trade. I got a beautiful '41 DeSoto limousine outside." Guy goes, "Whaaat? You got cash?" John says, "No, we don't have the cash, but we'll take the car now. You have my '41 limousine and my word that I am John Malangone. Don't believe me? You call the New York Yankee organization and they'll back me up. Anything you want, they'll back me up. We'll take the car now."

The guy says, "Wait a minute, we have to wait three or four days for that." John said, "I can't wait three or four days, I am in the army. I gotta get home." The guy says, "You can't take the car outta here, I am telling you right now."

Ok, so we walk outta there with no new car and I said to John, "Whatta we do now?" John says, "I dunno." We stop at a Chevrolet auto parts place. We saw a ratchet machine that makes a machine gun sound, rattattattattat... Boom, that disappears out the door and into the car. We go a few miles down the road and sell the machine. Got a good buck for that one. Now we have some money and we can get something to eat. Now we're headed for New York, going over the Triborough Bridge, with twenty-six cents. Good thing, because we paid a quarter for the toll. I left my house weighing one hundred fifty pounds. When I came back, my mother said, "What concentration camp were you in?" I lost twenty pounds on that trip!

I said to John, "What about the car?" John says, "Don't worry about it. I'll take it to Fort Dix." He takes it to Fort Dix and they impounded it because it was now on the base and there was no registration, no license, no paperwork... John then says to me, "Gary, the car is gone." John was in trouble for skipping the base for thirty days and confined to his bunk. John thought they were gonna send him to Korea after that.

Like Ron Weiss always said, you can't make this stuff up.

Chapter 33
Resiliency

Little Ferry
Northern New Jersey
2012-2013

John commented in the *Long Road Home* documentary, "The worst day of your life will pass. It's true. If you can hold on, the worst day of your life will pass."

Orlando Panarese's death in 1937 was only the beginning of those worse days for John. He reflected on one of many of those moments...

When I went to the army, I had a death wish. I figured that I was never coming back. Never figured on coming back.

The setbacks did not stop at any point in John's life; they kept coming at him. He just managed to go around them and survive. Going into the army with a death wish resulted in a comeback of sorts...

All of a sudden, I am saving somebody's life. It was a miracle. After that, I felt untouchable. My batting average in the army was over .400.

At the age of eighty, John had intestinal surgery to remove a blockage. He also endured back surgery to repair a herniated disc. Malangone was issued a wheelchair upon discharge from a hospital, only to fall out of the chair before leaving the facility. The attendant assigned to wheel John out of the hospital did not apply the brake of the wheelchair properly, and the chair slipped out from under John.

The operation on the back, the accident with the wheelchair, the pain hit like lightning. I was being released. Plus the surgery on the intestine...

Despite the surgery and the accident, John continued to

move around Little Ferry, with the occasional use of a cane. He attended baseball games played by his friends in A League Of Our Own; nothing was going to slow the man down. He continued greeting everyone he met with a smile and saying "How we doin' today?" John continues to sport his legendary grin and to evoke humor with his stories and observations about people.

In late October of 2012, Hurricane Sandy swept ashore in New Jersey, wreaking havoc and earning the nickname "Frankenstorm." Sandy was considered the most destructive hurricane of the 2012 season. The storm's tremendous size created ruin and devastation along the New Jersey and New York coastlines. Initial U.S. damage estimates were near $50 billion, making Sandy the second costliest violent storm (after Hurricane Katrina) to hit the United States. One hundred and forty-seven direct deaths in the Atlantic basin were attributed to Sandy, with seventy-two deaths occurring in the mid-Atlantic and northeastern United States. According to the National Oceanic and Atmospheric Administration (NOAA), Sandy caused the greatest number of U.S. fatalities that were directly related to a tropical storm outside of the southern United States since 1972.

Little Ferry, New Jersey, flanking the Hackensack River, was hit hard by Sandy. On the evening of October 29, tidal water, up to eight feet high in some neighborhoods, surged from the riverbanks onto the streets, swamping the community and inflicting massive devastation. Local residents were shocked and unprepared to deal with the floods. Little Ferry's most famous resident, John Malangone, did not escape the swirling waters that engulfed the streets of the town, and neither did his home...

We were told to evacuate before the storm hit because no one would come for us if anybody stayed. I stayed anyway. Dogs were barking on the steps. They wouldn't come down... water had come up two steps. I thought it was the last step. I looked down the street. All the lights in town were out. It was pitch black. I thought I saw a Hummer coming down the street with no lights on. I stepped again and something hit me. That humpback was a wave. It knocked me down. I didn't know what to do. I couldn't see anything and my flashlights were in the cars. I put on my Mickey Mouse boots and walked back through the house.

The electricity was out for weeks. The basement was filled up with water. Everything was destroyed. Had to start ripping out all the sheetrock and clean up the mold. Had to replace the boiler and hot water heater and everything the dishwasher, dryer, washing machine. Had to rip all the walls out.

Now if we wanna get a FEMA loan, we gotta get flood insurance. This happened ONE time!! [raising a finger] One time! In fifty years I never had a drop of water. What if I got hit with an airplane? [grinning] Do I need airport insurance, too?

Following the storm, a building inspector visited the house and concluded it was unfit for occupancy. Malangone refused to leave and gradually restored the home, despite ongoing problems for months afterward.

Little Ferry's celebrity athlete did not go unnoticed. After the storm, Steve Politi, columnist for *The Star-Ledger*, a New Jersey-based newspaper, visited John and surveyed the damage to the house. John, also concerned about the loss of some baseball memorabilia that were stored in the basement, told Politi, "I don't want this to set me off again." Malangone had felt the onset of a panic attack and had tried climbing onto his roof to shake it. Eventually it passed.

Life is not easy when you're gettin' old. I am very surprised that I handled it. I didn't think I would come out of it that good.

The medical issues continued to bother John.

I wasn't feeling good. My daughter [Christina] took me out for Father's Day. But I wasn't feeling well, so she took me to the emergency room. I told them I couldn't get my shoe on or off. They cut open the shoe and my foot looked like a balloon, ya know? They said, "My God, it's infected. You gotta stay here." They pumped antibiotics in me for hours. I was there about five or six days.

Despite the various issues, the aging ballplayer refuses to quit on any curveballs that life keeps throwing at him.

I can't stand too long because of my back and neck. Now that it is over with, and I am this far, there is a lot more to go. I feel better, the way I handled all this, the way I did. Once in a while I get a flashback, ya know, asking myself why me, why now? When I got the house, the VA [Veteran's Administration] told me nothing could ever happen to this house. It would withstand everything.

Fueling the resiliency that characterizes John is the realization that he is loved and needed by others, and that there is an ongoing purpose for his life. Hugging and embracing his granddaughter, Jackie, is a joy, as hugging his own children was something unthinkable while raising them during the early years of his marriage. The man is no longer fearful of hugging and showing affection to others, especially children.

I feel blessed, thank God. He's been good to me. I know I had a cross to bear, but he's been good to me.

Daughter Christina explained the change in her father:

I just wanted to put something into perspective. My father is loving towards Jacqueline, his granddaughter, in a way that he could not express to us when we were children. This is a far cry from his past. I wanted to express and convey my father's relationship with Jacqueline. Whenever I come home to visit him, he's usually sitting at the kitchen table, watching TV. He always greets Jackie with a great big smile, saying, "There's my girl," and giving her a very loving hug. And Jackie likewise.

Despite all the tragedy and heartbreak that John has suffered over the course of his lifetime, he continues to survive because of a strong inner core that does not allow him to quit.

Epilogue

Moonachie, New Jersey
Craig's Deli
Little Ferry, New Jersey
Present Day

For little kids and big league ballplayers and everyone in between, the arrival of spring every year signals a fresh start and raises hopes of a better and more promising baseball season. The annual revival of baseball activity begins indoors, in numerous gyms and batting cages, and eventually spreads outdoors on sandlots and diamonds, despite unpredictable weather in March and April. This is accompanied by continual monitoring of major league teams and their stars through the newspapers, talk radio, and other outlets. People begin making plans to buy tickets to see their favorite professional teams. Parents acquire mitts and baseballs to play catch with their youngsters and encourage them to enlist in various baseball youth programs. Baseball's time-honored ritual of opening day festivities, from youth leagues to the professional level, celebrates the joyous inauguration of a new season of competition. Mother Nature complements the occasions with welcomed warm weather and the annual blossoming of plants in a riot of colors. On a spiritual level, for baseball fans and participants, the arrival of spring brings to mind English essayist Alexander Pope's phrase, "Hope springs eternal."

For John Malangone, the spring of 2013 arrived with life's promise of renewal in nature, baseball, and himself. While I was recently taking a tour with John of local baseball fields in Foschini Park, in nearby Hackensack, New Jersey, John reminisced about everything from clutch hits to sleeping on park benches while waiting for a big game. We stopped at the John Stevens Field complex in Moonachie, and John pointed out all of the fields. Enthusiasm for baseball is alive and well here, despite the fact that only John and I were present at the time, barely tolerating the March winds. John suggested getting out of the car to set up a throwing net I had in the trunk. After warming up and throwing into the net, I was subjected to the coaching side of the ex-Yankee, who was eager to pass along his observations.

Watch your release point...
Move back a few steps...
Throw from a stretch position...
You're too high...
Too much Kentucky windage...

John was in full baseball mode now, grabbing a bat and telling me to pitch to him so that he could start bunting. John was grinning and having fun, instinctively reacting and lowering the bat and making that distinct sound that is heard when a thrown baseball makes contact with the sweet part of the bat. This activity for him was a piece of cake.

All of the pain that John had ever suffered was gone at the moment, while he was seemingly embraced by invisible baseball gods. All of the anguish, heartaches, and tragedies that have been etched in the lines on his face simply vanished. There was a sense that Orlando, Paulie, Anthony, and the others were present in spirit, but there was no demon this time.

My practice session with John in Moonachie was over, but the good memories continued to live on as John headed back to Little Ferry to Craig's Deli, a short walking distance from John's home. The eatery is regarded as John's home away from home. The proprietor, Craig DeFazio, is proud of Little Ferry's famous resident.

I have known John for eighteen plus years and it's been nothing but a pleasure. Nice guy, always a smile on his face, a twinkle in his eye. He's more than a customer. John is like an uncle who would come over to your grandma's house for Sunday dinner. That is what it is like when you see John. His stories always captivate us. Every time he comes in, I purposely send customers to him, after they see his picture on the counter, just so that I can hear more of his stories, and get more details, while I am taking care of more customers. It's kinda like multitasking in my own way. I always enjoy seeing John come in. I told him way back, "You're always welcome."

Decorated in the colors of the Italian flag, the walls in Craig's Deli are lined with red, white, and green tiles. One wall is adorned with framed photos and artwork of famous celebrities and athletes from bygone eras. Ghostlike sketches of Yankee greats, including Joe DiMaggio, Mickey Mantle, and Yogi Berra, peer down from the wall and serve as reminders to John Malangone of another time and place and lost opportunity. John is not haunted by them, but is instead comfortable knowing that he was one of them—a professional ballplayer.

Customers approaching the deli counter will always notice, besides several framed *Sports Illustrated* covers, the 1955 Yankee photo of John posing with Hall of Fame catchers Bill Dickey and Mickey Cochrane. For John, the accent is always on the positive when he is reminiscing with fellow patrons about his past.

While Craig was speaking, a typical encounter between John and a local patron was taking place.

Customer: *Nice hat* [referring to John's ancient Yankee cap].

John [with a big grin]: *Nice jacket* [referring to the man's Yankee jacket].

While talking aloud about a baseball memory, John caught the attention of another patron, whose curiosity led her to ask John what he was talking about. John responded with typical flourish about his past by saying,

I was with the Yankees. Do you know my story? I have a copy of it [Damned Yankee] in the car. I'll be right back.

Upon his return to the deli, I asked John about a brawl between the Dodgers and Padres that resulted in an injury to Dodger pitcher Zack Greinke, after he hit batter Carlos Quentin with a pitch during a game; an irate Quentin charged Greinke near the pitching mound and the collision between the two men resulted in Greinke's collarbone being broken. What would John have done if he were the pitcher? His reply was simple.

First of all, I never hit a batter, even when I was told to do so. No matter what happened, I woulda stayed on the mound. I don't move. He [the batter] has to climb the mound. That's not easy to do. You're gonna lose your footing, ya know? They don't come swinging, wrestling most of the time. Baseball players are strong, but they are not fighters. I woulda hit him with a left hook and it woulda been over right there. He would still be there...

Ron Weiss was right. You can't make this stuff up...

But the discussion about fighting did not end there. John had watched a documentary on ESPN entitled *Playing for the Mob*. The story was about several college athletes who were recruited by mobsters to fix point spreads on college basketball games. The athletes received cash payments for shaving points on designated games; physical threats and intimidation were employed by mob figures to ensure cooperation by the ball players. The show brought back unpleasant memories for John, who recalled the pressure placed on him by Dom Bepp and Father Joseph to box. John recalled how once he cooperated with Dom Bepp, he would feel obligated to do bidding for the mob.

The documentary used clips from a film called *Goodfellas,* based on the life of a real-life mobster, Henry Hill. The man was heavily involved in the point shaving scandal, which took place at Boston College in 1979. John always said that *Goodfellas* was the only movie that accurately portrayed Mafia culture.

Despite all of the past troubles, the man is blessed. And more importantly, at eighty-three years of age, he is still kicking. He spends most Sunday mornings giving advice to the Bergen Yankee ballplayers, whether they are working out in the NJ Sports Advantage facility or playing on the local ball fields. On occasion, during weeknights and weekends, John talks to local organizations about his career and the *Long Road Home* documentary.

Like Craig DeFazio noted, there is always a smile on his face and a twinkle in his eye.

His occasional visits to the old haunts in East Harlem are now happy ones for John. He regales interested bystanders with old stories about the neighborhood. He can be found in Patsy's Pizzeria on First Avenue, chatting with firemen and police officers and regular customers during their lunch hours. Old-timers remember John as one of their own, holding legendary status as a baseball and boxing athlete. He has posed for pictures with patrons and tells them how he cleaned spittoons and swept sawdust off the same floor nearly seventy years ago. He can also be found chatting with employees and local Pleasant Avenue residents in Rao's Restaurant about people, places, and events from another era.

Prior to the publication of this book, John's old roommate from the 1955 Yankee rookie camp, Johnny Kucks, passed away at the age of eighty-one. Kucks had a signature moment in the 1956 World Series, pitching and winning a 9-0 shutout against the Brooklyn Dodgers in game seven, and clinching the series for the Yanks. While Kucks and Malangone went in different directions with their careers, the two remained in contact with each other over the years. John attended church memorial services and reminisced about his old friend:

I knew him at Fort Dix in the army before we went to rookie camp in 1955. He was a great roommate. He and Blanchard were the same way. Kucks became like Paulie to me, ya know? He and Blanchard accepted me. Kucks never put me down. He would say [as a pitcher], "I'll take Malangone. He'll bring in more runs than he'll let in." It sounded good. I realized he was giving me a compliment. Other pitchers would say, "I don't want that moron catching me."

Following the conclusion of funeral services, John, tears in his eyes, told members of the Kucks family, "I am sorry he is gone."

Stories about John seeking solace in various houses of worship are well known, and this led me to ask him if he felt a religious experience in baseball. His face lit up, and he exuberantly replied,

Are you kidding me?? Absolutely!! I have been waiting eighty-two years to say this without being ashamed. I always thought somebody would laugh at that idea and look down at me. Yes, the ballpark [old Yankee Stadium] gives me that feeling. Now I feel that way just being in any ballpark. But the religious miracle for me was Paul Krichell coming to Jefferson Park. How would anybody have spotted me? I never woulda even thought of a tryout. If Krichell hadn't shown up, nobody woulda spotted me for professional baseball. It saved me and Paulie from being in the mob. I once said to Paulie, "Where would we be?" Not in the army. Paulie woulda been kicked out, 4F because of his face, and they woulda caught my age [seventeen]. Me and Paulie needed a miracle and we always prayed hard for it. We figured if we combined our prayers, the two of us together, we had a better chance of getting that miracle. The real miracle was signing the contract with the New York Yankees, the team on the radio.

I never woulda been able to go back to 114th Street, because the mob woulda looked for me. If I stayed there, I mighta been going all the way with the mob, I don't know.

Baseball is a religious experience for me. Baseball makes me close to God. The signing was one of the miracles. The Roy Hobbs World Series in 1994 was a miracle. It was the closest thing to professional ball. That winning hit in the last inning gave me new life. What did I say in the documentary [Long Road Home]? What did I say? Professional ballplayers, including me, have a gift from God.

New York University president John Sexton, author of *Baseball as a Road to God*, discussed in his book how baseball can be deeply spiritual and religious for some people. There can be more than just hope and faith that spring eternal for followers of the game. Baseball includes other elements of religion for its faithful followers. The author expounds on how the game of baseball has sacred icons in its stadiums, its players, and memorable events that include miracle moments and continuing curses. Prayers were answered in Brooklyn in 1955, as the Dodgers finally defeated the Yankees in the World Series in a climactic game seven. For Chicago Cub fans, the famous Billy Goat curse of 1945 is still in effect, but this has not discouraged the faithful fans from continually rooting for their team. Perhaps at some point in the future, the prayers of loyal Cub fans will be rewarded with a miracle when the team wins a World Series.

For John, the miracle is his annual involvement with Ronnie Weiss on the fields of A League Of Our Own; the league's spring, summer, and fall seasons of 2014 have been a source of additional memories for both men. Prior to the publication of this book, the pair had called in one afternoon to the *Alan Hahn* show on ESPN Radio. The topic involved doing or changing one thing to speed up the game of baseball. Weiss explained, "The game is not played against the clock." John offered a suggestion about a rule involving catchers blocking the plate, but did not stop there. He then advocated eliminating pitch counts, video replay, and said he had "thirty more things..." At that point, the station invited him to call back the following week...

Somewhere the gods of baseball (and perhaps some boxing gods as well) are smiling down on a man who, despite all the sadness, has emerged as a strong survivor in life. Each and every day, John Malangone is still able to smile at everyone around him and say, "How we doin' today?"

A recent visit by John to Our Lady of Mount Carmel Church in East Harlem brought him some comfort and solace; during this visit, John reminisced with a parish priest who was unaware of his neighborhood background. John left the priest with a copy of "Damned Yankee" and proceeded to light candles in the vestibule at the front of the church. Reflecting on his childhood and the death of Orlando, he commented, "I am ready to meet Orlando again."

I asked, "What would you say to him?"

He answered back with a broad grin, "Let's play ball."

Endnotes

Despite the numerous demographic changes that have occurred in East Harlem over the past fifty years, Patsy's Restaurant still remains an icon in the neighborhood.

No one understood John's reading disability, because a diagnosis for dyslexia was not utilized during his school-age years. Although the dyslexia was coined as a phrase in 1887, it would take decades of research to acquire additional scientific knowledge and testing procedures in this subject area.

Dom Bepp is the only fictional name used in the story. Dom Bepp passed away several years after meeting John for the last time in the downtown bakery. Suffering from cancer, Jerry, the chauffeur, also passed away.

Mike Dash, author of *The First Family*, describes in well-researched detail the birth of the American Mafia and its first boss named Giuseppe Morello.

Despite the nickname "hoodlum priest," Father Joseph took a liking to the Malangone boy and supported him whenever possible.

Besides the brief encounter with Joe DiMaggio (Chapter Six), the other Yankees that John would chance upon that day were Joe Page, Pete Sheehy, Gus Mauch, and Charlie Silvera. John learned the names through conversations with a number of Yankee personnel after joining the organization. Joe Page was a lefty reliever, known as "Fireman" Joe Page. Page's career with the Yankees ended after the 1950 season. Although John did not know Page at the time, Malangone remembered the lefty's motion as the bullpen gate opened, and he was able to learn later the player's identity.

Coming to Yankee spring training sessions over the years, John would get to know Pete Sheehy. Sheehy was the Yankee equipment manager and clubhouse attendant for over seven decades. Sheehy's career spanned the Ruth-Gehrig Murderers Row era, and ended in the early eighties with stars that included Manager Billy Martin, Don Mattingly, and Willie Randolph. Pete

Sheehy was beloved and admired by John during his years with the Yankee organization.

Yankee assistant trainer Gus Mauch also happened to be in the bullpen when John made his exit out of the playing area. Mauch became head trainer for the team in 1948 and remained until 1961. A year later Mauch joined Casey Stengel as trainer for the New York Mets. Mauch retired in 1969 after the Mets won the World Series.

Charlie Silvera, Yankee backup catcher, observed John that day while sitting in the dugout. Silvera eventually developed a supportive relationship with Malangone, which lasted long after John's Yankee career was over.

John's experience in Canada in 1952 was one of his most memorable baseball highlights. He and Paulie Tine traveled to St. Joseph's Cathedral on several occasions before Paulie's death in 1980.

An athlete possessing a combination of professional baseball and boxing skills is a rare occurrence in the world of sports.

The rescue of Corporal James Parker was the most memorable of all the experiences John had encountered during his service at Fort Dix.

Robert Bonebrake and John later reconciled. Bonebrake got a laugh out of John's offer to buy a "live alligator" and Paulie Tine's offer to wander into a Florida swamp and catch one.

Ron Weiss also enjoyed playing stickball in his Yorkville neighborhood in Manhattan. He was profiled in 2011 for his stickball abilities in a local NYC newspaper (Pryor 2011).

The destruction of John's trophies and memorabilia was costly; the psychologist's recommendation did not solve John's mental anguish but rather, it erased records of John's past athletic accomplishments. This documentation included a priceless scrapbook that contained rare boxing and baseball articles and neighborhood photographs. Some newspaper clippings and a 1957 8mm film of John hitting a homerun were not destroyed.

The original Malangone residence on East 114th Street in Harlem was torn down for a housing project in the 1950s. A residential building nearly identical to John's tenement still stands in the neighborhood on 119th Street. A photograph of the alleyway from this building shows how the original on 114th Street was constructed.

The Roy Hobbs Tournament has attracted many ex-major leaguers, including Bill Lee, Mike Marshall, Ron LeFlore, and Rick Miller, to the rosters of participating teams. John had the opportunity to play against some of these big leaguers, decades after squandering the opportunity to do the same in the 1950s.

Weiss initially wrote a piece that he entitled, "The Yankee Who Never Was." The story was never completed. Weiss decided to contact Wayne Coffey and ask him to write a column about John Malangone instead.

Following Gary Smith's retirement in 2014 from *Sports Illustrated*, many observers have stated the opinion that "Damned Yankee" was one of the most memorable pieces Smith has ever written.

A DVD copy of the *Long Road Home* documentary can be obtained through Bruce Spiegel's website of the same name.

John Malangone kept his story from extended family members for years after his secret was first publicized by Wayne Coffey in the *NY Daily News* in 1994. John Panarese's comment in Chapter 30 merely reinforced that fact.

John has attended the annual Robins reunion game for the past twenty years; Dick Caswell's Robins teams have always held special memories of him.

Bibliography

"1955 Birmingham Barons Statistics." *Baseball-Reference.com*. Sports Reference LLC, n.d. Web. 23 Dec. 2011. http://www.baseball-reference.com/minors/team.cgi?id=598733bd

"100,000 Italians Mark Saint's Day in Harlem." *New York Times* 17 July 1937: 16. ProQuest Historical Newspapers. Web. 05 Apr. 2011. http://atjg64.tripod.com/articlesjuly 171937.pdf

"A League Of Our Own." *A League of Our Own-Over 40 Hardball*. N.p., n.d. Web. 12 Jan. 2012. http://www.aleagueofourown.org/aboutourleague.htm

"A Look At Mob Hits, Misses, Disappearances, and Deaths In America." *Rick Porrello's AmericanMafia.com*. PLR International, Jan. 2004. Web. 27 Oct. 2013. http://www .americanmafia.com/Mob_Hits/1996_04_update.html

"AAABA Tournament History." *Johnstown Pennsylvania Information Source Online*. N.p., n.d. Web. 02 Mar. 2011. http://www.johnstownpa.com/History/hist23.html

Aggarwal, Karthik. "Malangone's Journey Is a Long Road." *NorthJersey.com*. North Jersey Media Group, 27 Sept. 2010. Web. 14 Mar. 2011. http://www.northjersey.com/ news/103691489_Malangone_s_journey_is_a_long_road.html

Alumni Varsity Association. *City College of New York 42nd Annual Hall of Fame Dinner*. 26 Apr. 2007. Induction Program. National Arts Club, New York City.

Appel, Marty. "Scouting Story." *Marty Appel Public Relations: Sports, Corporate, and Consumer PR Agency*. Yankees Magazine, 2003. Web. 31 May 2011. http://www.appelpr.com/ ARTICLES/A-scout.htm

Barry, Ellen. "The Streets of Queens Where Rizzuto Played." *New York Times* 16 Aug. 2007. Web. 02 Mar. 2011. http://www.nytimes.com/2007/08/16/nyregion/16phil.html

Beagle, Burt. "On the Sandlots." *Unknown* [NY] 15 Sept. 1966: n. page. Print.

Bellis, Mary. "The History of Penicillin." *About.com*. IAC, n.d. Web. 14 July 2012. http://inventors .about.com/od/pstartinventions/a/Penicillin.htm

Bevis, Charlie. *Mickey Cochrane: The Life of a Baseball Hall of Fame Catcher*. Jefferson, NC: McFarland, 1998. 170-71. Print.

"Bill Dickey Statistics and History." *Baseball-Reference.com*. Sports Reference LLC, 2013. Web. 25 Oct. 2011. http://www.baseball-reference.com/players/d/dickebi01.shtml

Blanchard, John. Letter to John Malangone. Summer 1956. MS. N.p.

Boone, Ruschell. "East Harlem Holds Annual Stickball 'World Series'" *NY1 News*. Time Warner Enterprises LLC, 05 July 2008. Web. 12 Feb. 2012. http://www.ny1.com/content/ top_stories/83450/east-harlem-holds-annual-stickball—worldseries-

Brewer, Caroline. "Victory, at Last." *The Record* [Woodland Park, NJ] 01 Mar. 1998: L1-2. Print.

"Brooklyn's Semipro Fields." *Covehurst.net*. N.p., n.d. Web. 01 Mar. 2011. http://www.covehurst
.net/ddyte/brooklyn/semipro_parks.html

Broome, Spencer. "The Athletic Standard: *Sports Illustrated's* Gary Smith of Charleston Profiles
Big Game and Big Picture." *Charleston Mercury* 10 Mar. 2009. Web. 30 Mar. 2013.

Carlino, Frank. "From Coffee House to Movie House." *Mahopac News*. Linear Publishing, 08 May
2012. Web. 15 Feb. 2013.

Cavanaugh, Jack. "For 30 Years, a Manager Travels the Back Roads of Baseball." *New York Times*
05 Aug. 1990 Web. 12 Jan. 2012. http://www.nytimes.com/1990/08/05/nyregion/for
-30-years-a-manager-travels-the-back-roads-of-baseball.html?pagewanted=all

Certificate of Death for Orlando Panarese. Rep. no. 16326. NY: Bureau of Records Dept. of Health,
1937. Print.

"Charlie Silvera Statistics and History." *Baseball-Reference.com*. Sports Reference LLC, n.d. Web.
26 May 2011. http://www.baseball-reference.com/players/s/silvech01.shtml

Coffey, Wayne. "How a Dad Deals with Son's Death; Baseball's His Peace." *NY Daily News*. N.p.,
27 Nov. 1998. Web. 27 Apr. 2013. http://www.nydailynews.com/archives/sports/dad
-deals-son-death-baseball-peace-article-1.821167?pgno=1

Coffey, Wayne. "The Yankee That Never Was." *NY Daily News* 11 Dec. 1994: n. page. Print.

Coffin, Phil. "Houk, One of Berra's Backups, Didn't Do Much." *New York Times* 21 July 2010. Web.
26 May 2011. http://bats.blogs.nytimes.com/2010/07/21/houk-one-of-berras
-backups-didnt-do-much/#more-31228

"Current and Former Player Nicknames." *Baseball-Reference.com*. Sports Reference LLC, 2013.
Web. 24 Oct. 2013. http://www.baseball-reference.com/friv/baseball-player
-nicknames.shtml

Daley, Arthur. "Sports of the Times; A Good Scout." *New York Times* 10 June 1957. Web. 25 May
2011. http://query.nytimes.com/mem/archive/pdf?res=F5091EFB3F5D157A93C2A81
78DD85F438585F9

"Do People, Who Make a Tragic Mistake That Alters Their Lives, Deserve a Second Chance?"
Maury. NBC. NY, Dec. 1997. Television.

"Dodgers Timeline." *Los Angeles Dodgers*. MLB.com, n.d. Web. 28 May 2013. http://losangeles
.dodgers.mlb.com/la/history/timeline.jsp

Durso, Joseph. *The Days of Mr. McGraw*. Englewood Cliffs, New Jersey: Prentice Hall, 1969.
Print.

"Ed Randall." *CBS New York*. CBS, n.d. Web. 18 June 2013. http://newyork.cbslocal.com/
personality/ed-randall/

Effrat, Louis. "Oldest Yankee Employee in 36th Year as Scout: Krichell Is Man Who Shelled Out
$1,500 Bonus for Gehrig." *New York Times* 07 Mar. 1955: 32. Print.

Effrat, Louis. "Silvera Is Eager to Show Wares." *New York Times* 15 Mar. 1957. Web. 26 May 2011.
http://query.nytimes.com/mem/archive/pdf?res=F20B12FB3D5D167B93C7A81788D
85F438585F9

"Elston Howard Statistics and History." *Baseball-Reference.com*. Sports Reference LLC, 2013. Web. 25 Oct. 2011. http://www.baseball-reference.com/players/h/howarel01.shtml

Feldman, Jay. "Make Scouts Eligible for Cooperstown." *Sports Illustrated* 05 Feb. 1990 Web. 25 May 2011. http://sportsillustrated.cnn.com/vault/article/magazine/MAG1123111/index.htm

Fleming, Frank. "New York Giants (1883-1957)." *The Sports E-Cyclopedia*. USA Today Sports Media Group, 15 Apr. 2012. Web. 17 Apr. 2012. http://www.sportsecyclopedia.com/nl/nygiantsb/nygiants.html

"Ft. Dix Nine Takes Title." *Pacific Stars and Stripes* [Fort Dix, NJ] 29 Aug. 1954: 13. Print.

Fox, John W. "Mainini and Malangone: Trips' Dizziest Battery." *Binghamton Press* 29 Mar. 1955: 17. Print.

Fox, John W. Personal Notes on John Malangone. Spring 1955. Print.

Francis, Bill. "Story of John Malangone and His Childhood Tragedy Wins Best Film Honors." *Long Road Home*. The National Baseball Hall of Fame & Museum, n.d. Web. 01 May 2013. http://longroadhomefilm.com/wp-content/uploads/2012/10/hallOfFame.pdf

Francis, C. Philip. "Satch." *Chatter From The Dugout*. N.p., n.d. Web. 25 Dec. 2011.

"Frank Home Run Baker Quotes." *Baseball Almanac — The Official Baseball History Site*. Baseball Almanac, n.d. Web. 24 May 2011. http://www.baseball-almanac.com/quotes/frank_baker_quotes.shtml

Friedman, Jon. "Meet America's Best Magazine Writer." *Marketwatch.com*. MarketWatch, 25 Apr. 2008. Web. 01 Apr. 2013. http://www.marketwatch.com/story/sis-gary-smith-is-americas-best-magazine-writer

Fuchs, Marek. "A Life Devoted to Robins Who Dreamed of Being Cardinals or Orioles." *New York Times* 22 May 2005. Web. 12 Jan. 2012. http://query.nytimes.com/gst/fullpage.html?res=9C03E7D81539F931A15756C0A9639C8B63

Gay, Timothy M. *Satch, Dizzy & Rapid Robert: the Wild Saga of Interracial Baseball before Jackie Robinson*. New York: Simon & Schuster, 2010. Print.

Gittleman, Sol. *Reynolds, Raschi and Lopat: New York's Big Three and the Great Yankee Dynasty of 1949-1953*. Jefferson, NC: McFarland, 2007. Print.

Goldstein, Richard. "Art Rust Jr., Pioneer in Sports Talk Radio, Dies at 82." *New York Times* 13 Jan. 2010. Web. 23 May 2011. http://www.nytimes.com/2010/01/14/sports/14rust.html

Gonzalez, David. "Stealing Home From the Old Neighborhood." *New York Times* 08 Sept. 2008. Web. 12 Feb. 2012. http://cityroom.blogs.nytimes.com/2008/09/08/stealing-home-from-the-old-neighborhood/?pagemode=print

Greene, Moe. "THE JOHN MALANGONE STORY." *The Rye Chronicle*, Vol. 102, Number 28, 21 Sept. 2006, p.6.

Haneles, Lou. "My Earliest Recollection of John Malangone." Letter. 20 Feb. 1995. MS. Author's Possession, Freeport, NY.

Harper. *Tom Peoples Is Shown Hitting the Canvas*. 1953. Photograph. Fort Dix Publication (unknown), n.p.

Hillerich & Bradsby Co. Louisville Slugger. Mar. 1955. Agreement to use John Malangone's name on baseball bats and promotions.

"History." *Katz's Delicatessen*. Katz's Delicatessen, n.d. Web. 16 Sept. 2011. http://katzsdelicatessen .com/history/

"HHC Bellevue - History." *HHC Bellevue*. NYC Health and Hospitals Corporation, 2014. Web. 11 June 2014. http://www.nyc.gov/html/hhc/bellevue/html/about/history.shtml

Israel, Steve. "Steve Israel: With the crack of the bat, life is right again." *Recordonline.com*. Dow Jones Local Media Group, 04 Aug. 2011. Web. 04 May 2013. http://www.recordonline .com/apps/pbcs.dll/article?AID=/20110408/NEWS/104080380/-1/NEWS14

"Javelin accident kills German athletics official." *BBC News*. BBC, 27 Aug. 2012. Web. 27 Mar. 2013. http://www.bbc.com/news/world-europe-19391807

"John Kucks Obituary." *Dignitymemorial.com*. Becker Funeral Home, 04 Nov. 2013. Web. 04 Nov. 2013. http://obits.dignitymemorial.com/dignity-memorial/obituary.aspx?n=John-Kucks &lc=4025&pid=167807303&mid=5725256&locale=en_US

"John Malangone a Remporte Le Trophee Lord Calvert." *Le Nouvellste* [Quebec] 1952: n. page. Print.

Kaltenbach, Evelyn. "Lefty Mike." Letter to Mike Harrison. 13 July 2012. MS. Bronx, NY.

Kepner, Tyler. "The Scout in the Back of the Press Box." *New York Times* 12 June 2008. Web. 26 May 2011. http://bats.blogs.nytimes.com/2008/06/12/the-scout-in-the-back-of-the-press -box/

"Kid Elberfeld's Influence - Casey Stengel." *Norman "The Tobasco Kid" Elberfeld and Elberfeld Genealogy*. N.p., n.d. Web. 22 Dec. 2011. http://www.kidelberfeld.com/www/Kid Elberfeld/Influence/StengelLifeTimes.htm

Kilgannon, Corey. "Burt Beagle, Ever-Present Sports Statistician, Dies at 73." *New York Times* 26 Feb. 2007. Web. 11 June 2013. http://www.nytimes.com/2007/02/26/sports/26beagle.html

Koppett, Leonard. *The Man in the Dugout: Baseball's Top Managers and How They Got That Way*. Philidelphia: Temple UP, 2000. *BaseballLibrary.com*. Excerpt. Web. 03 Oct. 2012. http://www.baseballlibrary.com/excerpts/excerpt.php?book=the_man_in_the_dugout

Krichell, Paul. "Invitation to Work out with the Yankees." Letter to John Malangone. 16 June 1954. MS. N.p.

"Letters." *Sports Illustrated* (17 Nov. 1997): 21. Print.

"Like father, like son." *Streetplay.com*. N.p., n.d. Web. 12 Feb. 2012. http://www.streetplay.com/ spotlight/spotlight009.shtml

"Little Italy East Harlem." *Ephemeral New York*. N.p., 14 Feb. 2011. Web. 05 Apr. 2011. https:// ephemeralnewyork.wordpress.com/2011/02/14/manhattans-one-time-biggest-little-italy/

Long Road Home: The John Malangone Story. Prod. Bruce Spiegel. 2004. DVD.

"Lou Haneles—BR Bullpen." *Baseball Reference.com*. Sports Reference LLC, 03 Apr. 2012. Web. 13 Apr. 2012. http://www.baseball-reference.com/bullpen/Lou_Haneles

Madden, Bill. *Pride of October: What It Was to Be Young and a Yankee*. New York: Warner, 2003. Print.

McGaw, Jeff. "Why Not? A Look at the MSBL's Origins." Men's Senior Baseball League, 2012. Web. 09 July 2013.

Meyer, Gerald. "Italian East Harlem." Vitomarcantonio.com. N.p., n.d. Web. 05 Apr. 2011. http://vitomarcantonio.com/eh_italian_east_harlem.html

Meyer, Gerald. "When Frank Sinatra Came to Italian Harlem: The 1945 'Race Riot' at Benjamin Franklin High School." *Political Affairs*. 03 May 2010. Web. 01 Apr. 2012. Originally appeared in *Are Italians White? How Race is Made in America*. Ed. Jennifer Guglielmo and Salvatore Salerno. New York: Routledge, 2003. 161-76. Print.

"MSBL/MABL Adult Baseball League." *MSBL/MABL Adult Baseball League*. N.p., n.d. Web. 09 July 2012. http://www.msblnational.com/

Murtha, Bill. "Show All for the USO." *NY Daily News* 22 Feb. 1942: n. pag. Print.

Mushnick, Phil. "PRIMETIME." *New York Post* 18 Nov. 2007. Web. 14 Mar. 2011. http://nypost.com/2007/11/18/primetime-2/

"My Dad and Jackie." Message to the author from Christina Malangone. 23 June 2013. E-mail.

Nathan, Steve. "The Best Baseball Player (No One's Ever Heard Of)." *Cigar Magazine* Spring (2007): 101-08. Print.

"New Rochelle Sports Hall of Fame." *New Rochelle Sports Hall of Fame*. N.p., n.d. Web. 12 Jan. 2012. http://nrshof.com/1993.php

O'Connell, Jack. "HOF Film Festival Kicks off Friday." *Major League Baseball*. MLB.com, 7 Nov. 2007. Web. 18 June 2013. http://mlb.mlb.com/news/article_entertainment .jsp?ymd=20071107

Old Timer. "Tigers' Home Was The Arctic Oval, But Grable Could Cause It To Thaw." *Times Newsweekly* [Queens, NY] 24 May 2007. Ridgewood Times. Web. 01 Mar. 2011. http://www.timesnewsweekly.com/sites/www.timesnewsweekly.com/files/archives/ Archives2007/Apr.-Jun.2007/052407/NewFiles/OURNEIGH.html

Pérez-Peña, Richard. "The Sports Whisperer, Probing Psychic Wounds." *New York Times* 16 Sept. 2008. Web. 15 Mar. 2013. http://www.nytimes.com/2008/09/16/books/16smit.html

Politi, Steve. "With one wave from Hurricane Sandy, years of demons rush back for former Yankees prospect John Malangone." *The Star-Ledger*. NJ.com, 11 Nov. 2012. Web. 17 June 2013. http://www.nj.com/yankees/index.ssf/2012/11/former_yankees_prospect _john_m.html

"Polybius Quotes." *Polybius Quotes (Author of The Rise of the Roman Empire)*. Goodreads, n.d. Web. 20 Feb. 2012. http://www.goodreads.com/author/quotes/39941.Polybius

Powell, Robert A. "Lou's Last Pitch." *Miami New Times* 22 Oct. 1998. Web. 13 Apr. 2012. http://www.miaminewtimes.com/1998-10-22/news/lou-s-last-pitch/

Pryor, Thomas. "Yorkville Stickball Champ at 73." *Our Town* 19 May 2011, p. 6.

Raterman, David. "Fitness Profile: Making His Pitch." *Sun-Sentinel* [Fort Lauderdale, FL] n.d.
: n. p. Print.

"Redwings." *New York Greasers, Gangs and Clubs From New York, Boppin Gangs From New
York.* N.p., n.d. Web. 22 Mar. 2012. http://www.stonegreasers.com/greaser/newyork
.html

Resner, Moe. "Westchester County... Be Proud of Our Own Yankees." N.p., Feb. 2003. Web.

Resner, Moe. "The John Malangone Story." *Martinelli Publications* 21 Sept. 2006: 6. Print.

Robinson, Eddie, and Paul C. Rogers. *Lucky Me: My Sixty-five Years in Baseball.* Dallas: Southern
Methodist UP, 2011. Print.

Rocchio, Lisa. "Our Lady of Mount Carmel." *Fordham University.* Fordham University, n.d. Web.
08 Apr. 2011. http://www.fordham.edu/halsall/medny/rocchio.html

Ruck, Rob. "Chicos and Gringos of Beisbol Venezolana." *Society for American Baseball Research.*
Research Journal Archives, n.d. Web. 04 Oct. 2012. http://research.sabr.org/journals/
chicos-and-gringos-of-beisbol-venezolana

"Sal Malangone and Family Violence." Personal interview. 21 June 2012.

"Sandy retired from list of Atlantic Basin tropical cyclone names." *NOAA National Oceanic
Atmospheric Administration.* United States Department of Commerce, 11 Apr. 2013
. Web. 20 June 2013. http://www.noaanews.noaa.gov/stories2013/20130411
_sandynameretiredt.html

Sexton, John Edward, Thomas Oliphant, and Peter J. Schwartz. *Baseball as a Road to God: Seeing
Beyond the Game.* New York: Gotham, 2013. Print.

Sigle, Fred. "Don't Allow Your Past to Rob Your Joy" *SermonCentral.* Outreach, Inc., Feb. 2007.
Web. 14 Mar. 2011. http://www.sermoncentral.com/sermons/dont-allow-your-past
-rob-your-joy-fred-sigle-sermon-on-peace-102482.asp

Simon, Tom. *Deadball Stars of the National League.* Washington, D.C.: Brassey's, 2004. Print.

Smith, Gary. *Beyond the Game: The Collected Sportswriting of Gary Smith.* New York: Atlantic
Monthly, 2000. Print.

Smith, Gary. *Going Deep: 20 Classic Sports Stories.* New York: Sports Illustrated, 2008. Print.

Smith, Gary. "Damned Yankee." *Sports Illustrated* 13 Oct. 1997. Web. 20 Dec. 2011. http://
sportsillustrated.cnn.com/vault/article/magazine/MAG1011129/index.htm

Spiegel, Bruce. *Long Road Home.* Homepage. N.p., Spring 2013. Web. 06 Sept. 2013. http://
longroadhomefilm.com/

"Steve Sigler" *Growing Bolder.* N.p., 11 Mar. 2007. Web. 13 Dec. 2014. https://www.growing
bolder.com/steve-sigler-905/

Superstorm Sandy Public Presentation – Monday, November 19, 2012. Rep. Borough of Little
Ferry, 19 Nov. 2012. Web. 20 June 2013. http://www.littleferrynj.org/file
storage/159/1302/superstormsandychangesaftermeeting.pdf

Turnow, Brad. "www.HistoryOfTheYankees.com." *Brad's Ultimate New York Yankees Website*. N.p., n.d. Web. 23 May 2011. http://www.ultimateyankees.com/history.htm

Van Overloop, Mark. *A League of Our Own: 2000 Fall League Statistics*. Rep: n.p., n.d. Print.

Varmecky, Brian. "About." *Aaabatournament.com*. N.p., n.d. Web. 07 Mar. 2011. http://www .aaabatournament.com/about.html

Verhovek, Sam H. "PRO FOOTBALL; A Friend Dies, and Oiler Kills Himself." *New York Times* 15 Dec. 1993. Web. 28 Apr. 2013. http://www.nytimes.com/1993/12/15/sports/pro -football-a-friend-dies-and-oiler-kills-himself.html

Warren, James. "Hiding From His Past, He Missed A Great Future." *Chicago Tribune*. N.p., 17 Oct. 1997. Web. 07 May 2014.

Weber, Bruce. "Johnny Kucks, Who Pitched Yanks to Title, Dies at 81." *New York Times* 11 Nov. 2013. Web. 11 Nov. 2013. http://www.nytimes.com/2013/11/02/sports/baseball/ johnny-kucks-who-pitched-yanks-to-title-dies-at-81.html?_r=0

Weintraub, Robert. *The House That Ruth Built: a New Stadium, the First Yankees Championship, and the Redemption of 1923*. New York: Little, Brown, 2011. Print.

Weiss, Ron. "More Than a Game" N.d. TS. Unpublished.

Weiss, Ron. "The Yankee Who Never Was." N.d. MS. Unpublished.

White, Bill, and Gordon Dillow. *Uppity: My Untold Story about the Games People Play*. New York: Grand Central, 2011. Print.

"Yankees' Sheehy Dies." *New York Times* 14 Aug. 1985. Web. 19 Dec. 2011. http://www.nytimes .com/1985/08/14/sports/yankees-sheehy-dies.html

Sources

Belli, Anthony. Personal / video interview. 07 Feb. 2012.

Benedetto, Dan. Personal / video interview. 10 June 2014.

Caswell, Dick. Personal / video interview. 20 July 2011.

Charles, Ed. Personal / telephone interview. 04 Apr. 2013.

Coffey, Wayne. Personal / video interview. 06 Dec. 2012.

Crihfield, Glenn. Personal / telephone interview. 07 Aug. 2014.

DeFazio, Craig. Personal / video interview. 24 Feb. 2013.

DeRosa, Mike. Personal interview. 16 May 2013.

Fiorello, Silvio. Personal / video interview. 01 Oct. 2010.

Fox, John. Personal / telephone interview. 19 Apr. 2012.

Goldsholl, Bob. Personal / telephone interview. 01 Sept. 2011.

Grasso, Guy "Ozzie." Personal / telephone interview. 25 July 2013.

Grasso, Guy "Ozzie." Personal / video interview. 13 Aug. 2013.

Kaltenbach, Evelyn. Personal / video interview. 13 July 2012.

Lane, Floyd. Personal / video interview. 13 July 2012.

Lentini, Mike. Personal / video interview. 11 June 2014.

Malangone, Anna. Personal / video interview. 03 Sept. 2011.

Malangone, Christina and Mary. Personal / video interview. 16 Oct. 2011.

Malangone, John. "John Malangone and Boys Club, Childhood, and Dyslexia." Personal interview. 04 Apr. 2011.

Malangone, John. "John Malangone and Fatherhood." Personal interview. 16 June 2012.

Malangone, John. "John Malangone and Johnny Kucks." Personal interview. 25 Nov. 2013.

Malangone, John. "John Malangone and Silvio." Personal interview. 20 Sept. 2011.

Malangone, John. "John Malangone and Sylvia Panarese." Personal / telephone interview. 04 Apr. 2011.

Malangone, John. "John Malangone and the Accident." Personal interview. 14 July 2012.

Malangone, John. "John Malangone and the Army." Personal interview. 08 Apr. 2012.

Malangone, John. "John Malangone and the RKO Incident." Personal interview. 24 Nov. 2011.

Malangone, John. "John Malangone and the Yankee Signing." Personal / telephone interview. 20 Apr. 2011.

Malangone, John. "John Malangone, Hurricane Sandy and the wheelchair accident." Personal interview. 19 June 2013.

Malangone, John. "John Malangone Recalls Paulie Tine Part 1." Personal interview. 16 June 2012.

Malangone, John. "John Malangone Recalls Paulie Tine Part 2." Personal interview. 16 June 2012.

Malangone, Sal. "Casey on the Radio." Personal / video interview. 08 Aug. 2011.

McElroy, Jim. Personal / video interview. 23 Sept. 2011.

Panarese, Margaret and Yolanda. Personal / video interview. July 2012.

Panarese, Margaret and Yolanda. "The Accident." Personal / video interview. 10 July 2012.

Preston, George. Personal / video interview. 07 Feb. 2012.

Resner, Moe. Personal / video interview. 05 Feb. 2010.

Roque, John. Personal / video interview. 21 Sept. 2013.

Sacino, Gary. Personal / telephone interview. 04 June 2013.

Sacino, Gary. Personal / video interview. 25 June 2013.

Santarpia, Joe. Personal / video interview. 05 Feb. 2013.

Smith, Gary. Personal / telephone interview. 27 Mar. 2013.

Spiegel, Bruce. Personal / video interview. 17 Feb. 2012.

VanOverloop, Mark. Personal /video interview. 02 Oct. 2011.

Weiss, Ron. Personal / video interview. 29 Jan. 2011.